Families and households in post-apartheid South Africa:
Socio-demographic perspectives

Edited by Acheampong Yaw Amoateng & Tim B Heaton

HSRC PRESS

Published by HSRC Press
Private Bag X9182, Cape Town, 8000, South Africa
www.hsrcpress.ac.za

First published 2007

ISBN 978-0-7969-2190-1

© 2007 Human Sciences Research Council

Copy-edited by Vaun Cornell
Typeset by Robin Taylor
Cover design by comPress
Print management by comPress
Printed by Creda Communications

Distributed in Africa by Blue Weaver
Tel: +27 (0) 21 701 4477; Fax: +27 (0) 21 701 7302
www.oneworldbooks.com

Distributed in Europe and the United Kingdom by Eurospan Distribution Services (EDS)
Tel: +44 (0) 20 7240 0856; Fax: +44 (0) 20 7379 0609
www.eurospangroup.com/bookstore

Distributed in North America by Independent Publishers Group (IPG)
Call toll-free: (800) 888 4741; Fax: +1 (312) 337 5985
www.ipgbook.com

CONTENTS

LIST OF TABLES AND FIGURES

Figures

PREFACE

Because of the devastating effect apartheid-induced policies such as migratory labour, influx control, the Immorality Act and so on, had on families and communities before the democratic transition in 1994, concerns about families and their well-being have come to occupy centre stage in the post-transition period both by policy-makers and the general public. One indication of this increasing concern about families and their social and economic circumstances is the rapid rate at which social and economic data on families and the households they occupy are becoming available for the purpose of planning to meet their needs.

The idea for the present publication originated in 2002 when I joined the Human Sciences Research Council (HSRC) from the University of the Western Cape. In this new position the Executive Director, Professor Linda Richter put me in charge of an in-house project called the Strengthening Families Project. Essentially, this project involved secondary and descriptive analyses of the various survey and census data that had proliferated in the country in the immediate post-transition period. Even though before 1994 sociologists and other social scientists had documented the nature of changes in families and households in the country, limitations of such studies in terms of coverage and scope had made works like the present monograph imperative. In other words, the idea was to take advantage of the myriad large-scale, quantitative socio-economic data sets that were increasingly becoming available to the South African public to describe the changes that families and households were experiencing as a result of the political, economic, and social transformations that were engulfing the broader society. Moreover, because of the multifaceted nature of domestic organisation, such a study was to be multidisciplinary.

The idea to write the monograph was communicated to social science colleagues both in and outside the HSRC, many of whom readily welcomed the challenge and agreed to attend a workshop in the Pretoria offices of the HSRC in November 2003, to discuss issues such as chapter outlines, data sources and timelines.

At the workshop, consensus was reached on important issues. Firstly, we agreed to use secondary data sources in the form of the two censuses and sample surveys (the October Household series, the South African Demographic and Health Survey, the General Household Survey series and so on). Secondly, we agreed that the analyses for the respective chapters would be essentially descriptive to render the study accessible to both undergraduate and postgraduate students in the family field, academic researchers, policy-makers and the lay public at large.

The present publication has been a protracted and combined effort of patient and diligent authors, critical readers, and a supportive and wise publisher. Thus, it is expected that some of the information in the study may be out of date, especially given the rapidity with which quantitative socio-economic data are being generated in the country. Even though alteration of established patterns of social interaction takes time, if the need to update the information contained in this study serves as a basis for further works of this nature, then our initial purpose in producing the monograph would have been served. The development and completion of this publication was due to the indefatigable efforts of friends and colleagues. First, we would like to thank the Executive Director of the Child, Youth, Family and Social Development Research Programme (CYFSD) of the HSRC, Professor Linda Richter, who gave me carte blanche in my research and the support for this work in particular. The authors of this monograph deserve a very special thank you for their thoughtful and well-written contributions. But for their enthusiastic timely revisions, it would have been impossible to complete the project. Over the years, we have been blessed with various interns and research assistants in the Cape Town office of CYFSD who all contributed enormously to the development of this publication: Ms Thandika Gana, Ms Mihloti Mushwana, and Mr Anthony Burns. Finally, we would like to thank the staff at the HSRC Press, for their diligence.

Acheampong Yaw Amoateng
Human Sciences Research Council, Cape Town

ACRONYMS AND ABBREVIATIONS

CPR	contraceptive prevalence rate
CRC	United Nations Convention on the Rights of the Child
DHS	Demographic and Health Survey
EA	enumerated area
GHS	General Household Survey
IES	Income and Expenditure Survey
IMR	infant mortality rate
LFS	Labour Force Survey
OHS	October Household Survey
PSU	primary sampling unit
SADHS	South African Demographic and Health Survey
SAYP	Survey of Activities of Young People
SMAM	singulate mean ages at marriage
SNA	System of National Accounts
Stats SA	Statistics South Africa
TMFR	total marital fertility rate
TN	total natural fertility rate
TF	total fecundity rate
TFR	total fertility rate
TUS	Time Use Survey
VIP	ventilated pit latrine

Note: *Names of South African population groups*
During the apartheid regime, legislation divided the South African populace into four distinct population groups based on racial classification. Although the notion of population groups is now legal history, it is not always possible to gauge the effects of past discriminatory practices, and the progress of policies designed to eradicate them, without reference to it. For this reason, the HSRC continues to use the terms black/African, coloured, white or Indian/Asian people where it is pertinent to the analysis of data.

CHAPTER 1

Social and economic context of families and households in South Africa

Acheampong Yaw Amoateng & Linda M Richter

Introduction

This study uses some of the most recent quantitative datasets generated in the country to look at families, and their residential dimension, households. It essentially uses a socio-demographic perspective to examine aspects of family life in South Africa in light of the transformation in the society's social structures since the democratic transition in 1994. We begin this task by examining the social structure of the country both before and after the transition to serve as the broad context for the substantive analyses of families and households. Even though we make the implicit assumption in this study that the prevailing political, social and economic conditions before the democratic transition were not conducive to a more objective analysis of family and household structures, to the extent that we focus on developments with regard to changes in family and household structures in the post-apartheid era, the present work is duly informed by family scholarship prior to this period.

Family and household structures in pre-transition society

The institution of the family is essentially multidimensional in nature in that it affects and is affected by the various social, economic, cultural and political institutions which together form the social structure of any society. Thus, changes in the structure and functions of the family are fundamentally occasioned by changes in other institutions in the family's environment. More broadly, social change is a function of two main sets of factors, namely, endogenous and exogenous factors. Writing about the heterogeneity of pre-colonial African social organisation, Adegboyega (1994), for example, has traced the source of the variation in family forms to the variations in environmental conditions.

Specifically, Adegboyega has argued that ecological factors seemed to have played a major role in determining the form the family assumed in different parts across the continent. For example, he has observed that among pastoralists like the Masai of eastern Africa, the family tended to be nuclear in form compared to the extended family form found among the more sedentary horticulturalists like the Akan of western Africa. Moreover, the mere fact of the existence of different rules of primogeniture observed amongst indigenous African peoples is a clear indication of the diversity observed in the pre-colonial African family. But, aside from these internal strains and stresses, there are other exogenous factors that engender family change. For instance, there appears to be consensus among writers of the African social experience that the incorporation of African societies into the international capitalist economy through the colonial project has been one of the major causes of family change on the continent (see, for example, Mazrui 1986; Russell 2002).

Some of the family patterns often cited as evidence of the immense economic, demographic, political, legal and religious innovation that occurred consequent to confrontation with the international capitalist order, are not only changes in the rules of kinship, which were essentially the political backbone of society itself, but also changes in relationships between husbands and wives, parents and children, and between members of the conjugal family and their kin. These changes were facilitated by such mechanisms as formal education, wage employment and adoption of Western belief systems, the direct transposition of the Western nuclear family system through the European settlers.[1] Several Western scholars concur with this general observation about changes in social institutions as a result of increased interactions of different cultures. For example, they have observed that throughout the period of modernisation and especially in the early stages of globalisation, major changes in social institutions have taken place across the world (for example, see Giddens 2000; Turner 2002).

Among the social institutions that have received considerable attention are the family, the economy, polity, and educational and religious institutions. Anthony Giddens, for instance, has argued that globalising forces are impacting on the family in ways such as the emergence of more egalitarian relationships between men and women, the increasing participation of women in work outside of the home and in public life, the separation of sexuality from reproduction, and the growing tendency for family relations to be based on the sentiments of love rather than economic or social concerns, with the intimate couple being the primary family unit. In South Africa, colonisation and its natural extension in the form of apartheid were institutionalised through such mechanisms as land expropriation, political disenfranchisement of the majority indigenous populations, and the institutionalisation of wage labour through industrial development.

These developments resulted in significant alterations in the social structures of the society. For instance, large numbers of people – resident Africans, imported labourers and settlers – left family homesteads and migrated to earn cash income to meet imposed taxes and supplement declining agricultural resources and to support their relocation. The massive movement of people from the countryside to urban centres following the development of industries led to the rapid urbanisation of South Africa. These patterns of socio-economic development were exacerbated by the institutionalisation of racism through the apartheid policy of separate development. Through a series of legislation, the life chances of the non-white groups in the

---

1 In South Africa, the importation of Indian and Malay indentured slaves by the white settlers to work in Natal and the Western Cape respectively brought in other family systems, while the interracial marriages that led to the creation of the coloured population group added yet another dimension to this diversity of family systems in the society.

society became severely restricted, while whites were given advantages in such critical domains as agriculture, education, employment, housing, and healthcare.

For instance, as a result of the 1913 and 1936 Land Acts, African ownership of land was restricted to only 13 per cent of South Africa's land area (Wilson & Ramphele 1989), thus considerably limiting opportunities for African farming.[2] In the area of education, the country's education system was racialised with the ultimate aim of providing inferior education to the non-white groups, especially the African majority under the Bantu Education Act (Fedderke et al. 2000; Naicker 2000). In their study of the country's different education systems based on data from 1910 to 1993, Fedderke et al. (2000) observe that white people's educational opportunity was consistently and considerably better than black people's educational opportunity.

On the specific issue of pupil–teacher ratios, Fedderke et al. found that while the white public school pupil–teacher ratio never rose above the mid-20 level, the best black pupil–teacher ratio provided by the private schooling system in 1941 was 31:1; the pupil–teacher ratio for black public schooling remained in the range from 50:1 to 70:1 for the period from 1957 to 1993. Moreover, under this unequal education of the races, Fedderke et al. found that the real expenditure on the schooling systems for white people was far larger than the absolute level of expenditure on any other race group until the mid 1980s; white per pupil expenditure remained at least seven times the level of that of black pupils between 1972 and 1992. Besides these indicators, black schools had inferior facilities, teachers and textbooks; although 96 per cent of all teachers in white schools had teaching certificates, only 15 per cent of teachers in black schools were certified.

The same pattern of unequal distribution of resources to the various race groups prevailed in the area of housing where, in terms of both quantity and quality of housing, white people had the greatest advantage. For example, research conducted by Real Estate Surveys between January and May 1992 showed that of the 11 500 formal houses built in the country, the distribution was as follows: Africans 23 per cent; coloureds 17 per cent; Indians 6 per cent; and whites 54 per cent. In terms of the average cost of the houses, the research revealed the following racial variations: Africans R36 290; coloureds R33 661; Indians R83 882; and whites R132 613 (*The Natal Mercury* 9 February 1993; *Business Day* 10 February 1993). Moreover, the Central Statistical Services (1992) reported that between January and June 1992, there was a 45 per cent decrease in the number of formal houses built for Africans, while there was a 31 per cent increase in those built for white people during the same period.

Thus colonialism-induced processes such as urbanisation, industrialisation and subsequent apartheid-imposed restrictions affected family and household formation patterns in the society, especially among Africans, who bore the brunt of such policies. Among Africans, the limitations on geographical mobility reinforced dual

---

2 Other notable pieces of legislation include the Group Areas Act of 1950, the Immorality Act of 1949, the Population Registration Act of 1950, the Bantu Education Act of 1953 and the Industrial Conciliation Act of 1956 (Mbeki 2001; Sampson 1987).

urban–rural homesteads and circular migration as organisational mechanisms of economic and social adaptation (Okoth-Ogendo 1989). With limitations on geographical mobility came limitations on social mobility in areas such as education and employment which, in turn, had profound implications for family life. For instance, urban-bound migration, which resulted from the lack of opportunities for farming in the country, impacted the family life of Africans in a number of ways.

First, in rural areas the absence of males, who predominated in the migratory labour system, meant either the postponement or complete avoidance of marriage among Africans.[3] Second, in cases where marriages were contracted, economic necessity meant that the husband/father left his wife and children behind to participate in the migratory labour system, a situation that led to such family patterns as female-headed households, out-of-wedlock births, and unstable household composition, especially among Africans in the rural areas (see, for example, Pasha & Lodhi 1994; Oberai 1991; Pick & Cooper 1997; Seager 1994; Simkins & Dlamini 1992).

Similar economic rationale underlay other family patterns observed among the various groups in the society. One example is the formation of complex households, which is usually associated with Africans and often attributed to the communalist ethos found in many African cultures; that is, the wealthier the patriarch, the more complex the household tended to be in the pre-colonial systems. A wealthy powerful man would tend to have more wives, more children and other dependants than a poor man.

In fact, empirical studies in certain African societies have found that households of the elite in African towns and cities tend to be complex due to poverty and perhaps the high incidence of fosterage in these cultures (Oppong 1974).[4] However, empirical evidence based on studies conducted both in Africa and among other African populations outside the continent appeared to suggest that the formation of complex households was as much a function of poverty as it was of culture among Africans (Stack 1974). Specifically, it was argued that as formal education spreads, especially among Africans, the nuclear family replaced the complex or extended family as the modal family type among this educated elite. In fact, in the context of apartheid South Africa, political factors interacted with economic ones to prevent the formation of extended family households among Africans. Specifically, Section 10 of the Urban Areas Act of 1945 and a housing policy that facilitated single family units of three or four rooms tended to compel nuclear families.

Conversely, the establishment of independent households among white people upon marriage is as much a function of economics as it is of the Western cultural values of independence and privacy. Needless to say, under pre-colonial and apartheid South African conditions, white people's relative access to societal resources in the form of

---

3 Apart from the sheer physical separation of the sexes as a result of male migration, the meagre wages paid to African workers and the widespread unemployment among them in the face of increasing commercialisation of the lobolo (bride wealth) ensure that for a large number of African males marriage is simply unavailable.
4 In the South African case, apartheid-era restrictions on African housing may have contributed significantly to the formation of complex households, especially in the urban areas.

education, income and occupational status meant that this type of living arrangement was available to them.

Because of the institutional racism that prevailed during the apartheid era, it is often tempting to think that the political, social and economic conditions engendered by the state only affected African family life. Contrary to this belief, these same processes affected the family lives of other racial groups in the society, given the fact that apartheid was a zero-sum game. For instance, the deliberate strategy of drawing white people to towns and cities, and hence to the modern sectors of the economy, ensured that they possessed the requisite social and economic resources for a viable family life. Maconachie (1989), for example, has noted that a central constraint on white married women's employment was their responsibility for the care of their children, especially younger children. However, because of white women's ability to access domestic help (provided mostly by African and coloured women), their labour force participation rates were generally higher than both African and coloured women. It is important to note that job reservation as legislated by the apartheid state meant that very few jobs other than domestic work were open to African women in the so-called 'Coloured Labour Preference Area' in particular, and in towns in general. Even though the employment of African women was equally constrained by childcare responsibilities, in their case this constraint was removed largely by African mothers' ready accessibility to childcare through kin, including politically subordinate, unpaid extended kin.[5] Against this broad background of the political economy of South African society during the colonial and apartheid eras, how were families and households depicted by family scholarship?

Pre-1994 family scholarship in South Africa

In the 1950s and 1960s, modernisation theory became popular in the explanation of the evolution of families and households, especially among family sociologists (UN 1995). According to this interpretation, before industrialisation the size of the family was relatively large, usually extended by the presence of several relatives. However, as society developed, such an extended family gave way to the nuclear family, a process that naturally reduced the household size (Giddens 1987).

Using this theoretical perspective several early empirical studies of black and white domestic organisations in South Africa concluded that the family patterns of the two groups were converging in the direction of the nuclear family system (see for example, Clark & van Heerden 1992; Nzimande 1987; Steyn 1993). In a study examining the relationship between exposure to urban life and patterns of domestic organisation in an African township near Johannesburg, Marwick (1978) found that the patterns of domestic organisation change to resemble those normally found in industrial societies. Specifically, he found that 48 per cent of the households in his sample were of the nuclear family type.

---

5 In personal communication, Jeremy Seekings of the University of Cape Town's Departments of Sociology and Economics drew our attention to this point about black and white labour force profiles.

Also, Pauw (1953) found that 58 per cent of his respondents in a study of Duncan Village lived in extended family households. However, 12 years later he observed among his respondents that the incidence of extended family households had dropped significantly. It was in reference to these and other similar studies that led Simkins (1986) to suggest that newer African settlements appeared to have higher proportions of nuclear households (see for example, Preston-Whyte 1978; Steyn et al. 1987; Simkins 1986). However, in his own calculations based on the 1980 Current Population survey, he failed to see any significant difference in the household patterns of black people living in metropolitan, urban and rural areas.

The social structure of contemporary South African society

Following the end of apartheid and the establishment of democracy, there have been several visible changes in the political, social, and economic domains that without a doubt have profound implications for family and household structures and processes. In this section, we examine some of the specific changes in the broader South African society to serve as part of the context for our examination of families and households in the post-apartheid era.

The economy

The legacy of colonialism, coupled with racial oppression through apartheid policies, created a unique political economy in South Africa that could best be characterised as racial capitalism. In this setup, the dominant white group professed the free market ideology, bolstered by such institutional mechanisms as the lack of political pluralism and the unequal participation of all racial and ethnic groups in the economy which duly hindered the development of capitalism and hence the country's economic growth.[6]

The racial ideology of apartheid and the country's subsequent exclusion from world politics in the early 1960s led to several negative political, economic and social consequences (Ballard & Schwella 2000). Thus, on the eve of the transition to democracy the task that faced the new government was to ensure the meaningful participation of black people in the country's economy through a fundamental transformation of the society's social structures. It was against this background of facilitating the transformation process following several decades of the detrimental impact of apartheid policies that the newly elected democratic government embarked upon a much-needed process of economic reform. Essentially, the aim of this economic reform was to create an outward-oriented economy going hand-in-hand with efforts to improve social equity and income distribution (DoL 2000). The new government's economic reform was undertaken within the framework of the Reconstruction and Development Programme (RDP).

---

6 The racialised nature of the political economy indeed caricatured the 'invisible' hand of classical economic theory. In fact, the neo-conservative strategy, which was formulated by a group of Afrikaner economists and influenced PW Botha's reforms in the 1980s, argued for a more market-oriented economy as an efficient means of resolving the crisis in the apartheid state (Lombard 1978).

Several scholars have argued that the main objectives of the RDP were to create a stable socio-economic environment conducive to high economic growth while simultaneously reducing the social disparities and inequalities inherited from the apartheid regime (Terreblanche 1999). However, the neo-liberal critique of the RDP as hampering economic growth led to its replacement by a macroeconomic policy called the Growth, Employment and Redistribution strategy (GEAR) in 1996.[7] The aim of GEAR was to take advantage of the lifting of sanctions following the democratic transition for a full reintegration into the world economy. This has led to the removal of trade restrictions in the form of tariffs, relaxation of foreign exchange regulations, restructuring of state assets (or privatisation as is known in certain quarters), and the adoption of an industrial policy that focuses on the labour-intensive sectors of the economy (Economic Commission for Africa 2002).[8]

Even though the strenuous efforts to restructure the economy and ensure that economic and social benefits reach the majority of the country's citizens still leave much to be desired, there is very little doubt that the adoption of neo-liberalism as a tool for societal reconstruction has brought some dividends to South Africa, as the country's economy is arguably the strongest in the sub-Saharan region (Castells 1999; Jenkins & Wilkinson 2002; Rogerson 1996).[9] For example, towards the latter part of 2005, Statistics South Africa reported that the GDP grew 4.2 per cent in the third quarter for the 28th consecutive quarter of growth. In fact, when compared with previous data, the data showed that this was the strongest performance since 1984 (*Sunday Times*, 4 December 2005).

As one indicator of the success of the economy, the Department of Labour's annual report (2000) cited an International Labour Organisation report which referred to the presence of foreign investors in the Johannesburg Stock Exchange (JSE), a fact which illustrates the increasingly globalised status of the financial sector. According to this, foreign purchases of JSE equities increased nearly eighteen-fold between 1991 and 1997; the number of listed South African enterprises in some of the major international stock exchanges also increased during this period. Moreover, it has been estimated that the economy created in excess of 1 million jobs over the five years from 1995–1999, benefiting all race groups and both genders (Poswell 2000). Also, a study conducted by Hayter (1999) confirmed the improvement in the employment situation, with the highest increases in employment recorded in the trade and finance sectors, where nearly 460 000 jobs and 360 000 jobs were created respectively. However, these gains appeared to be offset by losses in the mining, agriculture and textiles industries. Unlike other African countries, in the late 1980s and early 1990s South Africa had not officially implemented IMF/World Bank structural adjustment programmes.

---

7 It was quite natural that big business would oppose the RDP because of the implicit socialist ideals in the programme. Interestingly, it is this rather minority view which held sway soon after the advent of democracy.

8 This desire to be a part of the international political-economic system led to South Africa becoming a signatory to the General Agreement on Tariffs and Trade and also joining the Southern African Development Community in 1994 (Economic Commission for Africa 2000).

9 With a per capita GNP of $3 160 South Africa is classified in the 1999 World Bank Tables as a middle-income developing country and ranked 86th of 206 countries (Jenkins & Wilkinson 2002).

While the country's adoption of the macroeconomic policy in place of the RDP might be construed as tantamount to structural adjustment, the facts on the ground show that this has been minor when compared to conventional IMF/World Bank programmes. For example, under the macroeconomic policy public expenditure was not slashed, as was made clear by a recent United Nations Development Programme report. According to the report, government expenditure on health increased from R366 million in 1995 to R373 million in 2002, while expenditure on welfare increased from R184 million to R214 million during the same period (UNDP 2003: 8). In fact, the 2003–2004 Budget allocations gave an indication of a major modification of the macroeconomic policy in favour of a Keynesian-type state intervention in the economy in the form of a massive public works programme as a means of alleviating the unemployment situation.[10]

Thus, overall, social spending increased – in real terms becoming markedly pro-poor. Moreover, the country had neither a debt nor foreign exchange crisis. However, these benefits notwithstanding, the macroeconomic policy has had some social costs because of the lack of response to GEAR by investors (Nattrass 2003). For instance, Nattrass and Seekings (2001) have observed that investment has not responded as quickly or as extensively to GEAR as expected; this is evidenced by the fact that between 1996 and 1999 private investment grew at about one-tenth of the rate expected by the GEAR modellers. Thus, despite the slight improvement in the GDP growth rate, employment performance over the past decade has been far from satisfactory, a situation which poses a major challenge for the country.[11] Altman (2003) used both the October Household Survey and the Labour Force Survey to show trends of employment and unemployment between 1994 and 2001. According to her study, the official unemployment rate rose by 10 per cent between 1994 and 2001, reaching almost 30 per cent of the labour force. Using Reserve Bank data, Nattrass (2003) observed that non-agricultural formal employment declined by over 20 per cent between 1990 and 2001, while Hayter (1999) found that the agriculture and utilities sectors showed job attrition of 3.3 per cent and 6.6 per cent respectively. In tandem with this rise in unemployment has been a concomitant rise in inequality between the top 10 per cent and the bottom 20 per cent.

The state

As in the economic domain, significant strides have been made in the political and social domains since the democratic transition in South Africa. Apartheid policies essentially denied access to the country's resources to a large number of its people. This politics of exclusion gave rise to a huge problem of dependency through engendering widespread poverty, and the new government's transformation agenda

---

10 There appear to be signs that some of these efforts are beginning to yield dividends as shown by the improvement in the employment outlook. According to the latest figures by Statistics South Africa, the official unemployment rate declined from almost 31 per cent to 26 per cent in October 2005.

11 The problem of job losses – which has been largely attributed to factors such as the strong rand, privatisation, and the failure to protect the economy from competition with heavily protected economies from both north and east as a result of globalisation – has been the main bone of contention between the ANC-led government and its Cosatu and Communist Party allies. The two left-leaning partners in the Tripartite Alliance want more state intervention in the labour market to ensure a social safety net; the macroeconomic policy, however, commits the government to a more flexible labour market.

centrally addresses the inclusion of previously marginalised groups. Through a series of legislative and administrative programmes the government continues to find ways of improving delivery in the areas of social security, education, welfare, health, housing and so on.[12] Social security, in the form of grants to older persons, children, and disabled people, has benefited families through the distribution of resources within the family and the alleviation of the costs of caring for dependants with special needs.

In South Africa, social assistance is provided in the form of: an old age grant; a disability grant; a war veterans grant; a care dependency grant; a foster child grant; a child support grant; and grants in aid and social relief of distress. Given their importance in the government's anti-poverty programme, social grants have received a major boost from the Department of Social Development with a projected expenditure of R20 billion in 2001/02. By February 2003, there were 5 620 802 beneficiaries of social grants, a figure which represented an increase of over 74 per cent over the last two years. Moreover, child support grants, which account for most of the rise in the number of social grants beneficiaries, increased from 348 532 to about 2.5 million between April 2000 and February 2003, a percentage increase of 2.1 per cent (DoSD 2003). According to the government's Social Cluster media briefing on 19 February 2003, 5.5 million people were receiving social grants. Over 95 per cent of older persons who were eligible are receiving grants and, as of October 2003, more than 3 million children were receiving the child support grant. The old-age grant was estimated to be worth about twice the median per capita income of African households (Case & Deaton 1998), and is used to purchase provisions within households, including the education of grandchildren.[13]

Even though the information available on the social and economic impact of HIV/AIDS on families and children in South Africa is very scanty, the epidemic represents another major challenge to the state, given the alarming rate at which individuals are infected. According to Shisana and Simbayi (2002), 11.4 per cent of South Africans (or 4.5 million people) are living with HIV/AIDS. Moreover, the study found that the highest prevalence rate of 15.6 per cent was in the age group of 15–49 years. In terms of gender, the prevalence rate for females was 12.9 per cent compared to a rate of 9.5 per cent for their male counterparts. In terms of race, the highest prevalence rate of 12.9 per cent was among Africans, compared to 6.2 per cent among white people.[14] In a follow-up to this study, all the indications are that both the incidence and prevalence rates continue to increase (Shisana et al. 2005). According to the latest study, the national HIV prevalence rate for persons aged 2 years and over is now 10.8 per cent with the rates for males and females being 8.2 per cent and 13.3 per cent respectively. In terms of race, the overall prevalence among African adults

12 As an administrative mechanism to ensure effective and efficient service delivery, the Mbeki administration has created the government clusters under the Presidency.

13 Old age pensions have been shown to be an important factor in the alleviation of poverty among older people and their households, and to promote the role of older people in social and economic activities (see, for example, Case & Deaton 1998; NCCPS 2001).

14 But, according to the study (Shisana & Simbayi 2002), this relatively low prevalence rate for white people in South Africa is considerably higher than countries with predominantly white populations such as the United States, Australia and France.

aged 15 to 49, who appear to be bearing the brunt of the burden of this disease, increased slightly from 18.4 per cent in 2002 to 19.9 per cent in 2005. Finally, of African females aged 15–49 years, the rate was 24.4 per cent (Shisana et al. 2005).

Furthermore, in an attempt to document the socio-economic impact on households affected by HIV/AIDS, a study by Smith et al. (1999) shows, among other things, how households cope with the financial impact of the epidemic. Based on a survey of 771 HIV/AIDS-affected households, the study revealed that affected households are on average spending a third of their income on medical care. Consequently, taking care of an AIDS-sick person is not only an emotional strain but also a major strain on household resources. According to Mampanya-Serpell (2000), the economic consequences of the HIV/AIDS pandemic at household level show that infected adults severely compromise household resources as their functional capacity to work and earn a living for their families is reduced, and their illness generates new financial demands to cover medical care, treatment and funeral expenses. All these factors threaten food security, healthcare and the education of surviving members of the household. These figures on the impact of the HIV/AIDS pandemic, coupled with the escalating rates of gender-based violence against women, which is highly correlated with the spread of the disease through new infections, pose a major challenge to the security of the state.

Moreover, according to the same study, household income falls by as much as two-thirds as a result of the impact of coping with the disease. Of the households surveyed, 29 per cent reported a change in household income through such mechanisms as reduced spending on necessities or cutting expenses on items such as clothing, electricity and other services (9 per cent) depending on the financial status of the family. Other indirect costs include travelling costs, travelling time and waiting time. A study by Kyazike et al. (1998) indicated that most individuals expressed concern about the difficulties they face in the care of AIDS-ill family members and were particularly worried about the reduction in family income, a situation which is most severe among already poor households as shown by other similar studies.

The demographic profile

Despite its appearance of omnipresence in social life, there appears to be a general consensus that the concept of race is exceedingly slippery. Even though contemporary theoretical views on race flow from understanding it as a social construction, and therefore situational, there are social scientists who treat race as a biological concept and therefore a fixed characteristic (for example, James 2001). In South Africa, because of the apartheid-induced Population Registration Act of 1950, the term *population group,* which has both social and biological connotations, has become the standard analytical concept in public discourse.[15] According to the 2001 South African population census, Africans are the largest group comprising 79.02 per cent of the total population. The African group is very diverse and of the 12 different major language groups in the country, nine of them are of African origin. White

15 The apartheid classification into 3, 4 or 17 named groups has been essentially maintained since 1994.

people constitute 9.58 per cent of the total population, and are descended from Dutch, English and other settlers who coalesced into a relatively homogenous group under the apartheid system. The third largest group is the coloured group comprising 8.91 per cent of the population. Coloured people are of mixed black and white ancestry and were given a separate racial status under apartheid. Asians comprise 2.49 per cent of the population and this category is composed primarily of persons from India and Pakistan, but includes people from a variety of Asian countries.

Aside from these four main population groups, South Africa has 11 official languages based on the 11 ethnic groups, made up as follows: Afrikaans 13 per cent; English 8 per cent; IsiNdebele 2 per cent; IsiXhosa 18 per cent; IsiZulu 24 per cent; Sepedi 9 per cent; Sesotho 8 per cent; Setswana 8 per cent; Siswati 3 per cent ; Tshivenda 2 per cent; and Xitsonga 4 per cent (Stats SA 2004). Thus South Africa is a multiracial, multi-ethnic society and, because of the racial policy of apartheid, the different racial and cultural groups have had differential access to the society's resources, with white people having had the greatest advantage. Differences in socio-economic resources such as education, income and household amenities, coupled with cultural preferences, have in turn affected both family structures and processes. For example, using a six-point additive index to analyse the 1999 October Household Survey in South Africa, the Department of Social Development (2003) found that African households possessed only two of six amenities compared to a median of four in coloured households and a median of six in Indian and white households. These amenities were flush toilet, telephone, electricity from the mains, refuse collection, tapped water, and ownership of a motor car.

Fifty-six per cent of the South African population lives in urban areas, while 44 per cent lives in rural areas (Jenkins & Wilkinson 2002; Stats SA 2004). But, with urbanisation have come rapid changes associated with increased pressure on employment, education, health, water supply, sanitation, housing, and transport facilities, especially among new migrants (Chetty 1992; Mathee & von Schirnding 1994; Meyer 1993; Seager 1994). For example, it is estimated that approximately half of all African people in urban areas live in informal housing (Dor 1994).

But at the same time large numbers of impoverished rural people depended and continue to depend completely on remittances from migrant workers. Some scholars have suggested that such a dependency may function to strengthen family ties (Gelderblom & Kok 1994). Smit (2001: 546), for instance, notes that culture plays a large role in the 'survival strategies to ensure that the oscillating nature of the migrant labour system does not completely uproot them from their traditional family life'. So, against this background of social, cultural, economic and political changes that have been taking place in the immediate period before and after the democratic transition, what is the state of families and households in the society?

Family in post-transition scholarship in South Africa

As the above review of family scholarship in South Africa in the pre-transition period and elsewhere illustrates, modernisation theory and different variants of it have been used quite extensively in South African family studies. However, this general interpretation of family and household change has been falsified on the basis of growing empirical evidence on living arrangements that has shown that the evolution of households is more complex than previously thought (see, for example, UN 1995). It has been demonstrated, for instance, that household size has not declined linearly with economic development. Several studies conducted in Latin America and other less developed societies have found that in the capitalist industrial sectors of these societies relatives often end up co-residing, and in the process forming complex family households, because they cannot afford to live separately (Friedman 1984; Selby et al. 1990; Schmink 1984).

In the ethnographic work by Stack (1974) in the city of Detroit in the United States, she found that multigenerational living was common among African-Americans as an adaptive strategy in the face of the extreme poverty faced by this ethnic group. More importantly, research has shown that throughout most of western Europe, the family had typically been closer to the nuclear than to the extended type for at least several centuries prior to the onset of industrialisation (Laslett 1983; Laslett & Wall 1972).

And, finally, as scholars like Kojima (1989) have argued, Japanese society remains strongly committed to multigenerational co-residence, due partly to cultural factors and partly to entrenched structures of economic, family and intergenerational obligations. In South Africa, the debate as to whether residents of 'traditional' African societies live in multigenerational households has centred on the so-called 'convergence' thesis of African and white family patterns and has argued, essentially, that far from African family patterns converging towards those of white families, Africans are still committed to extended family living (Murray 1987; Russell 1994, 2002; Siqwana-Ndulo 1998; Ziehl 1994). In fact, this is reminiscent of Goode's (1963) analytical distinction between the ideology of the nuclear family and the nuclear family itself. That is, while culturally Africans may have embraced the extended family system, the concrete conditions in the urban-industrial milieu may have compelled them to live in nuclear family units.[16] It is against this background of more nuanced family scholarship that we look at families and households in post-apartheid South Africa.

Defining family and household

The concepts *family* and *household* are two conceptually distinct terms, although in societies where the nuclear family system predominates, and the domestic group is co-terminous with the dwelling unit, there is a tendency on the part of scholars to use them interchangeably in the investigations of household structures and processes

---

16 It is because of this that some scholars have argued that the sole reliance on census and sample surveys which are not only limited in the limited substantive family issues they cover, but are also cross-sectional in nature, do not allow one to examine family process.

(see, for example, de Vos 1995). However, in the South African context, we can hardly paint an accurate picture of families by equating family with co-residence, for several reasons. First, South Africa is a multiracial and a multicultural society. Second, the majority of South Africans subscribe to a patrilineal kinship system that is based on unilineal descent. Amongst the several rules of family formation under this kinship system is patri-local residence, whereby upon marriage a woman does not only move to live with the husband's patri-kin, but is legally absorbed into this group (Russell 2002).

In addition to these cultural norms, several scholars have argued that in societies where gross inequalities between men and women persist, where extended families are maintained for reasons of cultural preference and survival in the face of poverty, and where migration, employment opportunities, and regional turbulence and war have resulted in the dispersal of families across national borders and stretched kinship networks across vast geographic space, the depiction of families as co-terminous with households or homesteads is problematic (Russell 2002; Seekings et al. 1990; Turner 2002). Moreover, even in societies where the nuclear family system predominates – and hence the domestic group or the family is likely to be co-terminous with the household – this might not always be the case because of the rapid changes in these societies. As the links between family and residence, or household, loosen – to such an extent that co-residence is no longer a defining feature of family – this situation challenges traditional approaches to family and household research, which tended to treat the family and household or homestead as co-terminous (Giddens 2000).

What is a family?

Given the problematic nature of the relationship between families and households even in societies which subscribe to the nuclear family ideal based on the conjugal unit, the question we pose in this introductory chapter is: What is family? Even though an adequate answer to this question is germane to a satisfactory examination of families and households, it continues to elude family scholars. And this task becomes even more problematic in a multicultural, multiracial, and modernising society like South Africa.

In an attempt to define the family, Rodgers and White (1993) have turned to developmental theory which, according to them, has traditionally been fairly clear about the components of the definition of a family. According to this formulation, first the family is a social group and second, a family social group is part of the institution of marriage and the family.

Thus, a family's roles and role relationships are constructed by institutional norms and the variations in this set of institutional norms frame these family relationships. On the basis of these considerations, White has suggested the following basic definition of the family: 'A family is an intergenerational social group organized and governed by social norms regarding descent and affinity, reproduction, and the nurturant socialization of the young' (1991: 7). Although this definition may not be adequate in light of current changes in society, its importance lies in the fact that it views the family as a social institution with both ideational and concrete dimensions.

Thus, one approach that has been used to address the definition of a family is to explicate assumptions about the family that tend to be taken for granted. William Goode is one scholar who has been quite emphatic about this multidimensional nature of the family institution. Goode (1963) draws an analytical distinction between the ideology of the conjugal family and the conjugal family itself, arguing that it is possible for the former to take root without the latter being in place. This distinction between the normative and concrete aspects of the family institution was clearly in his mind when Adegboyega (1994) outlined the following assumptions:

- The dominance of men in a family situation – men are the heads of families.
- It is the duty of the head to ensure the welfare of the members through the organisation of production and through the equitable distribution of resources among family members.
- Fathers, with mothers, have joint responsibility for their children's maintenance and upbringing.
- Parents support all of their children to some or other extent.
- When children are economically able, they will, in the absence of a formal social security system and even in conjunction with social security, provide for the economic welfare of parents.
- Family members reside together in the same household and function within a unified household economy.

Even though these are mere assumptions (which may or may not be true in the face of modern developments in domestic relations), the points outlined clearly show that the definition of the term 'family' has proven to be rather elusive. As a result of this difficulty, some family scholars have suggested using the term 'families' as a way of giving meaning to the shift in ideological positions and the empirical fact of diversity in domestic relationships (Berger & Berger 1983; Worsley 1977).

This critical revision, which is heavily influenced by Marxism, particularly the critical feminist scholarship variant of it, is credited with the current view that a family is what a group of people says it is; families are essentially self-defining. According to this view, families may be extended or multi-generational; nuclear families consisting of one or more parents and children; single parents with children; re-constituted families with step-parents and step-children; gay families, and so on (see for example, Bateman 1996; Edgar 1992; Goode 1964). Moreover, this critique suggests that a family need not necessarily consist of a legally married couple, and that such family patterns as illegitimacy, homosexual relationships, and adoptive families are not necessarily deviations.

But, despite these nuances, there appears to be a broad consensus that families are social groups that are related by blood (kinship), marriage, adoption, or affiliation with close emotional attachments to each other that endure over time and go beyond a particular physical residence. Thus, essentially, family groups share the following features: they are intimate and interdependent; they are relatively stable over time;

and they are set off from other groups by boundaries related to the family group such that one family is separate from another in a variety of ways. That is, families have an identity, which may change over time (Edgar 1992; Goode 1964). Moreover, a family is contextually defined. For example, my wife and my children form my family (of procreation), but my family includes my siblings and their descendants (of orientation) depending on the context in which I use the term.

What is a household?

Almost all social science disciplines have grappled with both the conceptual and empirical difficulties inherent in defining the structure and functions of the household, with each discipline approaching the subject on its own terms (Chen & Dunn 1996). For instance, since anthropologists have traditionally analysed the household chiefly through the prism of family, marriage and kinship they have been concerned about defining the relationship between the family and household.

On the other hand, because of economists' earlier focus on the individual as consumer and the firm as producer they have been primarily concerned with defining the household in relation to production and consumption, at the expense of the kinship group or the family. Finally, feminist scholars look at the household through the additional lens of gender, that is, through the socially defined and ascribed roles and relationships of men and women.

These disciplinary nuances have led to a situation where over the years three major models have become quite discernible in the literature with regard to household. The first is the unitary or cooperative model, which was popularised by Gary Becker in the 1960s and emphasises resource and labour time distribution within a household (Mattila-Wiro 1999). This model considers one person as representing the entire household and assumes that decisions within a household are made jointly and that the household maximises a single set of objectives for all its members. Viewed from this model, all household resources are pooled and social harmony without conflict is the main characteristic of the household (Ellis 1998; Mattila-Wiro 1999). Such a model would be more applicable in a traditional agrarian setting where the household is the unit of economic production, since 'production is carried out in the home or on the land adjacent to it, and all household members, often including children, contribute to productive activity' (UN 1995: 3).

In such a setting, the term household appears to be co-terminous with the family, where membership of the household may involve concentric circles of: (a) fulltime permanent residents; (b) relations with an unquestionable need to join and reside; (c) relations who cannot be refused hospitality for a limited stay; (d) relations who need to ask to be accepted into the unit. Thus from the sociological point of view at least, in such a setting the household also becomes a traditional institution for production, reproduction and child rearing. In fact, it is in this sense that the adjectives 'nuclear' and 'extended' are used to describe households, with the former referring to households consisting of a married couple and their unmarried children, or a single parent with unmarried children, while the latter comprises, in addition to a nuclear family unit, a broader set of kin and occasionally unrelated individuals like the life cycle servants in historical west Europe.

Moreover, the latter type of household can consist of two or more brothers and their wives and children as is the case in a joint family system (see Adams 1986). The increasing differentiation of society through the forces of modernisation has brought with it other models of the household. For example, the view that the household is a unit of economic production and hence consumption, was challenged by the emergence of the factory, which led to the separation of work from the home. And, as the industrial society gradually gives way to the so-called post-industrial society where services and information and communications technology predominate, production and consumption are further being moved away from the household.[17] Second, developments such as formal education, surrogate parenthood, childless marriages and childcare services have also challenged the conventional notion of the household as an institution of reproduction and child-rearing. These developments have led to the emergence of such non-cooperative models as the 'separate sphere bargaining model' which does not assume that household members enter into binding and enforceable contracts with each other. Rather, these models assume that individuals not only have differing preferences but also that they act as autonomous sub-economies. Moreover they assume that income is not pooled and that the net transfer between individuals is the only link between them. Informed by feminist scholarship, non-cooperative models assume that women and men have separate economies within a household: a wife's budget is separate from her husband's (see, for example, Alderman et al. 1995; Lundberg & Pollak 1993). The third development, which is not unrelated to the above developments in the literature on households, is that the notion that the household is co-terminous with the family has been challenged by the same and related modernising forces. In fact, in this regard anthropologists have been quite influential in contending that there is no necessary relation between the household and the family or the co-residence group or between units of collective production, consumption, investment, and ownership (for example, Goody 1996).

Moreover, at the empirical level, several scholars have observed that households can 'double up' in response to economic changes, as recent deterioration of economic conditions in several African and Latin American countries has demonstrated (UN 1995). Even in the United States, Ahlburg and DeVita (1992) have shown that the doubling up of families in the grandparents' home increased not only among single-parent families, but also among two-parent families in response to difficult economic conditions. This general trend towards a reconstitution of the extended or multi-generational family has been observed in places like the United Kingdom, where children are becoming independent of their parental home, on average, some ten years later than they did 30 years ago.

So, what is a household? In an attempt to standardise the concept of household, the UN recommended the following definition as a valid guide for both the 1980 and

---

17 Ironically, there appears to be a reversal in this trend as evidenced by the increasing tendency to work from home as a result of the availability of personal computers and laptops in the computer age.

1990 rounds of censuses (see for example, UN 1990). A household is:

> …either (a) a one-person household, that is, a person who makes provision for his or her own food and other essentials for living without combining with any other person to form a part of a multi-person household or (b) a multi-person household, that is, a group of two or more persons living together who make common provision for food and other essentials for living. (UN 1989: 4)

Two important functions of the household are underscored by the above definition of a household, namely that a household is a unit occupying all or part of a dwelling unit (the housing unit concept) and that it is a unit where persons share resources to provide members with food and other essentials for living (the housekeeping unit concept).

Despite these efforts made by the UN and other international statistical agencies to standardise the concept of household,[18] there are still variations in both the criteria stressed in defining the concept as well as in the wording used by countries, a situation which gives rise to the problem of comparability. For example, Keilman has demonstrated that while the dwelling unit concept alone might be sufficient for many studies in the housing field:

> all other things being equal, it gives a lower number of [small] households than the UN definition, since two or more households [according to the UN definition] which provide for their own housekeeping but which live in the same dwelling are counted as one household in the dwelling unit definition. (1995: 116)

In South Africa, the official statistical agency, Statistics South Africa, uses the UN's definition by defining as a household as consisting of:

> a person, or a group of persons, who occupy a common dwelling [or part of it] for at least four days a week and who provide themselves jointly with food and other essentials for living. In other words, they live together as a unit. People who occupy the same dwelling but who do not share food or other essentials were enumerated as separate households. For example, people who shared a dwelling, but who bought food and ate separately, were counted as separate households. (Stats SA 1996: 12).

From the above discussion of the definitions of household and family, we see that while often household and family are used as equivalent terms, they are not interchangeable, because whereas family members need to be related by blood or associated by marriage and adoption, members of households are not necessarily family members (UN 1995).

---

18 In fact, according to the UN (1989), by the time of the 1980 round of censuses, among the countries for which the definition of household was available, 83 had a definition that incorporated both the housekeeping and the housing unit concepts.

The aim of the present study

The foregoing depiction of the social structures of the country both before and after the democratic transition in 1994, and the existing body of knowledge with regard to the depiction of families and households relative to the two periods, is not meant by any means to focus attention on whether the society is associated with any particular family or household form. Rather, the aim has been to illustrate the importance of the symbiotic relationships between institutions that regulate domestic relations and those that govern other aspects of human existence which, together, form what is commonly known as the social structure of the society. In other words, social actors' simultaneous engagement in these different institutions of society is largely responsible for the observable processes of change and transformation in these institutions at any particular time.

Thus, the principal aim of the present study is to describe the social, economic and political changes that have taken place in South Africa since the political transition in 1994 and how such changes help us to understand family and household structures in the society. It is worthy of note that one of the interesting developments in the country since the democratic transition is the increasing availability of large-scale quantitative data sets in the country, especially, since the mid-1990s (see, for example, Seekings 2001). Clearly, the proliferation of such large-scale quantitative data as the two all-race population censuses, the 1994–1999 October Household Surveys, the 2000–2004 General Household Surveys, and the various Labour Force Surveys – all under the auspices of Statistics South Africa – has helped to offset the problem of scope, representivity, reliability and other methodological problems that beset earlier family studies in the country.[19] Moreover, the fact that policy-makers are increasingly requesting quantitative analysis and South African scholars' desire to reconnect with global academic networks are responsible for the increasing availability of quantitative data sets. And, besides the increasing availability of quantitative data sets, some family scholars are making continuing efforts to collect more ethnographic and longitudinal data because of their skepticism about the adequacy of quantitative and cross-sectional data to portray the dynamics of family life (for example, see Russell 2002 for a critique of quantitative studies of the family in southern Africa).

It is within the context of the broad socio-economic changes that have taken place in South Africa since the democratic transition and the simultaneous proliferation of quantitative data that have sought to capture such changes that the idea of the present study was conceived and written. The study is about families and households in post-apartheid South Africa and the chapters consist of descriptive and analytical work on family-related issues based on major national data sets in the form of population censuses and sample surveys that have been generated in the country since the democratic transition in 1994. To this effect, we make use of such data sets as the 10 per cent public use data from the 1996 and 2001 censuses, the 1994–99

---

19 This is no way meant to suggest that these recent data sets are completely bereft of methodological problems. Specifically, the fact that all of the above-mentioned data sets are cross-sectional constitutes a major limitation to their use in analysing such a dynamic processes as family and household structures.

October Household Surveys, the 2000–03 General Household Survey data series, the Labour Force Surveys, and the 1998 Demographic and Health Survey (DHS) data.

Thus, in our effort to paint a richer picture of families and households in the society, contributors were asked to be as flexible as possible and use data sources generated in the post-transition period. As already indicated, we are only too aware that the best means of capturing a phenomenon as dynamic as family life is through the use of longitudinal and or qualitative data sets; however, we also believe that the consistent manner in which some of the existing censuses and sample surveys have handled certain crucial family and household variables makes them useful time-series data which can be used to undertake the kind of descriptive work presented in this study.

The importance of such an undertaking and its timing cannot be overemphasised. For one thing, a study on families and households is sorely needed because, due to the fact that apartheid-induced policies excluded large sections of the population from the mainstream of the society, most data on families and households were unrepresentative of the population, especially the African majority. Second, the bulk of such family studies focused on a limited dimension of family life, namely the residential dimension or household composition. Yet, we know that as a major social institution, family life involves more than its composition; aspects of family life such as the incidence and the rate at which such central family events as marriage, childbearing, divorce, child survival, and family well-being are occurring were largely ignored.

In contemplating this work, we had two main types of audience in mind. The first audience is policy-makers. As a study of families and households in contemporary South Africa, it was intended to provide an assessment of the performance of society with regard to the welfare of the population. To the extent that most people live in families and households, we expected the study to make a valuable contribution toward assessing the performance of policy-makers with regard to the population's welfare by examining not only the rate at which families and households are being formed, but also the social and material resources and costs of families and households of different types in the population. This is especially so for those groups and communities that bore the brunt of apartheid's social engineering policies in the areas of housing, education, health care and employment. Thus, we hoped to provide empirical evidence about social and demographic dimensions of family and household lives that would form part of the growing knowledge base for the formulation and implementation of policies and programmes that seek to strengthen families and households in the society.

The monograph's second target audience is all students and practitioners of family life. As we have shown earlier in the review of family scholarship, even though some efforts were made to document family and household lives in the society before the watershed democratic transition, the dominance of ideological concerns rendered family scholarship in the pre-transition period anything but scientific. In other words, the Eurocentric view of social life that dominated social studies in general and family studies in particular during this period, is gradually giving way to the concept of cultural relativism or multiculturalism, whereby each cultural group in the society is accorded equal status.[20] Applied to the family, these developments have led to a more critical approach to family studies, an approach that simultaneously combines theory and methods to look critically at family and household structure and change. It was our expectation, therefore, that the present study would contribute immensely to the burgeoning literature on critical family scholarship in the society following the transition to democracy.

Specifically, in recent years serious doubt has been cast about the credibility of several such studies with regard to the structure and change of families and households. Second, even though we are still grappling with the problem to a limited extent, apart from the ideological preoccupations of many of these studies there were such methodological and logistical problems as coverage and hence the representivity of samples with regard to crucial socio-economic indicators. Following the establishment of the South African democracy, the need for all-inclusive social and economic data for the purposes of socio-economic planning has led to efforts by all levels of government and even the private sector to invest considerable resources in this endeavour.[21]

Organisation of the rest of the study

In line with our plan to look at families and households from multiple disciplinary perspectives, Chapter 2 looks at the theoretical framework of the entire work by examining selected theoretical approaches that scholars in the selected disciplines have used over the years to explicate family and household processes. Among the social science disciplines represented here are anthropology, economics, demography, and sociology, although this selection does not in any way suggest that such disciplines as history, political science or even geography have not dealt with issues of family and household. Specifically, such theoretical approaches as structural-functionalism, conflict theory, modernisation theory, demographic transition theory, the family life cycle and family life course theories are discussed within the context of the family and household.

In Chapter 3, the authors take up the issue of household types in the population and at the same time use the life course perspective to look at the living arrangements of children, young adults, adults and the elderly. Chapter 4 looks at the economic dimension of family and household life and, to that extent, examines such issues as changes in and sources of household income, employment patterns, the skip generation, housing and amenities available to the different segments of the population. Chapters 5 and 6 respectively deal with family formation and dissolution patterns in the population. Specifically, Chapter 5 discusses both the incidence and

---

20 Afrocentrism, which is an offshoot of this multiculturalist fervour, argues that Africans must not only be studied within the contexts of their cultures, but African scholars must be actively involved in this enterprise.
21 In fact, this was the *raison d'être* of the World Bank's sponsorship of the 1993–94 Integrated Household and Community Survey (SALDRU).

timing of marriage and divorce for males and females and for the different population groups, while Chapter 6 takes up the issue of fertility or childbearing. In Chapter 7, the authors discuss the neglected, yet important, issue of children's contribution to household work. Finally, in Chapter 8, the family is used as a context for the discussion of child survival or infant mortality in the population.

References

Adams BN (1986) *The family: A sociological interpretation* (4th edition). Orlando, Florida: Harcourt Brace Jovanovich Publishers

Adegboyega O (1994) The situation of families in East and Southern Africa. Unpublished manuscript

Ahlburg DA & DeVita CJ (1992) New realities of the American family. *Population Bulletin* 47(2). Washington D.C. Population Reference Bureau

Alderman H et al. (1995) Unitary versus collective models of the household: Is it time to shift the burden of proof? *The World Bank Research Observer* 10(1): 1–19

Altman M (2003) The state of employment and unemployment in South Africa. In J Daniel, A Habib & R Southall (Eds) *State of the Nation: South Africa 2003–2004*. Cape Town: HSRC Press

Ballard H & Schwella E (2000) The impact of globalisation on local government in South Africa. *Development Southern Africa* 17(5): 737–749

Bateman G (1996) Defining families for policy making. Paper presented at the AIFS Research Conference, 'Family Research: Pathways to Policy', Brisbane

Berger B & Berger P (1983) *The war over the family*. London: Hutchinson

Case A & Deaton A (1998) Large cash transfers to the elderly in South Africa. *The Economic Journal* 108(450): 1330–1361

Castells M (1999) *Information technology, globalization and social development*. UNRISD Discussion Paper No. 114, September

Central Statistical Services (1992) *1992 South African statistics*. Pretoria: Central Statistical Services

Chen MA & Dunn E (1996) *Household economic portfolios: Assessing the impact of micro enterprise services*. Office of Micro Enterprise Development, Economic Growth Center, Global Bureau, USAID

Chetty KS (1992) Urbanisation and health: Evidence from Cape Town. In DM Smith (Ed.) *The apartheid city and beyond: Urbanization and social change in South Africa* London: Routledge

Clark B & van Heerden B (1992) The legal position of children born out of wedlock. In S Burman & E Preston-Whyte (Eds) *Questionable issue: Illegitimacy in South Africa*. Cape Town: Oxford University Press

Daniel J, Habib A & Southall R (2003) *State of the nation: South Africa 2003–2004*. Cape Town: HSRC Press

DoSD (Department of Social Development, South Africa) (2003) *Social grants beneficiaries*. Available at http://www.welfare.gov.za

DoSD (2003) *Describing families for policy: Literature, archival and secondary research to support the development of family policy.* Pretoria: Human Sciences Research Council

De Vos P (1995) *Household composition in Latin America.* New York: Plenum Publishers

DoL (Department of Labour, South Africa) (2000). ILO report on the social impact of globalisation. *Annual Report to Parliament.*

Dor G (1994) New settlements, growing communities. *Critical Health* 46: 6–13

Economic Commission for Africa (2002) Economic report on Africa: Tracking performance and progress. Addis Adaba: UNECA

Edgar D (1992) Conceptualising family life and family policies. *Family Matters* 32: 28–37

Ellis F (1998) *Peasant economies, farm household and agrarian development.* New Castle: Cambridge University Press

Fedderke JW, Kadt RD & Luiz JM (2000) Uneducating South Africa: The failure to address the 1910–1993 legacy. *International Review of Education* 46(3/4): 257–281

Friedman K (1984) Households as income-pooling units. In J Smith, I Wallerstein & HD Evers (Eds) *Households and the world economy.* Beverley Hills, CA: Sage.

Gelderblom D & Kok P (1994) *Urbanization: South Africa's challenge. Volume 1: Dynamics.* Pretoria: HSRC

Giddens A (1987) *Sociology: A brief but critical introduction.* Orlando, Florida: Harcourt Brace Jovanovich Publishers

Giddens A (2000) *Runaway world: How globalization is shaping our lives.* New York: Routledge

Glenn ND (1977) *Cohort analysis.* Beverly Hills: Sage Publications

Goode WJ (1963) *World revolution and family patterns.* New York: The Free Press

Goode WJ (1964) *The family.* Harlow, Essex: Prentice Hall

Goode WJ (1982) *Explorations in social theory.* New York: Oxford University Press

Goody J (1996) Comparing family systems in Europe and Asia: Are there different sets of rules? *Population and Development Review* 22(1): 1–20

Hayter S (1999) Assessing the social impact of globalisation: Trade liberalisation and employment. *Trade and Industry Monitor* 9: 2–6

James A (2001) Making sense of race and racial classification. *Race and Society* 4: 235–247

Jenkins P & Wilkinson P (2002) Assessing the growing impact of the global economy on urban development in Southern African cities: Case studies in Maputo and Cape Town. *Cities* 19(1): 33–47

Keilman N (1995) Household concepts and household definitions in Western Europe: Different levels but similar trends in household developments. In EV Imhoff, A Kuijsten, P Hooimeijer & LV Wissen LV (Eds) *Household demography and household modelling.* New York and London: Plenum Press

Kojima K (1989) Intergenerational household extension in Japan. In FK Goldscheider & C Goldscheider (Eds) *Ethnicity and the new family economy.* Boulder, Colorado and San Francisco, CA: Westview Press

Kyazike AL, Namuyimbwa MN, Kajura CA, Mawanda GK, Senabulya M & Aboho A (1998) The effects of HIV/AIDS care on household resources in Uganda. Int conf AIDS 12:739 (abstract no. 34273), Taso Entebbe, Uganda

Laslett P (1983) Family and household as work group and kin group: Areas of traditional Europe compared. In R Wall, J Robin & P Laslett (Eds) *Family forms in historic Europe.* Cambridge: Cambridge University Press

Laslett P & Wall R (Eds) (1972) *Household and family in past time.* Cambridge: Cambridge University Press

Lombard JA (1978) *Freedom, welfare and order: Thoughts on the principle of political co-operation in the economy of Southern Africa.* Pretoria: Benbo (Bureau for Economic Research)

Lundberg S & Pollak R (1993) Separate spheres bargaining and the marriage market. *Journal of Political Economy* 101(6): 988–1010

Maconachie M (1989) Dual-earner couples: Factors influencing whether and when white married women join the labour force in South Africa. *South African Journal of Sociology* 20(3): 143–151

Mampanya-Serpell N (2000) HIV/AIDS and food and nutrition security. Available at http://www.ifpri.org/pubs/fpreview/pv07/pv07ch02.pdf

Marwick M (1978) Household composition and marriage in a Witwatersrand African township. In Argyle & W Preston W (Eds) *Social systems and tradition in Southern Africa.* Cape Town: Oxford University Press

Mathee A & Von Schirnding Y (1994) Environment and health in rapidly urbanising cities. *Critical Health* 46: 21–27

Mattila-Wiro P (1999) *Economic theories of the household: A critical review.* Tokyo: The United Nations University Press

Mazrui A (1986) *Africans: A triple heritage.* New York: Little Brown & Co

Mbeki T (2001) State of the Nation Address to Parliament. Cape Town, 9 February

Meyer C (1993) Migration patterns unravel the population, poverty, environment tangle. *Development* 1:12–16

Murray C (1987) Class, gender and the household: The developmental cycle in Southern Africa. *Development and Change* 24: 755–785

Naicker SM (2000) From apartheid education to inclusive education: The challenges of transformation. Paper presented at the International Education Summit for a Democratic Society, Wayne State University, Detroit, USA, 26–28 June

Nattrass N (2003) The state of the South African economy: A crisis of employment. In J Daniel, A Habib & R Southall (Eds) *State of the nation: South Africa 2003–2004.* Cape Town: HSRC Press

Nattrass N & Seekings J (2001) Two nations: Race and economic inequality in South Africa today. *Daedalus,* Winter: 45–70

NCCPS (2001) *Non-contributory pensions and poverty prevention in developing countries? A comparative analysis between South Africa and Brazil.* Available at http://idpm.man.ac.uk/ncpps/Papers/NCPPDleaflet1.pdf

Nzimande SV (1987) Family structure and support systems in black communities. In A Steyn, HF Strijdom, S Viljoen & F Bosman (Eds) *Marriage and family life in South Africa*. Pretoria: Human Sciences Research Council

Oberai AS (1991) *Population growth, employment & poverty in Third-World mega-cities analytical & policy Issues*. New York: St. Martin's Press

Okoth-Ogendo H (1989) The effect of migration on family structures in sub-Saharan Africa. *International Migration* 27: 309–317

Oppong C (1974) *Marriage among a matrilineal elite: A family study of Ghanaian civil servants*. London: Cambridge University Press

Pasha HA & Lodhi A (1994) Determinants of household formation in a Third World setting. *Urban Studies* 31(6): 947–957

Pauw BA (1953) *The second generation: The study of the family among urbanized Bantu in East London*. Cape Town: Oxford University Press.

Pick WM & Cooper D (1997). Urbanisation and women's health in Khayelitsha, Cape Town: An overview. *African Journal of Reproductive Health* 1(1): 45–55

Poswell L (2002) *The post-apartheid South African labour market: A status report*. Cape Town: Development Policy Research Unit, University of Cape Town

Preston-Whyte EM (1978) Families without marriage. In WJ Argyle & EM Preston-Whyte (Eds) *Social system and transition in Southern Africa*. Cape Town: Oxford University Press

Rodgers RH & White JM (1993) Family development theory. In PG Boss, WJ Doherty, R LaRossa, WR Schumm & SK Steinmetz (Eds) *Sourcebook of family theories and methods: A contextual approach*. New York and London: Plenum Press

Rogerson CM (1996) *Rethinking the informal economy in South Africa*. Development paper No. 84, Development Bank of Southern Africa, Halfway House

Russell M (1994) 'Do blacks live in nuclear family households? An appraisal of Steyn's work on urban family structure in South Africa. *South African Sociological Review* 6(2): 56–67

Russell M (2002) *Are urban black families nuclear? A comparative study of black and white South African family norms*. Centre for Social Science Research, Social Surveys Unit, Working Paper No. 17, University of Cape Town

Sampson A (1987) *Black and gold*. London: Hodder & Stoughton

Schmink M (1984) Household economic strategies: Review and research agenda. *Latin American Research Review* 19: 87–101

Seager JR (1994) Growing cities, new disease patterns: Urban health in the developing world. *Critical Health* 46: 14–20

Seekings J (2001) The uneven development of quantitative social science in South Africa. *Social Dynamics* 27(1): 299–312

Seekings J, Graaf J de V & Joubert P (1990) *Survey of residential and migration histories of residents of the shack areas of Khayelitsha*. Research Unit for Sociology of Development Occasional Paper No. 15, University of Stellenbosch

Selby HA, Murphy, AD & Lorenzen SA (1990) *The Mexican urban household*. Austin: University of Texas Press

Shisana O, Rehle T, Simbaye LC, Parker W, Zuma K, Bhana A, Connolly C, Jooste S, Pillay V et al. (2005) *South African national HIV prevalence, HIV incidence, behaviour and communication survey 2005*. Cape Town: HSRC Press

Shisana O & Simbayi LC (2002) Nelson Mandela/HSRC Study of HIV/AIDS. Cape Town: HSRC Press

Simkins C (1986) Household composition and structure in South Africa. In Burman S & Reynolds P (eds) *Growing up in a divided society*. Johannesburg: Raven Press

Simkins C & Dlamini T (1992) The problem of children born out of wedlock. In S Burman & E Preston-Whyte (Eds) *Questionable issue: Illegitimacy in South Africa*. Cape Town: Oxford University Press

Siqwana-Ndulo N (1998) Rural African family structure in the Eastern Cape Province, South Africa. *Journal of Comparative Family Studies* 29: 407–417

Smit R (2001) The impact of labour migration on African families in South Africa: Yesterday and today. *Journal of Comparative Family Studies* 32: 44–58

Smith M, Solanki G & Kimmie Z (1999) *The Second Kaiser Family Foundation survey of health care in South Africa*. Pretoria: The Health Systems Trust

Stack CD (1974) *All our kin: Strategies for survival in a black community*. New York: Harper & Row

Statistics South Africa (1996) *Census 1996: An overview*. Pretoria: Stats SA

Statistics South Africa (2004) *Census 2001: Community Profiles*. Pretoria: Stats SA

Steyn AF (1993) *Gesinnstrukture in die RSA. Co-operative Research Programme in Marriage and Family Living*. Pretoria: Human Sciences Research Council Report HG/MF-4

Steyn AF, Strijdom HG, Viljoen S & Bosman FJ (1987) *Marriage and family life in South Africa: Research priorities*. Pretoria: HSRC

Terreblanche SJ (1999) The ideological journey of South Africa: From the RDP to the GEAR macro-economic plan. Religion in public life. University of Stellenbosch

Turner L (2002) Book review: Anthony Giddens, Runaway world: How globalization is reshaping our lives. *Transcultural Psychiatry* 39: 394–415

UN (1989) *Demographic Yearbook 1987*. Sales No. E/F. 88.XIII.1 New York: United Nations

UN (1990) *Supplementary principles and recommendations for population and housing censuses*. Series M, No. 67/Add. 1 New York: UN Statistical Office

UN (1995) *Living arrangements of women and their children in developing countries: A demographic profile*. New York: UN Department for Economic and Social Information and Policy Analysis Population Division

UNDP (United Nations Development Programme, South Africa) (2003) *The Challenge of Sustainable Development*. Pretoria: UNDP

White JM (1991) *Dynamics of family development: The theory of family development*. New York: Guildford

Wilson F & Ramphele M (1989) *Uprooting poverty*. Cape Town: David Philip

Worsley P (1977) Introducing sociology (2nd edition). Harmondsworth: Penguin

Ziehl SC (1994) Social class variation in household structure: The case of a small South African city. *South African Journal of Sociology* 25(1): 25–34

CHAPTER 2

Towards a conceptual framework for families and households

Acheampong Yaw Amoateng

Introduction

In this chapter we put the entire work in a broader conceptual framework by looking at selected theoretical perspectives, propositions and approaches that the social science disciplines represented in this study have used to elucidate family and household structures and processes. Specifically, the chapter provides an overview of selected theoretical perspectives that family and other scholars in these and other related social science disciplines have employed to organise the growing and disparate empirical data on families and households in South Africa. Since a family is an example of social institutions, we begin the chapter with a brief look at the term *social institution,* by employing the 'organismic' analogy, which has been prominent in sociology. In this analogy, society or a social system is viewed as any other organism with different parts performing different functions to ensure the survival of the whole organism. In the case of a social system, these different parts are called social institutions. Classic examples of social institutions are: political institutions like the government, courts and parliament; financial institutions like banks and credit bureaus; and cultural institutions like schools and churches. To this effect, a social institution has been defined as:

> An interrelated system of social roles and norms organized about the satisfaction of an important social need or function…the social roles and norms comprising the social institution define proper and expected behavior oriented to the fulfillment of the particular social need such as the provision of food and other material goods. (Theodorson & Theodorson 1969: 206–207)

To understand a social theory in general, and family theory in particular, two issues with regard to the above definition of a social institution are significant. First, it means that the individual interacts with other individuals in a variety of institutions. Second, the definition suggests that every social institution has two dimensions, namely, the ideational/normative and behavioural dimensions with regard to the roles and actions that lead to the fulfilment of particular social needs. A norm is 'a patterned or commonly held behaviour expectation or learned response held in common by members of a group' (Bates 1956: 314). Thus, norms are the basic structural building blocks for all groups, including the family group (Rodgers & White 1993). In other words, as the concrete actors within these social institutions, these groups of individuals or the social collective are tied to one another by virtue of shared traditions. A pioneering work that illustrated the distinction between the ideal and statistical norms with regard to the family as a social institution is that of Paul Glick at the United States Bureau of the Census. As far back as 1947, Glick had used the United States population census to compare life cycle stages of families in 1890 and those in 1940, by estimating median ages of couples at first marriage, birth and marriage of the last child, and death of each spouse. In employing the family life cycle concept to study family trends, Glick had divided the history of the family into six main stages – formation, extension, completed extension, contraction, completed contraction and dissolution. These stages corresponded to seven family events – marriage, birth of the first and last child, departure of the first and last child from home, death of first spouse, and death of surviving spouse.

In anthropology, a similar notion, the 'domestic life cycle', was used to draw attention to the changing nature of households over the life course. In this scheme, the main stages were expansion, dispersion and replacement (see, for example, Goody 1958; Fortes 1970). The distinction between professed family ideology and actual family behaviours as illustrated by notions of family and domestic life cycles also found expression in Laslett's work when he formulated what he *perceived* as the essential elements of the West European family (1977: 13–20). Elements of the western European family identified included the popularity of nuclear/simple family households in conjunction with a relatively late age at marriage; relatively late age at childbearing with minimal age differences between husband and wife with a relatively high proportion of wives older than their husbands; and the presence of a significant proportion of life cycle servants in the households of, especially, the rich. Writing with the two dimensions of the family institution in mind, Goode has noted a distinction between the ideology of the conjugal family and the conjugal family itself, arguing that it is possible for the former to take root without the latter being in place; norms are the bases for predicting future family change (Goode 1970/1963: xiii). According to Goode, it is possible, in principle, for a society or a group within it to ascribe to the values associated with the conjugal family system, namely individual choice in marriage, egalitarian marital relationships and so on, and yet live in domestic situations that are very different from the conjugal family itself.

Russell (2002) employs the distinction between family ideology and family behaviours to distinguish the kinship system of societies of northern Europe on the one hand, and those of Southern Africa on the other. With regards to the west European family system, she notes two outstanding characteristics. First, the family household experiences a predictable developmental cycle from *establishment* (the couple), through *consolidation and expansion* (the bearing of children) to *fission* (adult children leave home to acquire independent means of subsistence while they search for a mate). At this juncture *decline* sets in. The original household diminishes, until ultimately only a single person is left (who may remarry or be reincorporated into an offspring's home). Second, marriage is only as durable as the mutual satisfaction of the contracting couple, especially the mutual sexual satisfaction. If being *in love* is the sign for marriage to take place, *not being in love* is the sign for marriage to end. In contrast to black South Africans, whose patrilineal kinship system is based on a unilateral descent, Russell (2002) notes certain unique features of the family system.

First, descent is through the father and the idea of a patrilineally-linked descent group informs people's householding behaviour, determining who may and may not live together, marry, bear children together, expect reciprocity. Second, marriages, which are ideally between mature men and younger women, are arrangements between kin groups within different lineages; bride wealth from one is exchanged for a bride from another. Third, since polygyny is the ideal form of marriage, it is always legitimate for men to be courting potential new wives; women bear children for their husband's lineage, so it is important that they live with his kin, in order that the children can be brought up properly.

Several family scholars have expressed dissatisfaction with this 'ideal typical' western and African family pattern as identified by Russell. Generally, these scholars have argued that while the cyclical assumption carried with it the comfort of a predictable and regular pattern to family histories, the empirical evidence pointed to families that varied widely in the paths they took, a problem which compelled the human development theorists to adopt the term 'life course' to deal with the experience of individuals. With regard to the depiction of the western family system, Rodgers and White (1993) have argued that such a view of the family was most certainly pro-marriage, pro-natal, pro-nuclear family, tended toward a class and ethnic bias and failed to recognise divorce, premature deaths of children and adults, remarriage, stepfamilies, or unemployment and other work life variations. And, feminist scholars in both economics and anthropology have criticised this view of the family by generating and presenting first systematic empirical evidence not only of economic conflict and inequality within the household (Barrett 1980; Harris 1981; Mackintosh 1979; Whitehead 1981), but also of gender differences in the allocation of time, resources, and power within the household.

Specifically, feminist scholars have called into question the universality and stability of the conjugal unit. They argue that even in those regions and among social groups where marriage is near universal, women may spend a considerable portion of their lives without a spouse in residence. They found, for example, that from the 1970s to the 1980s, the proportion of households headed by women rose from 11.5 per cent to 17.3 per cent in Morocco, 12.5 per cent to 21.6 per cent in Thailand, 20.7 per cent to 26.1 per cent in the Dominican Republic, and 14.7 per cent to 19.5 per cent in Peru (Reported by K Ono, United Nations, cited in Bruce, Lloyd & Leonard 1995). In South Africa, it is a well established fact that as a result of the higher rates of participation in the migrant labour system by African men, desertion and lower rates of marriage, the conjugal unit amongst Africans is unstable. According to estimates derived from the 2001 census, nationally 16 per cent of husbands live apart from their wives. And, of this, over one-fifth of African husbands live apart from their wives compared with 6 per cent, 6 per cent and 4 per cent of coloured, Indian, and white husbands respectively. Vogel (2003) has observed large differences between nations in the European Union with regard to demographic behaviour such as the size of families, the timing of the move from the parental home, the timing and spacing of partnerships, the timing of fertility, dissolution of partnerships and the elderly living in extended families. According to him, these differences reflect not only *family traditions* (social practice), but also variation in the current opportunity structure offered by the other welfare institutions. For example, he found that young adults move out of the parental home much later in the South and Ireland and much earlier in the Nordic countries, as compared to the intermediate central European countries. Moreover, he found that the proportion of unemployed adults included in parental households varied between some 13 per cent in Norway and 78 per cent in Italy.

In sub-Saharan Africa, Adegboyega (1994) has observed that the typical African family pattern of early and universal marriage is not observed in most southern African countries because of the migratory labour system. According to him, the need to participate in this economic activity takes mainly black men in the marriageable ages away from the marriage market, leading to such family patterns as late marriage and low incidence of marriage in the region. And, writing about southern African societies, Russell (2002) has noted the ambivalence of the social change that has taken place in these societies with regard to the rules of family formation. Specifically, she argues that despite the verbal commitment of urban black people to the nuclear family ideology, the descent-based consanguinal system of the African family has adapted well to the harsh demands of modern-urban industrial conditions leading to an array of householding arrangements, a fact which was supported by Seekings, Graaf and Joubert (1990) who found in a survey of Cape Town that what constituted a 'household' included people not sleeping under the same roof.

A review of family and household theories

In this section we outline some of the main theoretical orientations of families and households. If society is an interrelated set of institutions and institutions are systems of roles and norms that regulate social interaction, we can define a theory broadly as a set of propositions that purport to explain a social phenomenon. Writing from the demographic point of view, Burch (1995: 86) defines a theory as 'general statements about social, economic, cultural, and demographic interrelations, or about the behavioural underpinnings of demographic events'. A similar definition is provided by Ryder (1992: 162) from the point of view of formal demography: '...the deductive study of the necessary relationships between quantities serving to describe the state of a population and those serving to describe changes in that state, over time, in abstraction from their association with other phenomena'. The importance of these definitions of a theory lies in the fact that the characteristics which a family and household system may assume at any particular point in time are determined by political, demographic, economic, ecological and cultural factors (Adegboyega 1994; Laslett 1979; Wall 1995).

The arrival of the industrial-capitalist revolution marked a paradigm shift in family theorising from one dominated by traditional beliefs and philosophical speculations to one characterised by the use of the scientific method with its rigorous methodology (see, for example, Boss et al. 1993; Christensen 1964). The increased rationalisation of society led to the systematisation and formalisation of family theory, since the social group termed variously as the *family, household* or *domestic unit* continued to be regarded as one of the basic constituent institutions of the capitalist world economy (Martin & Beittel 1987). The end product of this process of systematisation and formalisation was the rebirth of two prominent, sociological theoretical traditions that have been used to analyse family structure and process, namely, structure-functionalism and Marxist conflict theory. These two broad theoretical traditions have been the point of departure for several sub-theories, or what Merton (1967) referred to as 'middle-range' theories of the family and household to distinguish them from their parent theories which were *grand* in terms of their levels of abstraction.

Structure-functionalism and the family

Even though several scholars in sociology and anthropology contributed to the development of functionalism as a theoretical perspective in the family field, the scholar who is regarded as the most 'modern' advocate of the structure-functionalist school of thought is the American sociologist, Talcott Parsons. In his first major work, *The Structure of Social Action* (1937), Parsons sought to weave together various strands of thought which viewed human action as goal-directed; as involving the selection of appropriate means among alternatives; as regulated by ideas; and as being circumscribed by physical-biological parameters.[1] But his real contribution to functionalism occurred after 1945 when he recognised the fact that actors do not exist in isolation from each other, but rather interact within social systems (Parsons 1951). This line of thought logically led to Parsons' contribution to family sociology during this period. For instance, he argued that the family is not an independent society but rather a subsystem of society, and that familial roles interpenetrate with roles in other societal structures. Moreover, Parsons viewed the nuclear family as a consequence of differentiation on the two axes of hierarchy/power and instrumental/expressive functions.

Expectedly, this evolutionary view of the family led to a popular generalisation in family sociology that, as a society industrialises and urbanises, the extended family withers away (see also Kephart 1966; Kirkpatrick 1963; United Nations Statistical Office 1959). Burch (1967) has noted that within societies this generalisation is taken to mean that extended families predominate in rural than in urban areas, while cross-culturally extended families are more prevalent in under-developed than in developed societies. Following Parsons, Goode (1970) wrote about the homogenising effects of industrial capitalism with regard to family patterns. Specifically, Goode's position was that the penetration of capitalist ethos around the world had led to the nucleation of the family in western and non-western societies alike.

Although structure-functionalism in general, and Parsons' contribution in particular, has been accused of conservative bias, the *systemic* view of society it emphasises, which also underscores Parsons' attempt at building a general theory of action, certainly represents one of the strengths of the theory since, as already mentioned, it forms the basis of several theories in sociology and other disciplines, especially psychology.[2]

---

1 This seemingly ambitious project led to a charge of 'grand theorising' by scholars like C Wright Mills (1959).
2 It is important to note that Parsons incorporated several intellectual traditions, notably, Freud's psychoanalytic theory. For instance, he argues in *The Social System* that the process of personality development is linked to the family structure, because the most essential feature of the oral dependency phase is the child's attachment to one or a class of social objects of which the mother is the prototype (Parsons 1951).

For example, by positing a functional relation between the family and other societal institutions, he underscores the fact that as they evolve, family and community structures adapt to the physical and social conditions of production. Several western scholars have used this systemic view of society to trace the source of recent family changes to the economic and political changes that are sweeping the world under the rubric of globalisation and democratisation (see for example, Castells 1997; Fukuyama 1999; Giddens 2000).

The egalitarian ethos in marital relationships and the gradual disappearance of the conventional nuclear family of a man, his wife and their dependent children, and the emergence of varied family forms throughout the world are traced to such economic and technological changes as the development and spread of modern communication technology. For example, changes such as mechanisation, electric power and access to higher education have all helped to reduce dependence on human muscle power and an expansion of employment opportunities for women and men alike, high labour mobility and relative increase in real wages. Moreover, these economic and political changes have in turn led to concomitant changes in the family in the form of higher rates of divorce, single-hood, childless marriages, postponement of marriage and childbearing – patterns which challenge the normative, patriarchal view of the family. However, not everybody agrees that this depiction of the family applies equally well in all parts of the world. For example, Turner (2002) has argued that the above depiction of the family does not apply in situations where, as a result of poverty, culture, migration, employment opportunities, wars and regional conflicts, the extended family is the preferred living arrangement.

This systemic view of the family has not lacked its proponents elsewhere in Africa. It has been observed that most herders and pastoral nomads tend to have patriarchal families and a tendency toward monogamy, while women's productive work tends to be limited to herding small animals, dairying, and food processing and preparation (see for example, Adegboyega 1994). Several scholars over the years have used the same approach to explain various family and household formation and dissolution patterns and other demographic phenomena in different cultures. For example, economic factors, specifically poverty, have been implicated in the formation of extended family households among African-Americans in the United States (see, for example, Stack 1974). Also, as Kammeyer and Ginn (1986) have observed, although political actions and events may at first glance seem far removed from demographic events, they often have profound effects on demographic behaviours, as, for example, governmental policies in the areas of housing and health can influence birth and death rates (Burch 1995; Oakley 1978).

In South Africa, a critical examination of family scholarship, at least until the early 1990s, reveals that the predominant theoretical approach posited a functional relationship between families and society, whereby families are seen as performing functions such as the socialisation of children, sexual and reproductive control, economic co-operation, social support, and so on, in ways that co-ordinate with broader social and political goals. Within this context, family theory and research from the middle to the late twentieth century can be understood in terms of its ideological roots. For instance, the independent and isolated nuclear family commonly identified with western societies was idealised. Family theory and research sought to define as *a family* a social unit that comprised a husband, his wife, and their dependent children living in the same dwelling. In several ways, the evolutionist-functionalist model of the family was used to justify the apartheid status quo through its commitment to western ideas about family life.

Through the prism of this ideological lens, the African family was portrayed as a morally declining institution, which deviated from the nuclear family in terms of two key defining features – marriage and co-residence of members. As a result, research on black families tended to focus on 'dysfunctional' family patterns such as polygamy, extramarital sexual relations, illegitimacy, delayed marriage, teenage pregnancy, and female-headed households. One pervasive view in the family literature was the so-called 'convergence' thesis, which argues, rather paternalistically, that the family patterns of black people are converging towards those of their white counterparts as black people are increasingly being exposed to urban-industrial conditions through migration and employment in the modern sectors of the economy (Amoateng 1997; Pauw 1963; Preston-Whyte 1978; Steyn et al. 1987; Steyn 1993a, 1993b). It was in the same spirit of functional analysis that Maconachie (1989) observed that the increase in white women's labour force participation rates was due to the declining security which marriage provided them.

Moreover, the relatively late age at first marriage and its resultant low marriage rates among Africans in southern Africa compared to their counterparts in other sub-Saharan countries have been attributed largely to their participation in the migratory labour system in the region (Adegboyega 1994; Bozzoli 1991).

The 'liberal' critique of structure-functionalist theory of the family

Even though structure-functionalism, as theorised especially by Parsons, made an important contribution to the family studies literature, this mode of analysis came under sustained attack from the late 1950s onwards, on several grounds, by scholars to the left of the ideological spectrum (for example, Mills 1959).[3] Branding the functionalist model of family change as conservative, critique has been mounted on both theoretical and methodological grounds. Specifically, in terms of the family, critics charge that functionalism not only seeks to idealise the western isolated nuclear family vis-à-vis other family forms, but also within the family it justifies inequalities between the sexes as well between the generations. Besides the ideological problem of political conservatism, functionalism's account of the evolution of the nuclear family system in western societies has been found wanting on historical grounds. Based on the analysis of parish records on births and deaths in several northern and western European countries in the sixteenth and seventeenth centuries, scholars from the Cambridge School of Historical Demography have contended that the nuclear family has always

---

3 Collins (1988) has argued that in his efforts to revive functionalism through his 'Neo-functionalist project', Jeffrey Alexander (1985) is interested in teasing out from Parsons hints of his early interest in conflict derived from Weber.

been the dominant domestic unit amongst westerners and that the so-called extended family, which according to the functionalists was the modal type in the past, is a myth (Laslett 1983; Laslett & Wall 1972). Moreover, some scholars have observed that in pre-industrial societies the extended family was more common in urban than in rural areas, while others have still argued that economic and demographic constraints ensured that in no society could the extended family become the modal type (for example, Hsu 1943; Sjoberg 1960).

A fundamental problem with the structure-functionalist view of the family is the very narrow operational definition of the term it adopted. Several scholars have tried to overcome this limited view of the family implied by functionalism. For example, defining family as an 'aggregate comprising of persons related to one another by blood or marriage', Burch (1967: 348) suggested two types of family, namely the *family of residence* and the *family of interaction*, a distinction which simultaneously overcomes the ethnocentrism implicit in the Parsonian view and highlights the multidimensional nature of the family as a social institution. But still, Burch realised that this definition of the family was problematic as he expressed in the following statement: 'But it does not include all persons so related, and sometimes includes persons who are treated as if they were so related, as in adoption or fictive kinship practices' (Burch 1967: 348).[4] In seeking to clarify these dimensions of the family with the terms *conjugal, consanguineal*, and *residential*, this is what Ryder had to say:

> Residential distribution of personnel is implicit in the dual character of the family. Because it is a descent unit, it is exposed to the vagaries of demographic processes; because it is a residential unit, its cross-sectional composition must make economic sense day to day. (1992: 169)

In South Africa, the structure-functionalist paradigm of the family began to shift as the challenge to the apartheid state gathered momentum from the late 1970s onwards, reaching its apogee in the early 1990s. For analytical purposes, this period can be characterised as one of Marxist critique because of its underlying conflict orientation of family scholarship. Several writers have contested what is called the rhetoric of black family breakdown (Barrow 2001) and the portrayal of the black family as an illegitimate white family (Nobles 1979). Moreover, functionalist-inspired family scholars in South Africa have often fallen into the same trap as their European counterparts with their assertion that black family patterns are converging towards those of white families. Apart from the fact that the bulk of such studies of supposed 'family' patterns of black people were based on census or survey data on 'households', the value of the studies was circumscribed by the use of mainly urban samples (for a critique of these studies, see Ziehl 2001).[5]

---

4 Burch acknowledges the fact that even this definition of the family does not entirely avoid the ambiguity that the functionalist view presents, since 'different nuclear families may live in separate dwellings that are very close, even adjacent, to one another' (1967: 348). In fact Burch was merely re-echoing Murdock's (1965: 2) description of the patrilocal extended family: 'Three generations, including the nuclear families of father and sons, live under a single roof or in a cluster of adjacent dwellings.'

5 Burch (1995) has argued that empirical work in the area of household/family structure based on census data faces serious problems because of the lack of detail in such data on families. He recommends Todd's (1985) geographically broader and even more refined typology based largely on ethnographic data.

Other scholars used the same sources of data and found that African families were not evolving into an assumed universalistic nuclear form with modernisation in a linear and unproblematic way (Murray 1987; Russell 1994; Siqwana-Ndulo 1998; Ziehl 1994). Both structure-functionalism and conflict theory have contributed immensely to family studies through works by sociologists and anthropologists and demographers. Even though demography per se deals with a limited number of variables – fertility, mortality, and migration – because of the interrelationships between these central variables and the social, economic, political, cultural, and even ecological organisation of society, most of the existing theories in sociology and the other social sciences have been used to explain demographic phenomena.

For instance, Adegboyega (1994) examined family formation patterns among several sub-Saharan African countries and observed that among some pastoral groups in eastern Africa, like the Masai of Kenya, the family tends to be nucleated, while among the more sedentary agricultural groups in West Africa, the extended family system appears to be the norm. Moreover, Laslett (1979) observed that increases in fertility and nuptiality and decreases in mortality raise the possibility of the co-residence of parents and married children, while improvements in the standard of living may reduce the necessity of such co-residence and cultural changes may make it less desirable. And, it has been observed that the decline in mortality in the developed countries was the direct result of the improved standards of living that accompanied industrialisation, while the historic decline in fertility is generally attributed to a complex set of factors related to economic development and societal modernisation (Mckeown 1976; UN 1973). Kuijsten (1995) has argued that since the middle of the 1960s there has been a third phase of the demographic transition which has occasioned several other changes in demographic behaviour that were not foreseen in the original model of demographic transition, and thus merit a separate concept called the 'second demographic transition'.

Van de Kaa (1988) has identified three dimensions based on the consequences of the mutual influences of *structural factors* that flow from the completion of the post-industrial society and the welfare state such as increased standard of living, social security, functional differentiation, social and occupational mobility, education, and female labour force participation; *cultural factors* such as a decrease of social inequalities, an increase in personal freedom and in democracy, value pluralism, individualisation and secularisation (Becker 1990; Inglehart 1977); and *technological factors*, including the introduction of effective contraceptive methods, and improvements in the means of transport, communication, and health care.

Writing about the European experience with regard to the causes of the shifts in household size distributions, Höpflinger (1991) distinguishes three factors affecting several changes in family and household structures:
- basic demographic changes observed in almost all European countries in the field of declining fertility levels combined with higher life expectancies, resulting in substantial population ageing;
- the rapid and sometimes spectacular shifts in family formation; and
- the increasing number of family dissolutions and reconstitutions.

One conceptual development in demography that has impacted on family studies is demographic modeling or Population Studies Type II in Kammeyer and Ginn's (1986) schema. In this line of work, instead of using socio-economic variables to explain demographic patterns like family and household formation and dissolution through the central demographic processes, family demographers have modeled the interrelations between the basic processes of fertility, mortality and migration and the formation, change, and dissolution of various family and household units (Bongaarts 1983; Burch 1995; Burch & Matthews 1987; Coale & McNeil 1972; Krishnan & Kayani 1976; Rogers & Castro 1981). For instance, Wall (1983) has shown that some earlier changes in the composition of the household, especially the increase in the number of resident children in eighteenth-century Europe, were due to the fall in marriage rate and the consequent increase in fertility.

And Burch (1967), by using age-standardised measures of the propensity to form households, demonstrated that the measure *average household size* is largely a reflection of fertility rather than household complexity. He has observed that family demography has been a leading beneficiary of the increasing availability of event history data and of the development of multi-state demographic techniques for their analysis. Also, Goodman et al. (1974) estimated kin numbers in a stable population given assumed levels of fertility and mortality, noting a strong dependence of numbers of kin on fertility, for all categories of kin, except ascendants in the direct line. This set of techniques has come to be known as the 'life course perspective'. Because of sociologists' and especially family demographers' concern with change, in recent years there has been increased emphasis on the development of more process-oriented frameworks such as the life course perspective and its accompanying dynamic statistical methods (see for example, Elder 1978; Hogan 1978b; Tuma & Hannan 1984). In a similar effort to describe family and household theories, De Vos (1995) calls this type of study the *American* approach and traces it to the pioneering work of Glick (1947, 1957) on the family life cycle to the continuing work of Sweet and Bumpass (1987, 1989) with regard to the analysis of the United States census data and their involvement in longitudinal sample surveys that collect and facilitate the analysis of event history data.

Because change implies temporal patterning, the dimension of time and time-based concepts such as sequence, duration, and transition of family and household events have become central to the life course perspective. The life course is historical by its very nature as a result of its origins in the sociology of ageing, the concept of cohorts and from the life history traditions in sociology and social psychology (Elder 1978). Events and associated changes in status provide the elementary building blocks for a conceptualisation of the family life course. Of particular concern to the life course perspective are the timing and sequence of events that are considered central to the family and household (Elder 1978). The life course addresses the issue of how people plan and organise their roles over their lives and how they time their life transitions on both the familial and non-familial levels in areas such as entering and leaving school, joining or quitting the labour force, leaving the parental home, migration, marriage, and parenthood (see, for example, Hareven 1978). Even though timing and occurrence are two aspects of the same process, timing is not a unitary concept, since different aspects of timing must be taken into account depending on the nature of the events in question. Age is the primary indicator of both the biological and social time of the individual life course. Socially defined roles are age graded and events are expected to occur within normatively specified age ranges (Heaton 1987).

Thus, the age at which events such as leaving the parental home, marriage, birth, divorce, migration and so on occur is the most commonly analysed aspect of timing, since the timing of the occurrence of such events has profound implications for the individual's future trajectory. Moreover, the collective timing of these events helps to define the nature of the family as a social institution. The life course perspective enables one to look at the duration both within and between events. Within event domains, duration within a given status such marriage is an important characteristic of the family. For instance, a marriage lasting a couple of years is very different from one lasting 30 or 40 years. Moreover, a one-year birth interval defines a very different family or household structure than a four-year birth interval. Across events domains, duration between marriage and first birth has important implications for the parenthood role and for early financial demands placed on parents. Ordering and sequencing are closely related to duration between events. In some cases events tend to occur simultaneously. For example, as Heaton (1987) has observed, marriage, formation of a new household, and initiation of sexual activity defined the creation of the normative (ideal) nuclear family in the United States for several decades. Thus, events such as cohabitation, unwed motherhood, and premarital sex describe sequences which do not conform to a normative pattern. Age, duration, and sequence are concepts that apply primarily to individuals and the individual thus is the primary unit of analysis. However, the term family indicates a collectivity. To this effect, synchronisation is the term used to describe the correspondence of time paths for individual family members. In cases such as marriage, divorce and marital birth, the event is experienced by husband and wife simultaneously and synchronisation is not problematic. Thus, the life course perspective provides a theoretical orientation for our understanding of the link between family time, individual time and historical time. Its influence on family history has been most powerful in three major areas: synchronisation of individual transitions and collective family changes; the interaction of both individual and collective family transitions with historical conditions; and the impact of earlier life transitions on later ones.

Conclusion

Our aim in this chapter has been to outline the theoretical framework for the examination of families and households in post-apartheid South Africa. The essence of the chapter is that family studies as an academic discipline is relatively young and therefore has had to borrow heavily from such established disciplines as sociology, anthropology, history, economics, and demography. In line with this multidisciplinary nature of family studies, we have reviewed the major theoretical orientations from each of these fields to help us make sense of not only family and household structure, but also family and household process. Among such theoretical orientations we have reviewed are the family life and domestic life cycle concepts popularised in sociology, demography and anthropology to draw attention to the reality of family and household change over time. These theoretical orientations, together with those of conflict theories and the life course perspectives, were necessary to complement the essentially static view of families and households under the functionalist theories of families and households. Through the prisms of these theories, and especially by showing the fact that the family as a social institution has both an ideational and a concrete dimension, we have shown the strengths and weaknesses of the various characterisations of the so-called western and African family systems. The analyses of the empirical data that follow in the subsequent chapters of this study will be informed by one or more these theoretical orientations that we have outlined in this chapter.

References

Adegboyega O (1994) The situation of families in East and Southern Africa. Unpublished manuscript

Alexander JC (1985) Introduction. In JC Alexander (Ed.) *Neo-Functionalism*. Newbury Park, CA: Sage Publishers

Amoateng AY (1997) The structure of urban black households: New survey evidence from a coloured and an African community on the Cape Flats in the Western Cape of South Africa. *African Sociological Review* 1(2): 22-40

Barrett M (1980) *Women's oppression today*. London: Verso

Barrow C (2001) Contesting the rhetoric of 'black family breakdown' in Barbados. *Journal of Comparative Family Studies* 32: 419–441

Bates FL (1956) Position, role and status: A reformulation of concepts. *Social Forces* 34: 313–321

Becker HA (Ed.) (1990) *Life histories and generations*. ISOR: Utrecht

Beutler IV, Burr WR, Bahr KS & Herrin DA (1989) The family realm: Theoretical contributions for understanding its uniqueness. *Journal of Marriage and the Family* 51: 805–816

Bongaarts J (1983) The formal demography of families and households: An overview. *IUSSP Newsletter* No. 17: 27–42

Boss PG, Doherty WJ, LaRossa R, Schumm WR & Steinmetz SK (1993) *Sourcebook of family theories and methods: A contextual approach*. New York: Plenum Press

Bozzoli B (1991) *Women of Phokeng: Consciousness, life strategy, and migrancy in South Africa, 1900–1983*. Portsmouth, NH: Heineman

Bruce J, Lloyd C & Leonard A (1995) Families in focus. New York: Population Council

Burch TK (1967) The size and structure of families: A comparative analysis of census data. *American Journal of Sociology* 32(3): 347–363

Burch TK (1995) Theories of household formation: Progress and challenges. In E van Imhoff, A Kuijsten, P Hooimeijer & L van Wissen (Eds) *Household demography and household modeling*. New York: Plenum Press

Burch TK & Matthews BJ (1987) Household formation in developed societies. *Population and Development Review* 13(3): 495–511

Castells M (1997) *The power of identity.* Oxford: Blackwell

Christensen HT (1964) *Handbook of marriage and the family.* Chicago: Rand McNally

Coale AJ & McNeil D (1972) The distribution by age of the frequency of first marriages in a female cohort. *Journal of the American Statistical Association* 67: 743–749

Collins R (1988) *Theoretical sociology.* New York: Academic Press

Council of Europe (1990) Household structures in Europe. *Population Studies* 22. Council of Europe: Strasbourg

De Vos P (1995) *Household composition in Latin America.* New York: Plenum Press

Elder GH Jr. (1978) Family history and the life course. In TK Hareven (Ed.) *Transitions: The family and the life course in historical perspective.* New York: Academic Press

Fortes M (1970) *Kinship and social order.* London: Routledge Kegan Paul

Fukuyama F (1999) *The great disruption: Human nature and the reconstitution of social order.* London: Profile Books

Giddens A (2000) *Runaway world: How globalization in shaping our lives.* New York: Routledge

Glick PC (1947) The family life cycle. *American Sociological Review* 12: 164–174

Glick PC (1957) *American families.* New York: Wiley

Goode WJ (1970) (First edition 1963) *World revolution and family patterns.* New York: Free Press

Goodman LA, Keyfitz N & Pullum T (1974) Family formation and frequency of various kinship relationships. *Theoretical Population Biology* 5: 1–27

Goody J (1958) *The developmental cycle in domestic groups.* Cambridge: Cambridge University Press

Hareven T (1978) Cycles, courses and cohorts: Reflections on the theoretical and methodological approaches to the historical study of family development. *Journal of Social History* 16: 73–109

Harris O (1981) Households as natural units. In K Young, C Wolkowitz & R McCullagh (Eds) *Of marriage and the market.* London: CSE Books

Heaton TB (1987) Methodological perspectives on the family life course. Unpublished manuscript

Hogan DP (1978) The variable order of events in the life course. *American Sociological Review* 43: 573-586

Höpflinger F (1991) The future of household and family structures in Europe. In Council of Europe *Seminar on present demographic trends and lifestyles in Europe.* Council of Europe: Strasbourg

Hsu LK (1943) The myth of Chinese family size. *American Journal of Sociology* 48: 555–562

Inglehart R (1977) *The silent revolution: Changing values and political styles among western publics.* Princeton: Princeton University Press

Kammeyer CW & Ginn H (1986) *An introduction to population*. Chicago, IL: The Dorsey Press

Kephart W (1966) *The family, society, and the individual* (2nd edition). Boston: Houghton Mifflin

Kirkpatrick C (1963) *The family: As process and institution* (2nd edition). New York: Ronald Press

Krishnan P & Kayani AK (1976) Model divorce tables. *Genus* 32: 106–126

Kuijsten A (1995) Recent trends in household structure. In E van Imhoff, A Kuijsten, P Hooimeijer & L van Wissen (Eds) *Household demography and household modeling*. New York: Plenum Press

Laslett P (1977) *Family life and illicit love in earlier generations*. Cambridge: Cambridge University Press

Laslett P (1979) The stem family hypothesis and its privileged position. In KW Wachter, EA Hammel & P Laslett (Eds) *Statistical studies of historical social structure*. New York and London: Academic Press

Laslett P (1983) Family and household as work group and kin group: Areas of traditional Europe compared. In R Wall, J Robin & P Laslett (Eds) *Family forms in historic Europe*. Cambridge: Cambridge University Press

Laslett P & Wall R (Eds) (1972) *Household and family in past time*. Cambridge: Cambridge University Press

Mackintosh M (1979) Domestic labour and the household. In S Burman (Ed.) *Fit work for women*. London: Croom Helm

Maconachie M (1989) Dual-earner couples: Factors influencing whether and when white married women join the labour force in South Africa. *South African Journal of Sociology* 20(3): 143–151

Martin W & Beittel M (1987) The hidden abode of reproduction: Conceptualizing households in Southern Africa. *Development and Change* 18(2): 215–234

Mckeown T (1976) *The modern rise of population*. New York: Academic Press

Merton R (1967) *On theoretical sociology*. New York: The Free Press

Mills CW (1959) *The sociological imagination*. New York: Oxford University Press

Murdock P (1965) *Social structure*. New York: The Free Press

Murray C (1987) Class, gender and the household: The developmental cycle in Southern Africa. *Development and Change* 24: 755–785

Nobles W (1979) The black family and its children: The survival of humaneness. *Black Books Bulletin* 6: 7–14

Oakley D (1978) American-Japanese interaction in the development of population policy in Japan, 1945–52. *Population and Development Review* 4(4): 617–643

Parsons T (1937) *The structure of social action*. New York: The Free Press

Parsons T (1951) *The social system*. New York: Free Press

Pauw BA (1963) *Second generation: A study of the family among urbanized Bantu in East London*. Cape Town: Oxford University Press

Preston-Whyte EM (1978) Families without marriage. In WJ Argyle & EM Preston-Whyte (Eds) *Social system and transition in Southern Africa*. Cape Town: Oxford University Press

Rodgers RH & White JM (1993) Family development theory. In PG Boss, WJ Doherty, R LaRossa, WR Schumm & SK Steinmetz (Eds) *Sourcebook of family theories and methods: A contextual approach*. New York and London: Plenum Press

Rogers A & Castro LJ (1981) *Model migration schedules*. Research Report 81-30, International Institute of Applied Systems Analysis: Laxenburg

Russell M (1994) Do Blacks live in nuclear family households? An appraisal of Steyn's work on urban family structure in South Africa. *South African Sociological Review* 6(2): 56–67

Russell M (2002) *Are urban black families nuclear? A comparative study of black and white South African family norms*. Centre For Social Science Research, Social Surveys Unit, Working Paper No. 17, University of Cape Town

Ryder N (1992) The centrality of time in the study of the family. In E Berquó & P Xenos (Eds) *Family systems and cultural change*. Oxford: Clarendon Press

Seekings J, Graaff J & Joubert P (1990). *Survey of residential and migration histories of residents of the shack areas of Khayelitsha*. Research Unit for Sociology of Development Occasional Paper No. 15, University of Stellenbosch

Siqwana-Ndulo N (1998) Rural African family structure in the Eastern Cape Province, South Africa. *Journal of Comparative Family Studies* 29: 407–417

Sjoberg G (1960) *The preindustrial city: Past and present*. Glencoe, Illinois: The Free Press

Stack CB (1974) *All our kin: Strategies for survival in a black community*. New York: Harper & Row

Steyn A (1993a) *Gesinslewe in die RSA*. Kooperatiewe Navorsingsprogram oor die Huweliks-en Gesinslewe, RGN Verslag HG/MF-4

Steyn A (1993b) Stedelike Gesinsruckture in die Republiek van Suid-Afrika. *South African Journal of Sociology* 24(1): 1–32

Steyn A, Strijdom H, Viljoen S & Bosman F (Eds) (1987) *Marriage and family life in South Africa: Research priorities*. Pretoria: Human Sciences Research Council

Sweet JA & Bumpass LL (1987) *American families and households*. New York: Russell Sage

Sweet JA & Bumpass LL (1989) *Conducting a comprehensive survey of American family life: The experience of the National Survey of Families and Households* NSFH Working Paper No. 122, Madison: University of Wisconsin, Center for Demography and Ecology

Theodorson GA & Theodorson AG (1969) *A modern dictionary of sociology*. New York: Harper & Row

Todd E (1985) *The explanation of ideology: Family structure and social systems*. London: Basil Blackwell

Tuma NB & Hannan MT (1984) *Social dynamics: Models and methods*. New York: Academic Press

Turner L (2002) Book review. Anthony Giddens, Runaway world: How globalization is reshaping our lives. *Transcultural Psychiatry* 39: 394–415

UN (United Nations) (1973) *The determinants and consequences of population change, Vol. 1*. New York: United Nations

United Nations Statistical Office (1959) *Handbook of population census methods, Vol. III: Demographic and Social Characteristics of the Population, Studies in Methods*, Series F No. 5, Rev. 1. New York: United Nations

Van De Kaa D (1988) *The second demographic transition revisited: Theories and expectations*. Werkstukken PDI, no. 109, Planologisch en Demografisch Instituut Universitteit van Amsterdam: Amsterdam

Vogel J (2003) The family. *Social Indicators Research* 64: 393–435

Wall R (1983) The household: Demographic and economic change in England, 1650–1970. In R Wall, J Robin & P Laslett (Eds) *Family forms in historic Europe*. Cambridge: Cambridge University Press

Wall R (1995) Historical development of the household in Europe. In E van Imhoff, A Kuijsten, P Hooimeijer & L van Wissen (Eds) *Household demography and household modeling*. New York and London: Plenum Press

Whitehead A (1981) 'I'm hungry, Mum': The politics of domestic budgeting. In K Young, C Wolkowitz & R McCullagh (Eds) *Of marriage and the market*. London: CSE Books

Ziehl SC (1994) Social class variation in household structure: The case of a small South African city. *South African Journal of Sociology* 25(1): 25–34

Ziehl SC (2001) Documenting changing family patterns in South Africa: Are census data of any value? *African Sociological Review* 5(2): 36–62

CHAPTER 3

Living arrangements in South Africa

Acheampong Yaw Amoateng, Tim B Heaton & Ishmael Kalule-Sabiti

Introduction

Ever since the first European settlers set foot on the soil of Africa, the domestic organisation of both the indigenous peoples and the settlers has been in flux as a result of the mutuality of influences (see, for example, Caldwell & Caldwell 1990; Ekeh 1990; Russell 2003). The introduction of formal education, systems of governance, worship and modern agricultural methods all contributed to transformations in domestic organisation. For instance, in South Africa, the modernisation process in the form of the expropriation of African agricultural land, the discovery of gold at the end of the twentieth century and the consequent development of industrial capitalism, and the importation of indentured labour from India and Malaysia, were all developments that significantly altered both kinship organisation and the living arrangements of every segment of the country's population. Writing about this alteration in domestic organisation, Russell notes:

> The new domestic strategies adopted by black people in South Africa to accommodate changed circumstances are *within the agnatic idiom,* which is proving no less resilient and adaptable than the Western *conjugal idiom* in providing a charter by which most black South Africans continue to order their radically altered domestic lives. (2003: 10)

Modernisation theory and different variants of it have invariably provided the conceptual framework for the bulk of the scholarship that has examined the issue of living arrangements in different cultures. Essentially, the theory posits that as society becomes differentiated through modernisation, the family changes from an assumed extended form to a more nuclear form through changes in household size. One interpretation of modernisation theory of the family is that within countries, nuclear family forms predominate in urban areas, while extended family forms are more prevalent in rural areas (Burch 1967). To a very large extent, this so-called *residence hypothesis* is an extension of the socio-economic argument, since there is nothing intrinsic about urban living that engenders this supposed transformation in family and household structures.

Urban areas generally tend to be selective of such socio-economic opportunities – education, wage employment, modern housing, better healthcare, leisure and recreation and so on – that are believed to encourage such 'modern' family and household patterns as lower levels of fertility, lower average household sizes, and independent or separate living. Similar economic argument is essentially at the heart of Stack's (1974) study of the living arrangements of African-Americans in the United States. She argues that the extreme economic circumstances under which most African-Americans live in American cities is the reason for the prevalence of extended families among them since they are compelled to pool their meagre resources to make ends meet. Following these apparent changes, the question of living arrangements has always been a subject of study by social scientists, especially family demographers (for a critical review of such studies see, for example, Ziehl 2001), although consensus on the magnitude and direction of the changes has thus far been elusive. For instance, until recently, the living arrangements of African and white people in the emerging towns and cities in South Africa were the subject of a raging debate in the family literature. According to one group of studies, the family patterns of Africans were converging towards those of their white compatriots (see, for example, Amoateng 1997; Nzimande 1987; Steyn 1993).

On the other hand, another group of studies argued that, consistent with their culture, Africans were still living in extended family households in spite of their exposure to the modernising influences of the urban-industrial complex. Thus, according to this argument, the so-called convergence thesis is a mere artifact of urban planning, which for so many years provided sustenance for the apartheid system (see, for example, Murray 1981; Russell 1994, 2002, 2003; Spiegel 1980a, 1980b, 1982). However, because of the peculiar history and politics of South Africa, the question of whether the family system among Africans has transformed as a result of contact with western culture has been the subject of speculation at best.[1]

Several social, political and demographic developments in the country in recent years have provided ample opportunities to revisit the issue of family change and the consequent living arrangements of the South African population. First, since 1994 the new government's transformation agenda in areas such as housing, education, and health is likely to have impacted not only kinship organisation but also the living arrangements of people in significant ways. Second, such demographic changes as decreases in fertility and mortality and recent reversals in declining mortality due to the HIV/AIDS pandemic (Sibanda & Zuberi 1999; Udjo 2001) and increasing rates of urbanisation (Jenkins & Wilkinson 2002; Stats SA 2001) are some of the factors that to all intents and purposes are likely to have affected family patterns and living arrangements. Finally, since the watershed democratic transition in 1994, there have been concerted efforts on the part of the state to generate more large-scale social and economic data sets which contain information about individual members of private households, their social and economic characteristics and the households in which they reside. Although limited in scope, the households and their characteristics are comparable in many respects and thus afford us the opportunity to examine possible changes in both household structures and the characteristics of the living arrangements of South Africans of all races and ages.

In this chapter we examine living arrangements by looking at both family and household structures and processes in South Africa using evidence from recent

---

1 Since 1936 South Africa has been conducting censuses, but because of the racial polarisations and the different methodologies used, the comparability and credibility of these data sources have been problematic (Noumbissi & Zuberi 2001).

empirical data from both censuses (Stats SA 1996, 2001) and surveys. To accomplish this goal, we will introduce a life course dimension to the examination of household composition at the micro level which will help us to have an idea about change and, on that basis, to speculate about the future trajectories of families and households. Since a household is basically a confluence of people at different points in their life courses, age becomes a crucial factor in the analysis of family and household change because the cumulative experiences of these individuals help to define the family as a social institution (De Vos 1995). Underscoring the importance of age and other life course characteristics of individuals in the composition of families and households over time, Hareven noted:

> It is important to realize that a profile of a household at a specific point in time obscures the constant movement of family members in and out of different household patterns over their life courses. People went through a series of life transitions which impinged not only on their own lives but also on the structure and membership of their families and households. (Hareven 1982: 154)

As a culturally diverse society, South Africans exhibit different household formation rules which ultimately affect the living arrangements of people over the life course, while factors such as politics, access to housing, health, education and other social and economic amenities would also be important in the decision about living arrangements. For example, because African cultures put a high premium on communal ethos, Africans and their descendants prefer to live in extended households. In fact, even in the face of modernisation, it has been observed in several parts of sub-Saharan Africa that a combination of a cultural ethic that puts premium on sharing the benefits of modernisation and widespread poverty has meant that the households of the elite of these societies tend to be complex rather than simple (Caldwell 1968; Oppong 1974).

Describing a typical household of the elite of the matrilineal Akan of Ghana, Oppong said:

> The Akan Senior Civil Servant's household in Accra generally includes his wife and most of his children, together with one or more relatives and in-laws and domestic helps. For instance in twenty of the households visited during the course of the study, which ranged in size from six to fifteen members and housed couples who had been married for an average of ten years with 3.2 children, there was found to be one wife's relative per household one husband's relative in every second household, as well as 1.2 paid domestic helps. (Oppong 1974: 73)

On the other hand, the present household living arrangements of white South Africans, and in fact all peoples of western European descent, has been characterised as the product of modernisation.[2] According to these 'evolutionists', the basis of the changes in the western household is the emergence of the industrial-capitalist civilisation, which

---

2 Laslett (1978) and scholars of the Cambridge Historical School have questioned this characterisation of the western European household, arguing that this type of household has always been of the 'simple' form.

has ushered in values such as separate living, independence and privacy (Blumberg & Winch 1972; Burch 1967, 1995; Caldwell & Caldwell 1977; De Vos 1995; Goode 1963; Martin & Beittel 1984; Ogburn & Nimkoff 1955; Parsons 1956). As a corollary to this type of 'civilization', Burch (1995) has observed that in such societies where separate living is valued, income may be positively associated with this lifestyle, since, as a luxury good, it is clearly expensive. Thus, in such contexts one can expect rises in separate living during good economic times when incomes generally rise and vice versa. Moreover, housing prices generally appear to be related to family and household formation in that when prices are high, they may discourage marriage and hence the formation of family households. Commenting on the role of culture on the changes in socio-demographic patterns in Europe, Burch notes:

> There is a widespread conviction, for example, that many of the patterns of family and household formation observed in the West since 1970 [part of the so-called 'second demographic transition'] may be bound up with a unique Western emphasis on the individual, and may not be repeated in the developing societies of Asia or Africa. (Burch 1995: 92)

Against this background of the cultural, economic, and technological forces in societies, we examine changes in the living arrangements of the South African population. Even though we draw on the empirical data that have proliferated since 1994, the bulk of the analyses are based on the 1996 and 2001 population censuses (Stats SA 1996, 2001).[3] In view of the fact that the 'household' serves as the unit for the collection of data on 'families' in conventional censuses, we are limited in our efforts to understand family structures and processes; family members do not necessarily co-reside, especially in a society with geographical mobility rates as high as South Africa's. In fact, several scholars have argued that because of the high rates of geographical mobility in the southern African region, it is rather difficult, on the basis of de facto household composition alone, to establish family relationships and the interdependencies thereof (see, for example, Goody 1972; Murray 1981; Peters 1983; Russell 2003).[4]

There have been several measures of household and family structures and processes in recent decades. For instance, some studies have used measures such as the mean household size (MHS), adult per household (A/H ratio), age-specific headship rate (ASHR), number of marital units (NMU) or generations in a household. While all these measures have been helpful in illuminating the nature of household and family structures and processes, in the present study we look at the distribution as a whole by using information on the 'relationship to the household head' variable recommended by the United Nations (Hammel & Laslett 1974; Shyrock & Siegel 1973). De Vos (1995) has noted that in its more complex form, the United Nations' scheme distinguishes among households in the four basic categories (UN 1980). Extended households are divided into: (a) a single family nucleus and other related persons;

---

3 The data provided in tables and figures in the chapter are drawn from the 1996 and 2001 censuses respectively (Stats SA 1996, 2001).
4 While we agree with this position, we do not think that it is entirely useless in providing insight into some of these dynamics. These methodological limitations notwithstanding, the data clearly depict the diversity of family forms in the country.

(b) two or more family nuclei related to each other; and (c) two or more family nuclei related to each other, plus other people related to at least one of the nuclei. Conventionally, in South Africa, the state's statistical agency, Statistics South Africa (Stats SA), has used the standard United Nations' nine relationship type approach in both the population censuses and sample surveys it conducts with slight variations. For example, the 1996 census listed nine relationship types, while the 2001 census listed 13 relationship types by differentiating between biological, adopted and step-children of the head and also included son/daughter-in-laws and brother/sister-in-laws of the head separately. We standardised the two censuses by recoding the relationship to head variable to create eight relationship types, namely:[5] head/acting head of household; spouse of head; child of head; sibling of head; parent of head; grandchild of head; other relative of head; and non-related persons.

The household type debate in the South African family literature

We now look at the household type in the South African family literature by examining living arrangements of the population. We do this by looking at the distribution of four broad household types – namely, one-person, nuclear, extended and non-related person households – while we also look at selected social, economic and cultural factors associated with the incidence of different types of households. Family sociologists have for centuries written about two broad family systems: an extended family system, which is associated with undifferentiated, rural societies, and a nuclear family system, which is associated with modern complex societies. At the level of culture, the two family systems are associated with north-western European and 'traditional' non-western societies respectively. In South Africa, several earlier family studies concluded that the extended family systems of the indigenous African peoples were evolving into the nuclear system of their white counterparts. Figure 3.1 shows the distribution of our four broad household types and depicts two fundamental issues. First, that most households in the society are occupied by family groups. Nearly eight out of ten households are occupied by family groups of varying types compared with less than one of four households that are occupied by either non-relatives or a single person. Thus, the vast majority of people in South Africa live with families as either head of the household, spouse, children, or grandchildren. So, despite the disruptive consequences of the migrant labour system and perhaps devastating effects of death due to HIV/AIDS, most people still find a family living arrangement, usually with close family members. Second, on the face of it, Figure 3.1 appears to lend credence to the view about the 'nuclearisation' of the family in the society as suggested by earlier studies; in fact, in 1996, almost one out of two households was of the nuclear family variety compared with less than one in three of extended family households, despite the marginal decline and increase in the proportions of nuclear family and extended family households respectively.[6]

5 Since the 1996 census also listed 'Other, unspecified relationship' but the 2001 census did not have this category, we omitted it from the present analysis.
6 To the extent that the nuclear family system revolves around the conjugal unit and is clearly identifiable with white people, the decline in the proportion of people who lived in such households between 1996 and 2001 could possibly be due to the out-migration of homogamous white and Asian couples. In fact, in a separate analysis, we found, for example, that between 1996 and 2001 the number of white/white marriages decreased by 25 per cent.

Moreover, if the position advanced by some family scholars that solitary living is a phase of the nuclear family system is valid, this apparent trend towards the nuclearisation of the family is indeed supported by the fact that the proportion of one-person households increased from 16.29 per cent to 21.05 per cent in the five-year period.

Figure 3.1: Distribution of household types in South Africa, 1996 and 2001

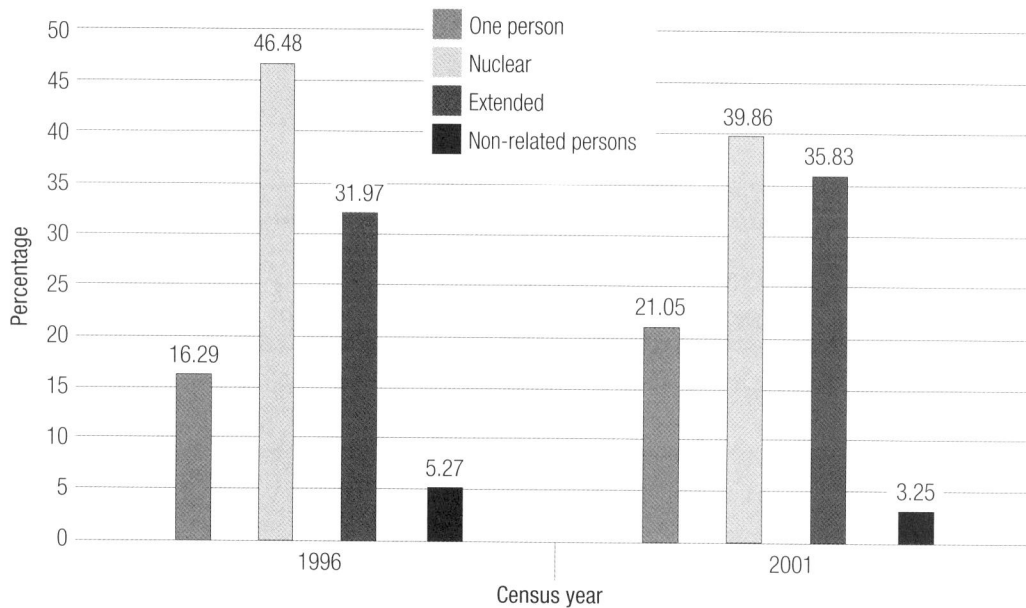

Source: Stats SA (1996, 2001)

As the residential dimension of the family, the structure of households and changes thereof are duly affected by a combination of cultural, political, demographic and economic factors. For instance, the prevalence of monogamy, relative affluence, cultural premium on the values of independent living and lower levels of fertility among white people have been conventionally associated with the nuclear family system. On the other hand, polygamy, higher levels of fertility, widespread poverty and communalist ethos amongst Africans have been associated with the extended family system. Thus, to the extent that socio-economic factors influence household living arrangements, it is critically important to take them into account in the examination of household types in South Africa. Figure 3.2a shows the distribution of household type by the race of the head of the household, while Figure 3.2b shows the detailed relationships within the household. On the whole, population groups show differences in living arrangements as demonstrated by the fact that Africans, followed by coloureds, are the most likely to live in extended family households, while whites and Asians are the most likely to live in nuclear family households.

Figure 3.2a: Distribution of household type by race of head

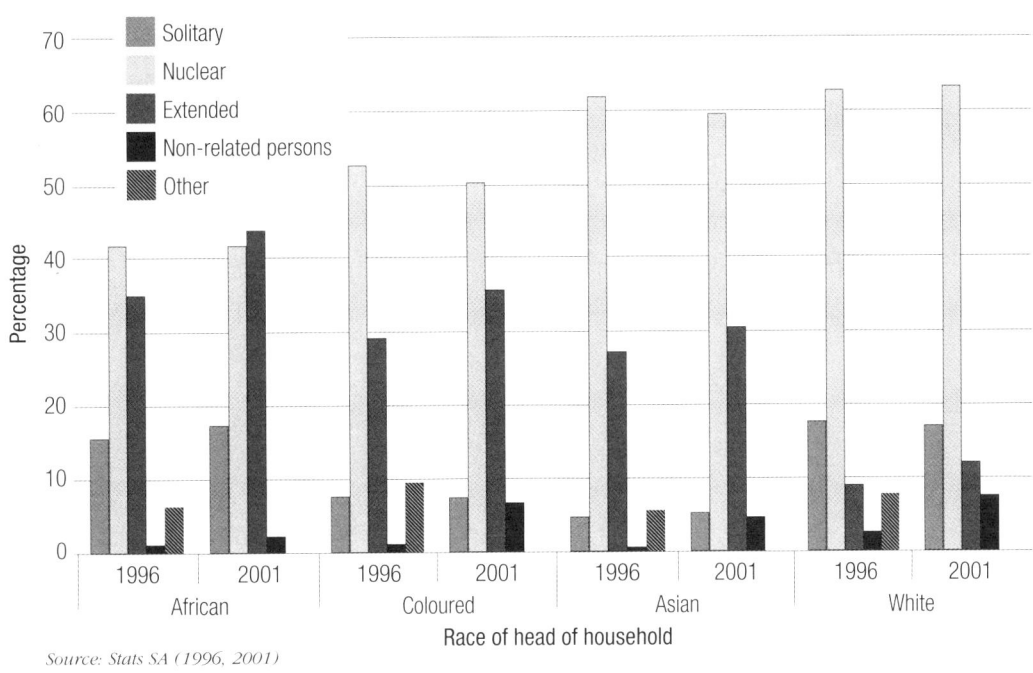

Source: Stats SA (1996, 2001)

Figure 3.2b: Distribution of household type by race of head

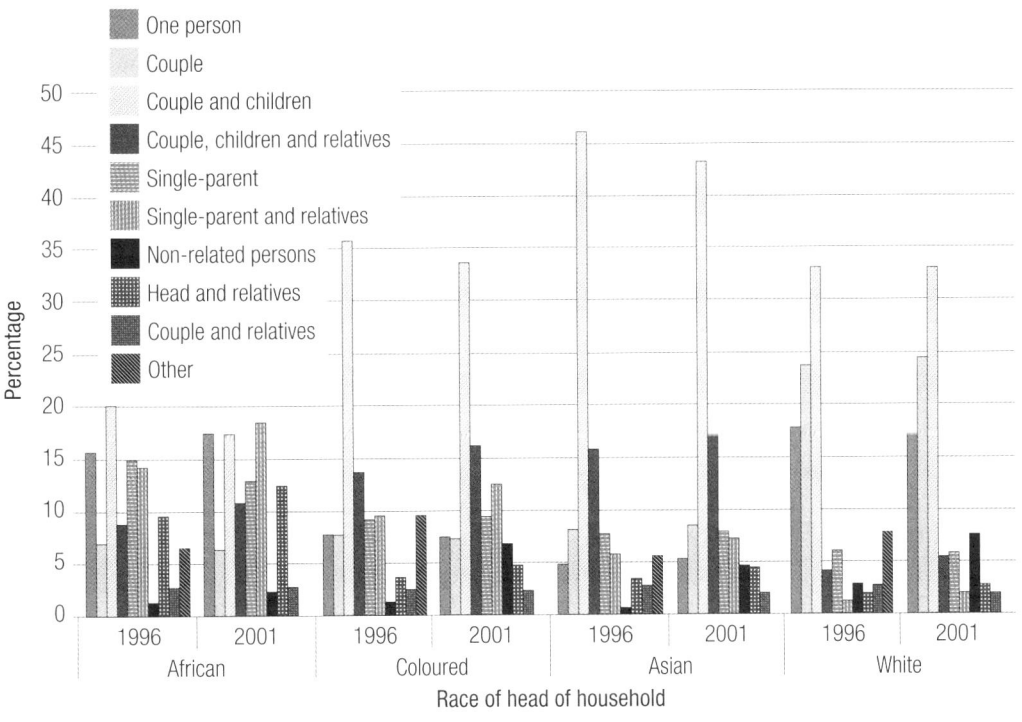

Source: Stats SA (1996, 2001)

Without a doubt, the racial patterns observed reflect differences in marriage, divorce and childbearing, along with different norms regarding co-residence with relatives. As already indicated, some family scholars have noted that solitary living is a phase in the nuclear family pattern and, to the extent that this is true, Figure 3.2b provides empirical support for this view. The proportions of single-person, couple and classic nuclear family households among white people are higher than among any other population group. These three household types respectively reflect the singlehood, marriage and childbearing phases of the life cycle of the nuclear family. The popularity of the nuclear family system is further supported by a separate analysis in which children under age 12 were compared with those between ages 12 and 17. While children under the age of 12 were most likely to live with parents and/or grandparents, the pattern varied by racial group; on average, about nine out of ten white children lived with parents, while only about half of African children lived with their parents.

Figure 3.3: Education and complex household living by race

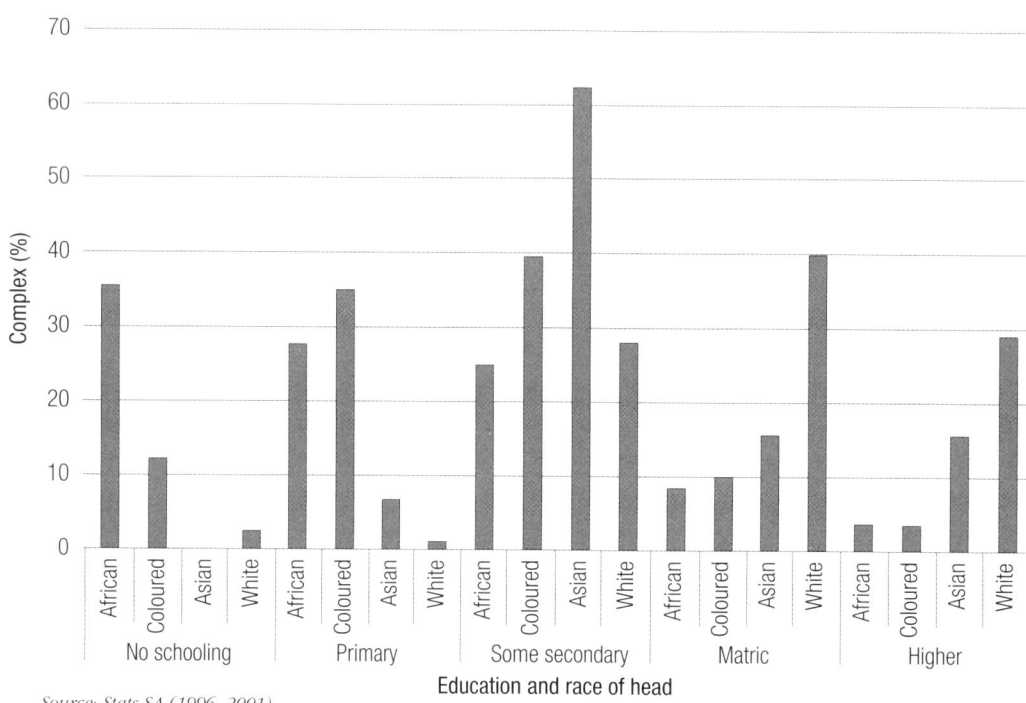

Source: Stats SA (1996, 2001)

Even though the nuclear family household is more common among whites and Asians, there are indications of an increase in the proportion of extended family households in white and Asian communities in recent years, especially among the well-educated and hence the affluent, as depicted by Figure 3.3. It is significant to note that, amongst Africans and coloureds, extended family living is more common among the least educated and poor, a fact which supports Stack's (1974) and others' observation that the poor are compelled to live together so as to pool resources. But, if whites and Asians are relatively better off than Africans and coloureds, what explains the increasing popularity of extended family living among whites and Asians in recent years?

Since 1915, with the introduction of the industrial 'colour bar' relating to apprentices and other forms of aid given to poor whites between 1920 and 1940 to enable white people 'to remain white and live white', successive Nationalist leaders like DF Malan constructed an economic safety net through the colour bar, the distinction between 'civilised' and 'uncivilised' labour, protectionist policies for companies that employed white people, and minimum wages laws that insulated semi-skilled white people from competition by unskilled black people (*Mail & Guardian* 7 August 2004). However, following the democratic transition and with the prevailing macroeconomic policy environment, the phenomenon of the poor white crisis of the 1930s is rapidly resurfacing. For example, according to the Institute for Security Studies (cited in *Mail & Guardian* 7 August 2004), white unemployment has nearly doubled since 1995. And, according to political analyst Lawrence Schlemmer, out of a total of 4.5 million white people, 430 000 (or 9.5 per cent) are 'too poor to live in traditional white areas' and 90 000 'are in a survival struggle' (quoted in *Mail & Guardian* 7 August 2004). One reason why a relatively high proportion of the white elderly was living independently was due to their access to old age facilities; however, with the more equitable distribution of these resources amidst the current macroeconomic climate, many, especially poorer, white people will not be able to afford to live alone. On the other hand, under the apartheid political economy, Africans were compelled to live in households which literally lacked the physical space to accommodate a large number of their kin and in the process discouraged extended family living.

As far as Asians, especially Indians, are concerned, even though on the face of it the nuclear family is quite popular among them, their living arrangement patterns largely show evidence of the continuity of the joint family system, since their communities exhibit a high prevalence of three-generational households. This family system ensures that two or more brothers, their wives and children live together in the same household, sometimes with their aging parents as well (Adams 1986; Jithoo 1983). Significantly, Indians forcibly relocated under the Group Areas Act were initially moved to houses designed for nuclear family living (Jithoo 1983), a fact which may explain the apparent popularity of the nuclear family system among them. Nonetheless, descendants of peoples from the East, Asians in South Africa still favour the joint family system.

But, compared to what seems to be a fairly consistent pattern for the stable and relatively wealthy Indian and white groups, and a cultural indication of the same for coloureds, the living arrangements of the African poor are much more varied and, of necessity, opportunistic, perhaps due to the impact of HIV/AIDS deaths, migrancy, marital instability, desertion as well as cultural choice. Some decades ago, Preston-Whyte (1978) used the term 'matri-focal' to characterise the urban African family in South Africa. According to her, relatively low rates of marriage and high rates of non-marital fertility, including out-of-wedlock births, have led to the co-residence of single parents with their mothers, leading to multigenerational living in African communities, especially in the cities. Coupled with this type of living arrangement, HIV/AIDS-related mortality has wreaked havoc among the middle-adult age group in poor communities in general and African communities in particular in recent years, and is forcing the elderly increasingly to play parental roles due to the increasing numbers of AIDS orphans. This is evidenced by the fact that a higher percentage of African children live with grandparents, compared with other race groups. Moreover, African children are also more likely to be living with a sibling or some other relative.

Table 3.1 shows that almost one-third of all households in the population are three-generational with important racial variations in rural and urban areas. The continuation of the age-old practice among young, unmarried African urban residents to send their children to their parents and grandparents in the countryside for care is shown by the fact almost one in four rural African households are three-generational compared to just about one-fourth of urban African households. Moreover, a combination of a relatively low marriage rate and high birth rate may be primarily responsible for the high incidence of three-generational households among coloureds, while the popularity of the joint family among Asians might be responsible for the fact that almost a quarter of all Asian households are three-generational. So, clearly to all intents and purposes Africans, followed by coloureds, prefer to live in extended family households, while their white counterparts, by every measure, followed by Asians, prefer to live in simple or nuclear family households. But, if this observation of living arrangements of the South African population is correct, what then was the basis of the earlier claim by some family scholars that African family patterns were converging towards those of their white counterparts?

Table 3.1: Distribution of household types by race of head in rural and urban areas

Household type	1996		2001	
	Skip-generational	Three-generational	Skip-generational	Three-generational
All households	5.10	27.32	5.14	30.64
Rural households				
African	7.61	33.50	8.08	38.90
Coloured	3.32	24.34	2.73	26.80
Asian	1.77	17.53	2.69	28.24
White	0.86	5.92	0.58	9.85
Urban households				
African	4.11	26.08	3.86	26.68
Coloured	2.96	29.93	2.53	32.91
Asian	1.02	21.15	1.00	25.21
White	0.71	6.51	0.71	9.38

Source: Stats SA (1996 & 2001)

To answer the question as to the basis of the earlier claim of convergence of family patterns between African and white people, it is important to note that on the face of it, the validity of this conclusion appears indisputable. For instance, even as late as 2001 the second all-race population census in the country (Stats SA 2001) revealed that nearly one out of five (20 per cent) of all African households were occupied by single persons, a figure which was comparable only to that of white people, among whom single-person households constituted 21 per cent of the total number of households. And, as far as the living arrangement of the conjugal unit goes, Table 3.2 shows the distribution of the proportions of husbands who live apart from their spouses by race according to the 2001 population census. According to Table 3.2, almost one out of every five African husbands was living apart from his wife compared with only 4 per cent of white husbands who did not live with their wives. Needless to say, this was some of the statistical evidence that has been used to draw the conclusion that Africans are increasingly living in nuclear families, but is this evidence sufficient to warrant such a broad generalisation about the African family? On the contrary, a critical interrogation of the census data reveals a very different picture of African living arrangements. In fact, some scholars of the western family have argued that solitary living is an important phase in the life cycle of that family system because the family begins and ends with this phase.

Table 3.2: Percentage distribution of husbands living apart from their spouses by race

	Husband living apart	
Race of wife	N	%
African	65 450	19.20
Coloured	3 350	6.29
Asian	1 201	5.83
White	3 130	3.74

Source: Stats SA (2001)

On the basis of the incidence of solitary living, then, it is tempting to conclude that increasingly Africans are living in nuclear families. However, a consideration of other factors shows that drawing conclusions about living arrangements based on de facto household data alone can be somewhat misleading. For instance, a critical examination of the data on housing type shows that while nationally 13 per cent of the population lived in informal housing or so-called shacks, 15 per cent of Africans lived in informal housing compared with less than 1 per cent of white people. Secondly, if as has been argued by several western family scholars, monogamy and hence the conjugal unit is the bedrock of the nuclear family system, in a context where many African married couples cannot live together – not by choice but by necessity – how viable is such a family system among them? It is beyond dispute that many Africans lived alone or with a few of their extended kin due to processes like housing constraints and other limitations imposed by apartheid-induced laws rather than a rational choice to live in 'nuclear' family households. The fact of the matter is that African South Africans are still attached to their cultural values and practices and nothing illustrates this more than their preference for extended family living. In fact, a close examination of the 1996 and 2001 population census data shows that while the incidence of extended family living registered a marginal increase among all race groups between the two periods, this was especially more profound among Africans. With access to education, employment, credit and so on, Africans are not only able to afford better and spacious housing, but they are also able to interact more with their extended kin in both the cities and rural areas.

Socio-economic factors and living arrangements

One of the central tenets of modernisation theory of the family is that household complexity declines with increasing differentiation of society. At the societal level, it is thought that extended family households are most common in pre-industrial agricultural societies, whereas the nuclear family household is most common in simple or modern societies (Blumberg & Winch 1972). Within society, extended family households are believed to predominate in rural areas, while nuclear family households are more common in urban areas. For example, in his work on the sociology of the family, Talcott Parsons observed that the classic nuclear family of husband, wife and children provided the best fit for modern urban life. Urban areas are selective of such factors as education, which is associated with the modernisation process.

In South Africa, living arrangements and household structures vary by level of urbanisation and education. These patterns are shown in Figures 3.4 and 3.5. For this analysis, education is calculated as the education of the head (if the head is not married) or as the average education of the head and spouse (if the head is married). Relationships between the frequency of household types and education are not always linear. For example, single person households are over-represented in households with low education (primary school) and high education (bachelor's degree or higher). Married couple and nuclear households increase with education, with the exception that these household types are less common in the most educated households. Nuclear family households are more common in urban areas, while more complex household structures are more common in low-density settlements. This pattern is consistent with the hypothesis that modernisation is associated with declining household complexity.

Figure 3.4: Education and household type

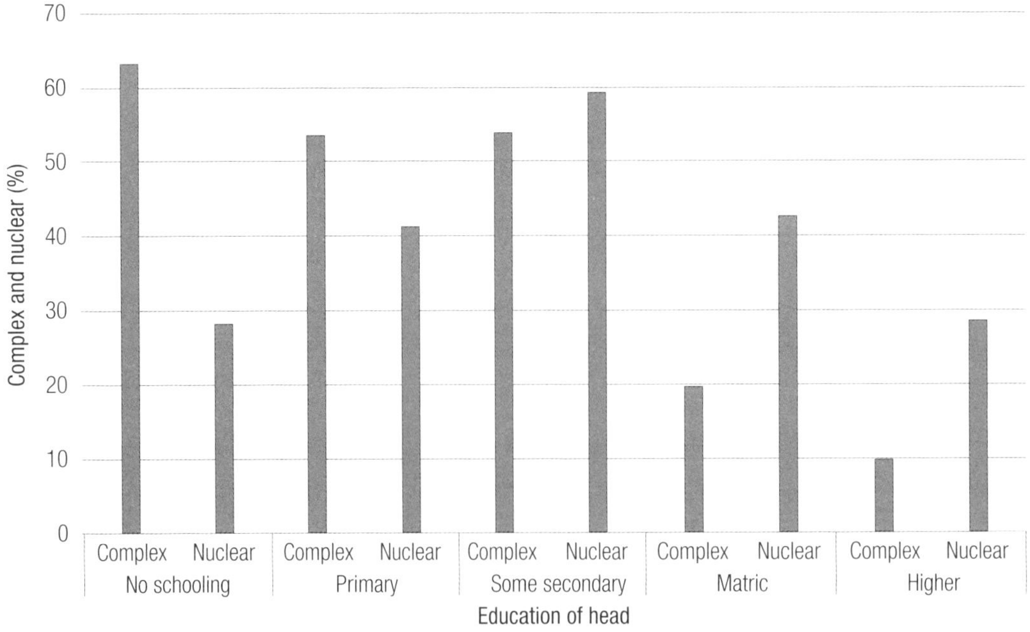

Source: Stats SA (1996, 2001)

Figure 3.5: Rural/urban residence and household type

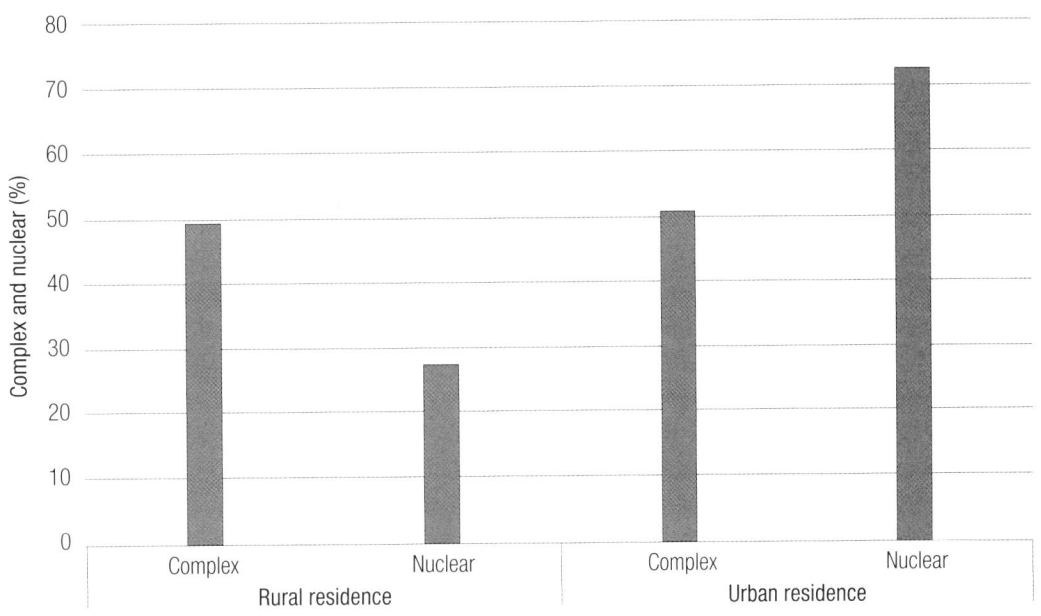

Source: Stats SA (1996, 2001)

Conclusion and discussion

Our aim in this chapter was to examine changes in households and the living arrangements of the people who occupy these households by using the 1996 and 2001 census micro data. Because households and the individuals who occupy them are part of the social and political environments, both modernisation theory and the life course perspective were employed to examine the question of change. Because households are an important component of a population, we also sought to document the effects of social and demographic characteristics, including race, urbanisation and education, on these households and the living arrangements of the individuals who reside in them. South Africa is a multicultural society and in the past, using various forms of evolutionary theory, several family studies, which assumed that families everywhere were transforming in a linear direction toward the nuclear family system conventionally associated with peoples of northwestern Europe and their descendants, concluded that the society was characterised by the nuclear family system.

More specifically, this position argued that the majority African population in South Africa, because of its exposure to such modernising influences as formal education, wage employment and urban living, was increasingly living in nuclear family households, a process which was inexorably moving the society towards a modal family system. The data presented in this chapter have shown that this conclusion about the family in the society as a whole, and Africans in particular, is rather misplaced. On the contrary, what the data show is that consistent with its multicultural character, and in line with the rapid social, economic and political changes taking place in the broader society, families and households are becoming more diverse. In fact, the society can be characterised as juxtaposing the nuclear and extended family systems.

The nuclear family system is clearly more popular among white, and to some extent, Asian people, while the extended family system is identified with Africans and coloured people. The popularity of the nuclear family system among whites is clearly demonstrated by the importance of the conjugal unit in their living arrangements. More simple household structures are also more common in urban areas and in more educated segments of the population. Moreover, the presence of children aged below 12, the relative absence of older children and the independence of the elderly in white households all demonstrate the popularity of the nuclear family system among white people. Conversely, the relative absence of the conjugal unit, the presence of children of all ages, siblings, other relatives, and the dependence of the elderly in African, Asian and coloured households demonstrates these groups' cultural preference for multigenerational living. As part of the explanation for the reconfiguration of living arrangements among Africans especially, several scholars (for example, Preston-Whyte 1978) have written about the matri-focal nature of African families due to such patterns as the absence and participation of men in the migrant labour system, high rates of premarital births and unpopularity of marriage amongst Africans as compared to other groups.

The fact that we are now witnessing an increasing tendency toward complexity of households, among Africans especially, is evidence of the limitations that the apartheid system placed on their cultural preference for multigenerational living. Under the myriad of apartheid laws, African males were temporary residents of the country's major towns and cities when they left the countryside to work as miners, domestics and factory hands. Because of this situation, coupled with the shortage of housing and other amenities, they could not live with either their immediate family members or relatives, who were in most cases left behind in the rural areas. But this situation in no way led to the 'disorganisation' of the African family, as some scholars have noted, since the extended family system was kept viable through such mechanisms as regular cash remittances, visits and fosterage of children. Family scholars in the west coined the phrase *nuclear hardship model* to describe the gulf between westerners' ideological attachment to the nuclear family system and the reality of some having to live in situations where they must pool resources as a survival strategy. In fact, if recent popular accounts and personal observations in South Africa are anything to go by, one can expect the incidence of multigenerational living amongst white people to increase, since most of the socio-economic privileges they enjoyed under apartheid are now falling away.

In conclusion, the present study found very little evidence to support the view that there is a single dominant family system identifiable with South African society, since the data pointed to the importance of the nuclear and extended family systems in the society. For reasons of both cultural preference and affordability, white South Africans have been able to maintain the nuclear family system characteristic of the west. The fact that African, coloured and Asian people are increasingly living in extended family households amid the rapid socio-economic transformation of the broader society shows the importance of culture and factors such as education and income, which are the basis of modernisation and dependency theories. If indeed Oppong's (1974) argument about the positive association between socio-economic status and the likelihood of living in an extended family household in West Africa is anything to go by, one can hazard a guess that as more and more Africans become empowered socio-economically, the incidence of extended family households will increase, especially in the face of reversals in the mortality declines in the African communities as we have already begun to witness. In fact, African people's relative access to such resources as education, high status occupations and housing has also meant that they can now afford to live with their kin from either the rural areas or elsewhere in the towns.

References

Adams BN (1986) *The family: A sociological interpretation* (4th edition). Orlando, Florida: Harcourt Brace Jovanovich Publishers

Amoateng AY (1997) The structure of urban black households: New survey evidence from a coloured and an African community on the Cape Flats in the Western Cape of South Africa. *African Sociological Review* 1(2): 22–40

Blumberg RL & Winch RF (1972) Societal complexity and familial complexity: Evidence for the curvilineal hypothesis. *American Journal of Sociology* 77: 898–920

Burch TK (1967) The size and structure of families: A comparative analysis of census data. *American Journal of Sociology* 32(3): 347–363

Burch TK (1970) Some demographic determinants of average household size: An analytic approach. *Demography* 7: 61–70

Burch TK (1995) Theories of household formation: Progress and challenges. In E van Imhoff, A Kuijsten, P Hooimeijer & L van Wissen L (Eds) *Household demography and household modeling*. New York: Plenum Press

Caldwell JC (1968) Population and family change in Africa: The new urban elite in Ghana. Canberra: Australian National University Press

Caldwell JC & Caldwell P (1977) The role of marital sexual abstinence in determining fertility. *Population Studies* 31(2): 193–217

Caldwell JC & Caldwell P (1990) Cultural forces tending to sustain high fertility. In GTF Ascadi, G Johnson-Ascadi & RA Bulatao (Eds) *Population and growth and reproduction in sub-Saharan Africa: Technical analysis of fertility and its consequences*. Washington: World Bank

Hammel EA & Laslett P (1974) Comparing household structure over time and between cultures. *Comparative Studies in Society and History* 16: 73–109

Hareven TK (1982) *Family time and industrial time: The relationship between the family and work in a New England industrial community*. Cambridge: Cambridge University Press

De Vos SM (1995) *Household composition in Latin America*. New York: Plenum Press

Ekeh PP (1990) Social anthropology and two contrasting uses of tribalism in Africa. *Comparative Study of Society and History* 32(4): 660–700

Goode WJ (1963) *World revolution and family patterns.* New York: Free Press

Goody J (1972) The evolution of the family. In P Laslett& R Wall (Eds) *Household and family in past time.* Cambridge: Cambridge University Press

Jenkins P & Wilkinson P (2002) Assessing the growing impact of the global economy on urban development in Southern African cities: Case studies in Maputo and Cape Town. *Cities* 19(1): 33–47

Jithoo S (1983) Indian family businesses in Durban. PhD Dissertation, Rhodes University, Grahamstown

Laslett B (1978) Family membership, past and present. *Social Problems* 25: 476–490

Martin W & Beittel M (1984) The hidden abode of reproduction: Conceptualising households in Southern Africa. In JI Guyer & PE Peters (Eds) *Conceptualising the household: Issues of theory, method and application.* Cambridge, MA: Harvard University Press

Murray C (1981) *Families divided: The impact of migrant labour in Lesotho.* Johannesburg: Ravan Press and Cambridge: Cambridge University Press

Noumbissi A & Zuberi T (2001) Household structure and aging in South Africa: A research note. Paper prepared for the Virtual Conference on African Households: An exploration of census data, African Census Analysis project, Population Studies Center, University of Pennslyvania, 21–23 November

Nzimande SR (1987) Family structure and support systems in black communities. In A Steyn, HG Strijdom, S Viljoen & F Bosman (Eds) *Marriage and family life in South Africa.* Pretoria: HSRC

Ogburn WF & Nimkoff MF (1955) *Technology and the changing family.* Boston: Houghton Mifflin

Oppong C (1974) *Marriage among a matrilineal elite: A family study of Ghanaian civil servants.* London: Cambridge University Press

Parsons T (1956) *Family: Socialisation and interaction processes.* London: Routledge & Kegan Paul

Peters P (1983) Gender, development cycles, and historical process: A critique of recent research on women in Botswana. *Journal of Southern African Studies* 10(1): 83–105

Preston-Whyte EM (1978) Families without marriage. In WJ Argyle & EM Preston-Whyte (Eds) *Social System and transition in Southern Africa.* Cape Town: Oxford University Press

Russell M (1994) Do blacks live in nuclear family households? An appraisal of Steyn's work on urban family structure in South Africa. *South African Sociological Review* 6(2): 56–67

Russell M (2002) *Are urban black families nuclear? A comparative study of black and white South African family norms.* Centre For Social Science Research, Social Surveys Unit, Working Paper No. 17, University of Cape Town

Russell M (2003) Understanding black households: The problem. *Social Dynamics* 29(2): 5–47

Shyrock HS & Siegel JS (1973) *The methods and materials of demography.* New York: Academic Press, Inc

Sibanda A & Zuberi T (1999) Contemporary fertility levels and trends in South Africa: Evidence from reconstructed census birth histories in Union of African Population Studies. In *The African Population in the 21st century: Third African Population Conference,* Vol. 1, Durban

Spiegel A (1980a) Rural differentiation and the diffusion of migrant labour remittances in Lesotho. In P Mayer (Ed.) *Black Villagers in an industrial society: Anthropological perspectives on labour migration in South Africa.* Cape Town: OUP

Spiegel A (1980b) Changing patterns of migrant labour and rural differentiation in Lesotho. *Social Dynamics* 6(2): 1–13

Spiegel A (1982) Spinning off the developmental cycle: Comments on the utility of a concept in the light of data from Matatiele, Transkei. *Social Dynamics* 8(2): 30–45

Stack CB (1974) *All our kin: Strategies for survival in a black community.* New York: Harper & Row

Stats SA (Statistics South Africa) (1996) *1996 Population census: Community profiles.* Pretoria: Stats SA

Stats SA (2001) *2001 Population Census: Community profiles.* Pretoria: Stats SA

Steyn A (1993) *Gesinslewe in die RSA.* Kooperatiewe Navorsingsprogram oor die Huweliks- en Gesinslewe, RGN Verslag HG/MF-4

Udjo OE (2001) A four-'race' model of mortality in South Africa. Communication présentée au Quatrième atelier du Projet d'Analyse des recensements Africains (ACAPO, Mutations Sociales et Démographie de l'Afrique: Enseignements tires de l'analyse des données des recensements, Dakar, Sénégal, 15–17 January

UN (1980) *Principles and recommendations for population and housing.* Censuses Statistical Papers M67. New York: United States Department of International Economic and Social Affairs

Ziehl SC (1994) Social class variation in household structure: The case of a small South African city. *South African Journal of Sociology* 25(1): 25–34

Ziehl SC (2001) Documenting changing family patterns in South Africa: Are census data of any value? *African Sociological Review* 5(2): 36–62

The economic well-being of the family: Households' access to resources in South Africa, 1995–2003

Daniela Casale & Chris Desmond

Introduction

When the ANC-led government came into power in 1994 it inherited a socio-economic environment characterised by widespread poverty, poor access to basic services and massive inequality in the distribution of resources across households. The urgent need for the new government to address this legacy of apartheid led to the implementation of various programmes and policies in the ensuing years aimed at improving the well-being of the previously disadvantaged. In this chapter, we attempt to evaluate how the economic well-being of households has changed in post-apartheid South Africa after just over a decade under the new dispensation.

There are many factors contributing to, and ways of measuring, the economic well-being of a household. In this chapter we have chosen to focus on an examination of trends in household income, expenditure, and access to housing and basic services. These trends are also analysed by race group and area type to give some indication of how different types of households have fared over the period under review.

In this study, we draw on data from the national census and household surveys conducted by Statistics South Africa (Stats SA) between 1995 and 2003.[1] While these surveys have collected a large amount of useful information on individuals and the households in which they live, it is important to note here that the analysis is often constrained by a lack of comprehensive and consistent data on key aspects of the economic well-being of households. In addition to the more general problems associated with collecting data on all types of income and expenditure for example, in South Africa, there is also the problem that the household survey and census instruments have changed from year to year. There have been changes to sampling methodology and questionnaire design, complicating the comparison of measures over time. In trying to examine how households' access to resources has changed in post-apartheid South Africa, a key feature of this chapter will therefore be the evaluation of the data available for the analysis.

---

1 October Household Survey 1995, 1997; South Africa Census 1996; Labour Force Survey (2) – 2000, 2001, 2002, 2003; General Household Survey 2002.

Data

The data used in this chapter are taken predominantly from three of the national household surveys conducted by Stats SA: the October Household Survey (OHS), the Labour Force Survey (LFS), and the General Household Survey (GHS). The 1996 Population Census data are also used in some cases where the questions asked were comparable to those in the surveys.[2]

The annual OHS, introduced in 1993, and the bi-annual LFS (February/March and September), which replaced it in 2000, consist of a sample of generally 30 000 households. One of the principal aims of both of these surveys was to provide a more reliable and detailed picture of employment and unemployment in the country. Entire modules in the questionnaires are devoted to labour market questions, allowing for more textured definitions of employment status and more in-depth analyses of labour market activity than is possible with the census data (Casale et al. 2004). For an analysis of *income* from employment, the household surveys therefore provide the most reliable data. Compared to the census, the OHSs and some of the LFSs also include far more comprehensive questioning on other socio-economic characteristics of individuals and the households in which they live.

As indicated above, there were differences in the way in which the surveys were conducted over the years. Since the data provided by the 1995, 1997 and 1999 OHSs appear to be most compatible in terms of sampling methodology and scope, only these three years of data from the OHS are used in this chapter.

Of the LFSs, we mainly use the September rounds: the LFS 2 (September 2000), the LFS 4 (September 2001) and the LFS 6 (September 2002). While all the LFSs contain a core set of questions on the personal and labour market information of the individuals on the household roster, only the September rounds of the LFS contain an additional household module, which provides important socio-economic information at the household level specifically (such as receipt of welfare grants, household expenditure, and access to services). However, we also make some use of the LFS 3 (February 2001), because it included questions on access to water,[3] and the LFS 7 (March 2003), as it was the most recent survey available at the time of writing, and can still be used to obtain information on income from employment.

The GHS was conducted for the first time in July 2002, and is also based on a sample of around 30 000 households. It contains, as with the LFS, a core set of questions asked of individuals on the household roster (including a module relating to labour market status, almost identical to that found in the LFS). The GHS was designed to include a set of additional questions relating to various social indicators that is far more extensive than that of the September rounds of the LFS. According

---

2 The results from the Census 2001 could not be included in this study as the individual and household level data files were not available at the time of writing.

3 The LFS 3, unlike the other February/Match rounds of the survey, included a limited number of questions directed towards the household specifically (mainly on access to services, and with a particular focus on water).

to Stats SA (2003: i), '[t]he main purpose of the GHS is to measure the level of development and performance of various government programmes and projects', and in this regard, '[t]he survey collected information on a variety of subjects including education, health, labour market, births, access to services and facilities, and quality of life'. Unfortunately, the GHS did not include any new, or at least more detailed, questions on household income and expenditure, two aspects of economic well-being on which the data collected are far from comprehensive in the household surveys. Nonetheless, it provides information on these measures similar to that in the September rounds of the LFS and so can at least be used in a comparison over time.

Before the descriptive statistics are presented, it is important to comment briefly here on the weights used to convert sample estimates to population estimates. The OHSs and the LFSs up to and including September 2002 have been published by Stats SA with both individual and household weights based on the 1996 census. The LFS 7 (March 2003) is the first to be released with updated weights based on the 2001 Census. However, because this survey did not include a household module, only individual weights are available in the data set. Stats SA has indicated that they are currently in the process of updating the weights for the earlier rounds of the LFS to the 2001 population census figures, but until these are available, one needs to be cautious when comparing the LFSs to the OHSs. The GHS 2002 has been published with *both* individual and household weights based on the 2001 census. When examining changes over the period in the analysis that follows, where possible the 1995 OHS and 2002 GHS are used as the endpoints, as these two surveys are weighted according to the closest census year.

Household income

Main sources of household income

Access to monetary resources is clearly essential to household welfare and to participation in a modern economy. In South Africa, the majority of households rely on income from employment, whether directly through salaries and wages of resident household members, or more indirectly through remittances from migrant workers or absent household members. This is evident in Table 4.1, which shows the main source of income for households in South Africa in 2002.

Table 4.1: Households' main source of income (percentage of households), 2002

	All	African	Coloured	Indian	White	Urban	Rural
Salaries and/or wages	59.4	54.7	76.3	81.2	73.5	69.6	44.3
Remittances	13.5	16.7	2.5	4.3	2.9	8.2	21.4
Pensions and grants	18.2	19.5	16.3	8.6	13.1	13.5	25.1
Sale of farm products	1.0	0.8	0.2	0.2	2.7	0.5	1.7
Other non-farm income	5.2	5.2	2.6	3.7	7.3	5.6	4.7
No income	2.7	3.1	2.3	2.0	0.5	2.6	2.9
	100	100	100	100	100	100	100

Source: Own calculations from GHS 2002

Although most households rely on earned income from employment as their main source of income, there are variations by race and by area type. Approximately three-quarters of white and coloured households and over 80 per cent of Indian households rely on salaries/wages as their main source of income, while only 55 per cent of African households are found in this category. A large percentage of African households instead report remittances (17 per cent) or pensions and grants (18 per cent) as their main source of income. Pensions and grants are also important sources of income for the other race groups, after income from employment. For the majority of households, this category would represent the social pension and other state welfare grants. For white households, however, it is more likely capturing reliance on private pension receipts (Case & Deaton 1998).

Very stark differences emerge between urban and rural areas. The majority of households in urban areas, close to 70 per cent, rely on employment earnings as their main source of income. In rural areas, a larger proportion of households rely on pensions, grants and remittances than on employment earnings; 47 per cent as opposed to 44 per cent. Interestingly, and despite the large numbers of individuals who report being engaged in small-scale farming in these surveys, income from the sale of farm products is not often stated as a main source of income for households, even in rural areas. While the sale of farm produce as a *main* source of income may not be common, probably because the cash returns to this activity are too low and variable, growing farm produce as an *extra* form of income is more common in households in which a member is engaged in small-scale farming (based on own calculations from the LFSs).

Whether the relative importance of these main income sources has changed over the period is not known from the data available (the question on which Table 4.1 is based was only asked in later survey years). One would expect that the rise in unemployment and the fall in average earnings since 1995 (Casale et al. 2004) would have led to the decreasing importance of salaries/wages and remittances as main sources of income. The equalisation of pension payments across all race groups by 1993 and the increase in the take-up rate of the child support grant (which replaced the state maintenance grant in 1999/2000), would suggest that non-earned income, and more specifically social grants, would have increased in importance over the post-1994 period.

To calculate the changing share of various income sources in total household income, or to calculate changing poverty rates among households, would require monetary values of the income received from all sources and by all individuals in the household over time. The survey data that we use in this chapter do not contain such comprehensive information. While estimates of income earned directly from employment are available in most of the household surveys conducted by Stats SA, the data on other sources of income – for example, rent, interest, dividends, pensions, remittances and state transfers – are far sketchier.[4] This is unfortunate as one of the

---

[4] For instance, in some years, questions are asked at the individual level; in others, at the household level. In certain survey years, only data on whether or not welfare grants are received is collected (mostly without requesting monetary values), while in others, information on additional income sources, such as private pensions and remittances, is collected.

most important aspects of the government's drive to redistribute resources and reduce poverty in post-apartheid South Africa has been through the increased provision of state transfers (DoSD 2003). Nonetheless, what information can be gleaned from the various surveys is presented in the sections below on 'earned' income (income from employment) and 'non-earned' income (income from other sources).

Earned income

As shown in Table 4.1, the most important source of income for the majority of households in South Africa is the earnings received or generated by resident members of the household through employment (whether working for someone else or in self-employment). The most reliable source of earnings data in South Africa is the OHS/LFS/GHS series, as the collection of employment information is the most efficient in these surveys. Also, over the years much emphasis has been placed on capturing *all* forms of employment, including small-scale and informal activities, which means that *earnings* from all types of work should be captured by the surveys.[5]

Table 4.2 presents estimates of household income from employment from 1995 to 2003. The distinct racial and urban biases in household income levels are apparent in all the years shown. In 1995, for example, average adult equivalent household income from employment in white households was almost five times that in African households, while in urban areas it was just over three times that in rural areas.

The data also show a clear downward trend in real average income from employment for all household types.[6] Using the weighted OHS 1995 and GHS 2002 data as the endpoints of the analysis, it is found that average adult equivalent household income fell by almost 33 per cent in real terms for all households. When analysed by race, the data suggest that white and African households experienced the largest declines in real average household income from employment over the period (27 per cent and 25 per cent respectively), followed by Indian (16 per cent) and coloured households (14 per cent). In urban areas, household incomes fell by 36 per cent on average between 1995 and 2002, compared to the 28 per cent decline experienced among households in rural areas.

The large decreases in average household income from employment are being driven by a number of factors. First, the proportion of households receiving income from

---

5 While it is possible to compare the information provided by the census on households' access to services to that provided by the OHS/LFS/GHS series, one has to be more cautious when comparing estimates of earnings from employment. Even if the same questions were asked in the census as in the surveys, the definition of the household (that is, who belongs to the household), differs between the two. In the census, all those present on census night are included in the household roster. In the surveys, only those who 'normally reside at least four nights a week in this household' are included in the roster. Because earnings from employment (and non-earned income such as grants) are received by individuals, which individuals are included in the roster would make a difference to the total household income estimate.

6 An obvious outlier to the trend is 1997. Household income from employment is unusually low given the estimates in the other years, as is the proportion of households receiving income from employment (see the lower frame of Table 2). It has been reported that employment estimates in this year were low compared to the overall employment trend that emerges over the period (Muller 2003; Casale 2004). If an employed individual was not classified as such in the survey, then no earnings information would be captured either for that individual, which would account for why household income from employment appears to be underestimated in 1997.

employment decreased over the period, as an increasing proportion of households report no members who are working (see also UNDP 2003: 21). In 1995, around 74 per cent of all households were receiving some income from employment; by 2002 this had fallen to 63 per cent (see the lower frame of Table 4.2). The most obvious reason for this change is the dramatic increase in unemployment over the period. According to the broad definition of unemployment (which includes also the non-searching unemployed), the unemployment rate increased from approximately 29 per cent in 1995 to 43 per cent in 2003 (Casale et al. 2004). Although not explored in this chapter, changes in household composition would also have an effect on the proportion of households with income from employment – there is some evidence, for example, to suggest that the unemployed tend to be clustered in households with other unemployed individuals (Dinkelman & Pirouz 2002; Wittenberg 1999).

Table 4.2: Household income from employment, 1995–2003

	1995 OHS	1997 OHS	2000:2 LFS	2001:2 LFS	2002:2 LFS	2002 GHS	2003:1 LFS
Real average monthly adult equivalent household income from employment (2000 rands)							
All	1 187	864	1 011	891	894	801	772
African	679	449	609	550	539	510	501
Coloured	910	782	1 041	942	823	785	742
Indian	1 743	1 416	1 538	1 624	1 555	1 465	1 632
White	3 377	2 657	3 510	2 911	2 811	2 470	2 457
Urban	1 699	1 230	1 359	1 190	1 231	1 083	1 046
Rural	533	293	410	374	359	383	400
Percentage of households with income from employment							
All	73.9	59.6	68.6	65.0	61.8	63.4	62.3
African	71.8	55.4	66.3	63.0	59.8	61.8	59.9
Coloured	85.7	78.9	82.4	75.5	75.9	74.8	76.7
Indian	87.5	76.3	81.9	78.7	81.5	76.6	81.5
White	74.7	66.0	71.5	67.4	60.0	63.8	61.2
Urban	81.1	70.9	76.6	71.9	68.6	70.0	68.2
Rural	64.9	42.1	54.8	53.1	51.1	53.7	54.3

Source: Own calculations using the OHSs, LFSs and GHS

Notes:
1. The data for 2003:1 are presented unweighted, as Stats SA did not provide household weights in this year. In the other years (and in all the following tables) the data are weighted using household weights provided by Stats SA.
2. To convert household size to adult equivalents, children under the age of 12 years were given a weighting of 0.5.
3. Nominal monthly earnings from employment were converted into real values using the average yearly Consumer Price Index published by Stats SA, with 2000 as the base year.
4. The urban/rural classification in the 1997 OHS is different from the other years. In 1997, Stats SA classified the category 'urban' to include semi-urban areas, while in the other years the category 'rural' is defined to include semi-urban areas.

Second, although not shown here, the survey data indicate that among those households containing at least one employed individual, household income also decreased on average over the period. This is not only because the average number of employed individuals per household fell, but also because, among the employed, average real earnings declined between 1995 and 2003. The fall in real earnings was particularly large among African workers and among those employed in informal sector employment, the type of work that has been growing at the fastest rate over the same period (for further discussion of employment and earnings trends between 1995 and 2003, see Casale et al. 2004).[7]

This is reflected in the rise in the number of working poor in South Africa. Casale et al. (2004) find that the proportion of the employed falling below a poverty line of $2 a day (R344 per month in 2000 rands) was just under 10 per cent in 1995 and by 2003 had almost doubled, reaching 19 per cent. Using a poverty line equal to the minimum wage of a domestic worker in an urban area (R584 per month in 2000 rands), the proportion of workers falling below this benchmark was 17 per cent in 1995 and 30 per cent in 2003. While these figures do not measure *household* poverty specifically, they suggest that a large and increasing proportion of the employed themselves cannot escape poverty through employment, let alone other household members they may support.

Some qualifications should be made here regarding the reliability of the data. The absolute values in each year are likely to contain considerable measurement error, particularly among very high earners and very low earners. Among very high earners, there may be reluctance to disclose high income values to the interviewer, and often high income earners choose rather to report an earnings bracket (in the households surveys the highest bracket is censored at R30 000 per month). Among very low earners, for instance, in-kind payments are likely to be important (especially among domestic and unskilled agricultural workers), and the household surveys do not collect information on these forms of remuneration. Given that the proportion of the employed reporting in brackets has remained relatively constant across the years, and assuming that the proportion of earnings received in in-kind payments has not changed significantly over the period, the data can still be used for comparisons over time.

However, as far as consistency over time is concerned, there is the problem that the employment information in the OHSs and the LFSs/GHS was not captured in exactly the same manner. In particular, with the crossover to the LFS in 2000, more emphasis was placed in the questionnaire on counting all forms of irregular work, including subsistence farming, as employment, even if the individual had engaged in the activity for only an hour in the previous week. It is likely therefore that some individuals engaged in informal and own-account activities would have

---

7 According to the survey data, household size has also been declining on average over the period – average adult equivalent household size fell from 3.80 in 1995 to 3.37 in 2002. This was for all household types except white households, among which no significant change was detected. Average adult equivalent household income from employment still fell significantly across all race groups, however, because the percentage fall in income was greater than the percentage fall in household size.

been classified as inactive or unemployed in the OHSs and thus not required to provide earnings information in the survey. This implies that household income from employment would be underestimated in the earlier OHS surveys (as would the decline in this measure over the years). Because this type of work is associated with very low returns and often subsistence farmers report zero cash earnings (see Casale 2004; Casale et al. 2004), the bias is unlikely to be very large.

Despite the various problems associated with measuring earned income, the data clearly suggest that households' access to income from employment declined on average over the period, among all race groups and in both urban and rural areas. Evidently, relying on growth in employment and earnings in South Africa as a strategy to reduce poverty among previously disadvantaged groups has not been sufficient in the economic environment of the post-apartheid decade.

Non-earned income

As explained above, reliable information on the monetary value of income received from sources other than employment, and by all individuals in the household, is not available in these household surveys. There is particularly limited information on private forms of non-labour income, or the income generated by wealth (such as rent, interest and dividends). These forms of income are generally more important among those in the higher-income brackets, and in South Africa, particularly among white people (UNDP 2003).[8] There is some information in the surveys on whether members of the household receive a private pension (shown in Table 4.3). The data indicate that, as expected, a considerable proportion of white households, unlike the other race groups, have members that draw from private pensions (almost 17 per cent in 2000).

Most of the surveys collect information on whether members of the household had received a welfare grant in the past year. Presented in Table 4.4 is the percentage of households with at least one member receiving a social pension, disability grant or child support grant.[9] The most important grant for households is the social pension, both in terms of the size of the grant (which, depending on the year, is between about four and five times the size of the child support grant) and take-up rates (DoSD 2003). Between 1995 and 2002, the proportion of households in which at least one social pension was received increased among all race groups and in both urban

---

8 While household access to wealth is not analysed any further here, due to the lack of data, it is important to point out that ownership of wealth is a key determinant of household welfare. It is estimated that the income from property and financial assets (including profits from non-corporate business enterprises) accounts for around 37 per cent of households' disposable income, mostly accruing to white households (from the 2002 national accounts, in UNDP 2003: 72–73). Not only does it generate its own income, but the ownership of wealth also acts as surety in the acquisition of loans (allowing the wealthy to amass further assets) and provides economic security to its owners. Ownership of wealth makes households better equipped to deal with temporary economic shocks, while the lack of wealth leaves households more vulnerable to being trapped in long-term poverty. The ANC government has made some attempts to change the distribution of wealth in favour of previously disadvantaged groups, through their policies relating to, for example, land reform, black economic empowerment, and small-, micro- and medium-sized enterprise development. Because Stats SA's household surveys do not collect information on financial and property asset values, it is not possible to measure how the distribution of wealth has changed across household types in post-apartheid South Africa. While more research is clearly needed in this area, the nature of these policies suggests gradual change, such that the ownership of wealth in South Africa would still lie predominantly in the control of the white segment of the population (UNDP 2003: 74).
9 In most of the survey years, the question asks if a member of the household received a particular type of grant – it is not known how many members in the household received that type of grant.

and rural areas. The social pension is a more important source of income among African, coloured, Indian, and rural households, however, with many white people excluded by the means test (Case & Deaton 1998).

Table 4.3: Percentage of households with a member receiving a private pension

	1997 OHS	1999 OHS	2000:2 LFS
All	4.8	3.1	4.4
African	1.8	1.6	2.4
Coloured	4.2	2.6	4.8
Indian	4.4	4.8	7.1
White	18.4	10.8	16.9
Urban	6.6	4.1	5.7
Rural	1.9	1.6	2.2

Source: Own calculations using the OHS and LFS

Table 4.4: Percentage of households with a member receiving a welfare grant

	1995 OHS	1997 OHS	1999 OHS	2000:2 LFS	2001:2 LFS	2002:2 LFS	2002 GHS
State pension							
All	9.4	23.3	16.5	16.9	19.0	19.9	18.3
African	10.7	26.3	18.3	18.0	19.6	20.5	19.1
Coloured	9.9	20.8	15.2	16.4	18.2	19.3	17.1
Indian	8.5	18.8	10.2	19.8	16.4	13.0	20.0
White	3.9	11.6	9.3	9.5	16.5	17.8	13.7
Urban	7.1	17.7	11.9	12.7	14.8	15.3	14.3
Rural	12.4	31.9	23.4	24.1	26.3	27.0	24.3
Disability grant							
All	3.9	4.1	3.1	2.9	4.0	4.7	4.3
African	3.8	3.5	2.9	2.8	3.6	4.7	4.1
Coloured	8.4	11.7	7.5	5.9	9.3	9.1	9.7
Indian	6.0	8.2	4.5	4.5	6.4	5.8	6.1
White	1.5	2.4	1.3	1.1	2.3	2.1	1.9
Urban	4.0	4.5	3.1	2.8	3.8	4.5	4.2
Rural	3.6	3.6	3.0	3.1	4.4	5.2	4.6
State maintenance grant/child support grant							
All	–	1.3	0.8	2.7	4.7	8.0	7.9
African	–	1.0	0.7	2.8	5.6	10.0	9.4
Coloured	–	4.9	2.4	4.0	4.1	4.7	7.1
Indian	–	3.3	1.4	2.4	1.2	1.7	1.5
White	–	0.6	0.3	0.6	0.4	0.2	0.3
Urban	–	1.7	0.8	2.5	3.7	5.6	5.9
Rural	–	0.7	0.7	3.0	6.6	11.8	10.8

Source: Own calculations using the OHSs, LFSs and GHS

Disability and child support grants are also more important sources of income among African, coloured and Indian households than among white households, and in the later years, among rural households compared to urban households. While the proportion of households with at least one member receiving a disability grant remained relatively stable over the period under review here, the proportion of households receiving at least one child support grant rose substantially after 1999, and especially for African and rural households. This followed the replacement of the state maintenance grant with the child support grant, which, although means-tested, was made available to more children under seven years of age in all race groups.[10]

Information on remittances, an important source of income for rural African households in particular, is collected less frequently than information on income from employment or social grants (see Posel 2003). While labour migration from African rural households seems to have increased in post-apartheid South Africa, and female labour migration in particular (Posel & Casale 2003), the proportion of households receiving remittance income has declined according to the household surveys (see Table 4.5). This may be both because fewer migrants are finding work and because average wages are declining.

Table 4.5: Percentage of households receiving remittances and average remittance value

	1997 OHS	1999 OHS	2002:2 LFS	1997 OHS	2002:2 LFS
	Percentage of households receiving remittances from migrant workers			Average annual adult equivalent remittance income per household with at least one migrant worker remitting (2000 rands)	
All	14.6	14.1	12.2	1 344.47 (21.8)	1 335.73 (128.9)
African	19.5	18.4	15.6	1 329.39 (21.6)	1 124.27 (34.0)
Rural	30.2	28.7	25.4	1 312.49 (22.56)	1 063.71 (31.0)

Source: Own calculations using the OHS and LFS

Note: Standard errors in parentheses

Average adult equivalent remittance income (in households with at least one migrant worker remitting) fell between 1997 and 2002 in real terms, among African and rural households. Although the number of adult equivalent household members fell in these households, the annual remittance income received by these households fell by a greater percentage. This occurred even though the average number of migrant workers per household in African and rural households increased over the period.

An important question is whether the increased provision of the various social welfare grants over the period has made up for the decline in household income

---

10 The data on foster care and care dependency grants are not shown here as less than one per cent of households received either of these grants over the period, regardless of race or area type.

from employment and remittances, particularly among African households. The Department of Social Development (2003) reports that by the beginning of 2003, 5.6 million beneficiaries were receiving social grants at a cost of R2.2 billion monthly. This would be expected to go some way towards alleviating poverty among households in South Africa (see Case & Deaton 1998, who show that the social pension was very effective in lifting households out of poverty in 1993).

Based on a number of simulations that attempt to estimate the impact of government grants on measures of poverty, the UNDP (2003) reports that the impact of the government's social security system is *not* sufficient in lifting a significant proportion of individuals out of poverty. The results of the simulations, based on 2002 data, indicate that, as expected, both the proportion of the population falling below a national poverty line of R569 a month per adult equivalent and the poverty gap were reduced following the distribution of grants to all age-eligible individuals. However, the effects are found to be limited, as a large part of the population, those of working age, is not captured by the social security net.[11] The report concludes that:

> The current social assistance system of grants in South Africa, although essential to addressing poverty, has limited impact on reducing head-count poverty or the poverty gap. The system is not designed to lift all or even the majority of the poor out of poverty. (UNDP 2003: 89)

Household expenditure

One way to avoid the problem of incomplete income information in the household surveys is to analyse changes in household expenditure over time. Expenditure data are collected in some of the surveys in a relatively consistent manner over the period. Households are asked in a single question to indicate what expenditure bracket their *total* monthly spending falls into.[12] Because the question did not include a very detailed prompt to individuals on which types of expenditure to incorporate in their total estimate, there is likely to be some underreporting. However, at least the *same* question is asked across the surveys, which suggests that any downward bias would exist in all the years. The main problem with the data is that household expenditure is reported in categories that have not been adjusted for inflation by Stats SA over the years. One would therefore expect an increasing number of individuals to shift into higher nominal expenditure categories over the years, as purchasing power decreases.

Table 4.6 shows, however, that even given nominal expenditure categories, the proportion of households falling into the lowest expenditure category of R0–R399

11 There is some information in the household surveys on whether a household member draws from the Unemployment Insurance Fund (UIF). In 1997, 0.6 per cent of households contained a member receiving UIF benefits; by 2000 this had increased to 2.7 per cent (own calculations from OHS 1997 and LFS 2000:2). That few households benefit from the UIF is not surprising seeing as only those unemployed who have worked in formal employment before and who have contributed to the fund, are eligible to draw from it. This means that most of the unemployed have no direct access to social security in South Africa and are supported mainly by other members of the household (who themselves may be eligible for one of the state welfare grants).

12 The question is phrased as follows: 'What was the total household expenditure in the last month? Include everything that the household and its members spent money on, including food, clothing, transport, rent and rates, alcohol and tobacco, school fees, entertainment and any other expenses.'

a month *increased* over the period 1997 to 2002, which suggests rising levels of poverty. In 1997 just under a quarter of all households were spending less than R400 a month; by 2002 the proportion in this expenditure category had increased to almost one-third of all households (an additional 1.5 million households). In 2002 adult equivalent household size was approximately 2.9 in households in the lowest expenditure category, implying that close to three people on average were surviving on a total expenditure of less than R400 a month.[13]

Table 4.6: Proportion of households in nominal total monthly expenditure categories

All	1997 OHS	1999 OHS	2001:2 LFS	2002:2 LFS	2002 GHS
R0–R399	24.5	27.1	32.5	30.5	32.4
R400–R799	30.6	28.5	27.8	27.5	28.2
R800–R1 199	15.6	14.3	12.6	12.6	12.4
R1 200–R1 799	9.2	9.2	7.6	7.9	7.3
R1 800–R2 499	5.8	6.3	5.8	6.2	5.7
R2 500–R4 999	9.2	8.4	7.8	7.8	7.4
R5 000 or more	5.0	6.3	6.0	7.4	6.6
	100	100	100	100	100
African					
R0–R399	31.5	33.6	39.4	38.0	39.5
R400–R799	37.2	33.5	31.8	32.1	32.7
R800–R1 199	16.4	14.7	12.9	13.2	12.5
R1 200–R1 799	7.6	8.4	6.6	6.9	6.4
R1 800–R2 499	3.5	4.3	4.0	4.2	3.9
R2 500–R4 999	2.9	3.9	3.8	3.7	3.4
R5 000 or more	1.0	1.5	1.4	1.8	1.6
	100	100	100	100	100
Coloured					
R0–R399	12.4	14.6	16.6	14.6	17.3
R400–R799	26.6	22.7	25.6	24.4	24.2
R800–R1199	21.1	18.9	16.7	17.0	16.7
R1200–R1799	15.1	14.1	12.9	12.7	13.0
R1800–R2499	11.0	11.1	9.3	10.6	11.1

13 Meth and Dias (2004), using data from the OHS 1999 and the LFS 2002:2, try to estimate the number of additional poor people in the lowest two expenditure categories (that is, R0–R799). After making various adjustments for inflation, adult equivalent household size, economies of scale, underreporting of expenditure and the impact of the social wage, they produce a range of estimates, but conclude that the number of people falling below a conservative poverty line increased over the three-year period by at least 2 million people.

	1997 OHS	1999 OHS	2001:2 LFS	2002:2 LFS	2002 GHS
R2500–R4999	10.8	13.7	13.0	12.5	11.8
R5000 or more	3.0	4.9	6.0	8.2	5.9
	100	100	100	100	100
Indian					
R0–R399	1.6	3.6	3.2	1.8	2.4
R400–R799	8.6	10.4	10.8	8.0	8.7
R800–R1 199	13.6	11.8	9.4	12.4	13.7
R1 200–R1 799	17.4	15.8	15.0	14.0	14.0
R1 800–R2 499	13.8	17.7	20.5	17.0	13.8
R2 500–R4 999	32.9	24.5	23.7	28.3	25.7
R5 000 or more	12.2	16.2	17.5	18.5	21.6
	100	100	100	100	100
White					
R0–R399	2.3	2.2	1.7	0.9	1.0
R400–R799	5.9	7.3	5.4	5.1	4.2
R800–R1199	9.7	9.2	8.6	6.2	8.5
R1200–R1799	12.6	9.1	9.1	9.3	8.6
R1800–R2499	12.7	12.1	12.5	13.4	13.0
R2500–R4999	33.5	27.6	27.9	26.0	27.4
R5000 or more	23.5	32.5	34.9	39.0	37.2
	100	100	100	100	100
Urban					
R0–R399	16.6	21.3	25.2	22.4	23.7
R400–R799	24.8	22.5	23.9	22.8	23.5
R800–R1 199	16.8	14.3	13.7	13.6	14.1
R1 200–R1 799	11.9	11.1	9.5	9.5	9.4
R1 800–R2 499	8.1	8.6	7.8	8.6	8.2
R2 500–R499	14.0	12.4	11.0	11.8	11.0
R5 000 or more	7.7	9.8	8.9	11.2	10.2
	100	100	100	100	100
Rural					
R0–R399	36.6	35.5	44.7	42.8	45.0
R400–R799	39.4	37.1	34.3	34.7	34.8
R800–R199	13.8	14.2	10.7	11.1	9.9
R1 200–R1 799	5.2	6.3	4.5	5.5	4.4

	1997 OHS	1999 OHS	2001:2 LFS	2002:2 LFS	2002 GHS
R1 800–R2 499	2.3	2.9	2.5	2.6	2.3
R2 500–R4 999	1.8	2.6	2.3	1.8	2.2
R5 000 or more	0.9	1.3	0.9	1.4	1.4
	100	100	100	100	100

Source: Own calculations using OHSs, LFSs and GHS

The racial and spatial biases are again clearly evident in expenditure levels. To point out just a few of the striking disparities: while over 70 per cent of African households in 2002 were spending less than R800 a month (falling into the two lowest expenditure categories), only 5 per cent of white households were spending less than R800 a month. Also, while a growing proportion of African households fell into the lowest nominal expenditure category over the period, the opposite was found among white households. Instead, there was a substantially larger increase in the proportion of white households compared to African households whose income fell into the top nominal expenditure category of R5 000 or more a month (as would be expected with bracket creep). For white households the increase was from about 24 per cent in 1997 to 37 per cent in 2002, while for African households, the increase was from 1.0 to 1.6 per cent.

There is also some evidence from Stats SA's Income and Expenditure Surveys (IES) which suggests that total household income and expenditure fell on average in South Africa between 1995 and 2000. Conducted every five years, the main aim of the IES is to provide weights for calculating the consumer price index, but in the process detailed information is collected on all sources of income (earned and non-earned) and on all types of expenditure. The survey found a 12 per cent decrease in real average household income, and a 3 per cent decrease in real average per capita income between 1995 and 2000. Real median income was also lower in 2000 than in 1995, suggesting that the poorest 50 per cent of the population were even poorer five years later (Stats SA 2002: 33). As far as spending is concerned, a fall of 22 per cent is recorded in real average household expenditure between 1995 and 2000. In per capita terms, expenditure fell by 15 per cent on average over the period. As with income, it was found that median expenditure was lower in 2000 than 1995, even taking into account inflation. Furthermore, the largest declines in these income and expenditure measures were recorded among African households (Stats SA 2002: 33).

While the 1995[14] and 2000 IESs should have provided the most accurate data to analyse changes in poverty in post-apartheid South Africa (because of the detailed questioning in these surveys), it must be cautioned that the results from the 2000 IES have been called into question by some researchers (for example, Meth & Dias 2004; Simkins 2003). Concerns have been raised that the figures from the 2000 IES may be downward-biased, as they contradict the national accounts, there are more

14 See Woolard and Leibbrandt (2001) for a detailed discussion of measuring poverty in South Africa, in which estimates are based on the linked OHS 1995 and IES 1995 data.

internal inconsistencies in the 2000 data set than in the 1995 data set, and there is evidence of significant under-enumeration of white people in 2000 (Simkins 2003). While the results from the IESs are noted here, because of these concerns, these data are not explored any further in this chapter (for more details, see Stats SA 2002, and Hoogeveen & Özler 2004[15]).

Access to housing and services

As is evident from the discussion thus far, collecting reliable information on income and expenditure in household surveys is associated with a number of problems. In South Africa further complications arise as the survey design has not remained consistent over the period. It is easier to collect reliable information on observable features of the household's access to resources, such as the type of dwelling the household lives in, or its access to electricity, water and other basic services. In South Africa, the data on household services are also generally collected in a consistent manner over the years. The census, all the OHSs and the September rounds of the LFS contain, in most cases, comparable information on access to housing, electricity, water, and sanitation. In this section we look at changing access to housing and certain key services as measures of the economic well-being of households over the period. These aspects of household welfare are particularly relevant in post-apartheid South Africa, as the ANC government has made concerted efforts to improve access to them over the past decade.

Access to services plays a significant role in determining the well-being of household members. In a recent study of the determinants of subjective well-being in South Africa, households identified housing, sanitation, water, energy, transport and education as important factors (Bookwalter & Dalenburg 2004).[16] There are, however, objective reasons why access to services plays a role in determining welfare, especially with regard to the determination of health status. The nature of households' access to water and sanitation has been shown to have a strong association with health, with a significant global burden of disease associated with poor access (Pruss et al. 2002). The association between health and water is particularly marked for children (Checkley et al. 2004). There are also health benefits associated with better access to electricity, particularly when used for cooking, as this reduces pollution levels within households (Ross et al. 1997).

The UNDP (2003) identifies seven basic areas of service as being important for the well-being of households: housing, energy for cooking, energy for lighting, energy for heating, water, refuse removal and toilet facilities. It is not possible in a chapter of this size to track changes in the provision of all seven of these services. This section examines the trends in access to, and, where possible, use of, a sample of services.

---

15 Using the linked OHS 1995/IES 1995 and LFS 2000:2/IES 2000 data, Hoogeveen and Özler (2004) find that there were an additional 2.3 million people living in poverty in 2000 compared to 1995 based on a $2/day poverty line.
16 Although not analysed here, it is recognised that improved access to, for example, public education, healthcare and welfare services (such as school feeding schemes) are also important determinants of well-being or quality of life. See UNDP (2003, Chapter 2) for trends in composite measures of human development such as the human development index and the human poverty index.

These include housing, piped water, mains electricity (for lighting and cooking), and toilet facilities. An examination of this subset of services will provide some indication of how living conditions of South African households have changed since 1994, as well as raise a number of key issues around the government's service provision programme in South Africa.

Data from the 1995 OHS show how unequal the access to, and in the case of electricity, the use of, services was across race groups and between urban and rural areas when the new government came into power (Table 4.7). According to these data, seven per cent of households in the country had an informal construction as their main living structure. Informal housing is used here as an indicator of household well-being because of the temporary and insecure nature of the dwelling as a means of shelter, and the close association between informal housing and poor access to other services.[17] Households living in informal dwellings in 1995 were predominantly African, with some coloured households living in similar circumstances. Informal housing is also primarily, although not exclusively, an urban phenomenon.

Table 4.7: Percentage of households with access to and making use of various services, 1995

	All	African	Coloured	Indian	White	Urban	Rural
Informal housing	7	10	4	0	0	9	5
Electricity for lighting	64	51	84	99	99	89	29
Electricity for cooking	57	44	75	99	98	83	22
Piped water	79	71	95	98	97	98	51
Flush toilets in dwelling	40	22	62	96	98	63	9

Source: Own calculations using OHS 1995

In 1995, only around half of African households were using electricity for lighting compared to almost all white and Indian households. There was also a considerable urban bias with less than a third of rural households using electricity compared to almost 90 per cent in urban areas. While for the wealthier white and Indian households there was little difference between the use of electricity for lighting and for cooking, for African and coloured households the use of electricity for cooking, a more expensive activity, was lower than for lighting.

The results for piped water show the percentage of households that have access either to a tap in the dwelling, to a tap in the yard, or to a public tap off-site, which they use for their main source of drinking water. Again, a clear racial bias is evident, as is an urban bias. Access to toilet facilities is dealt with in more detail later, but, as an indicator, the distribution of access to a flush toilet within the dwelling, as the best option, is shown to be highly uneven. Almost all white and Indian households had

---

17 The other common forms of housing captured in the surveys are various types of formal structures and traditional houses.

flush toilets within their dwellings, while African, and in particular rural,[18] households had very low access.

Faced with this extremely uneven access to services inherited from the apartheid government, increased provision of formal housing and basic services has been an important part of the ANC government's plans to ameliorate inequalities in living conditions. Considerable changes in legislation and policy have been made over the past ten years as part of the government's efforts to address the imbalances outlined above (UNDP 2003). The nature and appropriateness of these efforts is not the focus of this chapter; the chapter concentrates rather on their outcomes.[19]

Access to housing

Many of the issues raised in the following subsections on services relate to the nature of housing in the country. Access to services in informal dwellings is clearly going to be very different from access in formal housing, and changes in the percentage of households that live in informal dwellings will therefore affect levels of service provision. Table 4.8 outlines the observed trends in the percentage of households whose main living structure is classified as informal.

Table 4.8: Percentage of households whose main dwelling is an informal structure

	1995 OHS	1996 Census	1997 OHS	1999 OHS	2000:2 LFS	2001:2 LFS	2002:2 LFS	2002 GHS
All	7	16	11	12	14	13	12	12
African	10	21	15	16	17	17	16	15
Coloured	4	8	4	6	8	7	6	7
Indian	0	1	1	1	2	0	2	1
White	0	0	0	0	0	0	0	0
Urban	9	23	15	17	18	17	17	17
Rural	5	6	5	6	7	7	6	6

Source: Own calculations using the Census, OHSs, LFSs and GHS

The results suggest a rise in the percentage of households living in informal dwellings, although the 1996 census is an outlier.[20] The increase in informal housing appears to have occurred primarily among African and urban households, although there has also been an increase in informal housing among coloured households. The increase in informal housing has been the subject of some analysis and various causal factors have been identified, such as the movement from rural to urban areas related

---

18 Note that over 90 per cent of rural households are African households. This was the case in both 1995 and 2002, the two endpoints of the analysis.

19 For a detailed discussion and analysis of government policies in this area see UNDP (2003).

20 It is unclear why the census figures are so different from the survey figures, as the question changed little between 1996 and the surveys years. This higher proportion of informal dwellings captured by the census is also going to influence the results presented below relating to access to other services in 1996.

to job-search, as well as movement out of formal township areas initially sparked by violence (Nathan & Spindler 2001; Narsoo 2000; Todes 2001; UNDP 2003).

What is interesting to note is that, since 1999, the percentage of households living in informal houses has remained relatively constant. This suggests that while the number of informal houses is still increasing, the rate of growth may have slowed, possibly following an initial spurt of movement associated with the early stages of the political transition, and more recently related to the lower cost of living in rural areas (Klasen & Woolard 1998). The levelling-off of the proportion of households living in informal dwellings may also be related to increased access to formal housing as a result of the government's housing delivery programme.

The household survey data suggest that, during the same period, the proportion of households living in dwellings classified as formal did increase. It is the proportion of households living in dwellings classified as traditional or other which has been in decline (Stats SA 2002). The increase in formal dwellings has been boosted by the government's post-1994 housing delivery programme. Between 1994 and 2003, an estimated 1.5 million houses were built (Department of Housing statistics in UNDP 2003).

While this is, without a doubt, a notable achievement on the part of the ANC government, the quality of the low-cost housing provided has been called into question on a number of counts (BESG 2000; Tomlinson 1999; UNDP 2003). As the real value of the housing subsidy has fallen, many of the houses have been built in what has been described as a substandard manner: it has been estimated that 70 per cent of the houses did not meet the 35 square metre requirement and many offer insufficient resistance to cold and damp or have an interrupted electricity supply. Also, housing developments are often located on the urban periphery, increasing transport costs, and they have not provided the opportunity to receive rental income or to be used as collateral for loans as was anticipated (UNDP 2003). While a formal shelter is indisputably better than an informal shack, the observed increase in access to formal housing needs to be viewed in the context of the above-mentioned problems that have arisen in low-cost housing provision.

Access to and use of electricity

Electricity within a dwelling can be used for a number of different functions. These functions have different cost implications for, and benefits to, household members. Using electricity for lighting, for example, is far cheaper than using electricity for heating or cooking. For this reason, households that have access to electricity may still choose to use another fuel for cooking or heating, as cost may be a constraining factor. Examining connections to mains electricity only does not therefore give a full picture of the use of that electricity. To facilitate a more detailed understanding of trends, Tables 4.9 and 4.10 examine the use of, as opposed to simply the access to, electricity. Trends in two uses are outlined below: the use of electricity for lighting, a relatively cheap use; and the use for cooking, a more expensive application in terms of both initial investments and running costs.

As shown earlier, in 1995 the use of electricity for lighting was highly unevenly distributed along racial lines, as well as having a strong urban bias. Tracking the responses of households over seven surveys following the 1995 OHS shows a clear increase in the use of electricity for lighting (Table 4.9). In absolute terms, the rise in the number of households utilising electricity as their source of energy for lighting translated into an additional 2.5 million households, from 5.8 million households in 1995 to 8.3 million households in 2002.

Table 4.9: Percentage of households using mains electricity for lighting

	1995 OHS	1996 Census	1997 OHS	1999 OHS	2000:2 LFS	2001:2 LFS	2002:2 LFS	2002 GHS
All	64	58	65	69	72	75	76	76
African	51	44	54	61	65	69	70	70
Coloured	84	84	89	87	87	87	88	88
Indian	99	99	99	98	99	98	99	99
White	99	99	99	99	99	99	99	99
Urban	89	77	84	84	85	87	88	88
Rural	29	28	36	47	49	54	57	59

Source: Own calculations using the 1996 Census, OHSs, LFSs and GHS

The increase in the utilisation of electricity has come about largely as a result of increased access among African, and in particular rural, households. While around half of African households used mains electricity for lighting in 1995, by 2002 this had risen to 70 per cent. In rural areas utilisation doubled over the period, from just under 30 per cent to almost 60 per cent in 2002. Utilisation in white, Indian and urban households remained fairly constant, at high levels, over the period.

The large increase in the number of households using electricity for lighting is a positive trend and suggests that efforts to improve access to services are paying off. An examination of the percentage of households making use of electricity for cooking, however, suggests that the realisation of the benefits associated with increased access to electricity have, in some cases, been limited. Table 4.10 shows that among white and Indian households use of electricity for cooking has remained stable at high levels, while among African households use has remained relatively stable, but at *low* levels. Only among coloured households has the use of electricity for cooking increased significantly over the period.[21, 22]

21 Usage among households as a whole appears to have remained constant over the period despite increases in usage among coloured households. This is in part a rounding issue and in part a result of the weight of African households in the total (among whom a very small increase is recorded between 1995 and 2002).

22 Note that the results from the 1996 census in Tables 4.9 and 4.10 are lower than those of the other surveys. As mentioned above, the census differed in the proportion of households classified as inhabiting an informal structure, recording far higher rates. It is reasonable to assume that, *ceteris paribus*, those living in informal housing would have lower access to services than the average household, at least in urban areas. The lower levels of use of electricity would therefore be expected, given the higher proportion of informal housing observed. As noted earlier, the reason for the difference in the estimated proportions of households living in informal dwellings between the census and the surveys is unclear.

Table 4.10: Percentage of households using mains electricity for cooking

	1995 OHS	1996 Census	1997 OHS	1999 OHS	2000:2 LFS	2001:2 LFS	2002:2 LFS	2002 GHS
All	57	47	54	53	54	57	57	57
African	44	30	40	39	43	47	45	46
Coloured	75	76	82	78	79	83	84	81
Indian	99	98	99	97	98	98	98	99
White	98	98	98	98	98	99	99	98
Urban	83	69	76	73	72	76	78	77
Rural	22	15	20	22	23	24	25	27

Source: Own calculations using the 1996 Census, OHSs, LFSs and GHS

The increase in the use of electricity for lighting suggests that the number of households with *access* to the service has increased. The results on the use levels for cooking imply, however, that there are factors limiting the realisation of other benefits of access to electricity. This conclusion is reinforced by similar results obtained on use levels for heating (Stats SA 2002). Factors that may constrain the use of electricity for cooking and heating include the high relative cost of the investments required to perform these functions – the purchase of a stove or heater, for example. The running cost of uses other than lighting is also far higher. In addition, there may be constraints relating to the nature of the connection. In some cases, low-income households have been connected with low-amp connections, not powerful enough to support heating or cooking (UNDP 2003). Furthermore, illegal connections may not always be stable enough to support uses beyond lighting.

Access to water

The nature of access to water is clearly a key factor in determining the well-being of household members. Having access to clean piped water improves the quality of life of families, making basic tasks easier, freeing up time to perform other activities (especially for women), and promoting better health (Checkley et al. 2004; Pruss et al. 2002). As was described earlier, the level of access to piped water in 1995 was very uneven. White, Indian and coloured households appeared to have very high levels of access to clean water in 1995. African, and in particular rural, households in contrast had much lower levels of access.

Before examining the changes over the period, however, a more detailed understanding of the starting point is required. In Table 4.7, access to piped water included those households that had water piped directly into their dwelling, those that had direct access to water on the site of the dwelling/yard and those that had access to a public tap off-site.[23] Clean water can be obtained through other means, but the availability of piped water is tracked here as it is the most common form of access and it is also the type of access being promoted through the government's service delivery programme. In the following analysis trends in access to piped water are examined across household types, not only in aggregate terms, but also by the nature of that access. Table 4.11 presents the results on access to water in three cumulative steps, that is, they are reported as: 1) the percentage of households with a tap in the dwelling; 2) the percentage with a tap in the dwelling or a tap on-site/in the yard; and 3) the percentage with a tap in the dwelling, the yard, or a public tap off-site.

When access is disaggregated in this way its uneven distribution is far starker. In 1995, only 32 per cent of African households and 15 per cent of rural households responded that they used a tap within the dwelling as their main source of water, as opposed to 97 per cent of white and Indian households and 72 per cent of urban households. The situation among coloured households when portrayed in this manner shows a somewhat different situation from that suggested by the aggregate results. While access to some form of piped water was high among coloured households in 1995, at 95 per cent, only 71 per cent had access to water piped *directly* to the dwelling.

Overall access to some form of piped water increased over the period, rising from 79 per cent of households in 1995 to 86 per cent/83 per cent in 2002 based on the LFS 6 and GHS respectively. While the increase in overall access (the measure typically reported, see for example Stats SA 2002: 21) no doubt has a positive influence on the well-being of households, these aggregate figures mask important information.

Access to water for white and Indian households has remained high over the period with access almost entirely through direct supply to the dwelling. For coloured households, access has improved slightly over the period, largely as a result of increased direct access to water in the dwelling. The experience for African households, however, is markedly different. Aggregate access does appear to have improved, rising by about 10 percentage points over the period. This increase has not occurred through increased within-dwelling access though, but rather through increased access to public taps or other off-site sources. This in itself is an improvement compared to 1995, but it should be noted that non-direct access to piped water is associated with lower consumption per person and is a less hygienic alternative to direct access (Howard & Bartram 2003).

---

23 The remaining households used boreholes, rain water, streams, dams, springs or wells as their main source of water.

Table 4.11: Percentage of households with access to a tap in the household or yard, or a public tap, as their main source of water

	1995 OHS	1996 Census	1997 OHS	1999 OHS	2000:2 LFS	2001:1 LFS	2001:2 LFS	2002:2 LFS	2002 GHS
All									
Dwelling	48	44	42	39	39	40	40	39	39
Or yard	70	61	65	66	70	69	69	69	67
Or off-site	79	81	83	83	85	83	85	86	83
African									
Dwelling	32	27	23	21	25	25	26	23	25
Or yard	59	47	52	55	60	61	61	59	59
Or off-site	71	73	76	74	79	78	80	80	79
Coloured									
Dwelling	71	72	76	74	74	73	74	74	72
Or yard	92	91	93	92	92	90	92	92	91
Or off-site	95	96	97	97	97	95	98	97	96
Indian									
Dwelling	97	97	98	96	96	98	98	96	96
Or yard	98	99	100	96	99	99	99	99	99
Or off-site	98	99	100	97	99	99	99	99	99
White									
Dwelling	97	96	98	98	98	96	97	98	96
Or yard	97	97	99	99	99	97	98	99	97
Or off-site	97	97	99	99	99	97	98	99	97
Urban									
Dwelling	72	66	63	59	57	59	58	59	60
Or yard	94	85	88	89	89	90	90	91	91
Or off-site	98	98	99	98	98	98	98	99	99
Rural									
Dwelling	15	11	8	8	9	8	8	8	9
Or yard	36	25	27	31	33	32	32	33	33
Or off-site	51	54	57	61	59	55	58	61	60

Source: Own calculations using the Census, OHSs, LFSs and GHS.

Notes:
1. The question relating to access to water is asked relatively consistently over the period but with some important exceptions. In the OHS 1995 one question was asked on the main source of drinking water, and a second on the main source of water for other uses. In the other surveys, it is simply asked what the main source of water was. In the above table the main source of water for drinking is reported from the OHS 1995.
2. In the LFS 2001:1, households were asked whether they had access to piped water either in the dwelling, on the dwelling, or off-site. The other surveys had more options on water sources, but these have been collapsed into the three categories of the LFS 2001:1 for comparison.

What appears to have occurred over the period is an improvement in access to piped water, but a decline in the average quality of that access. A higher percentage of households now have access to some form of piped water as their main source of water, but a lower percentage have this access through direct supply to the dwelling.

Access to toilet facilities

Stats SA (2002: 26) has reported that access to flush or chemical toilets[24] has increased since 1995, although not significantly. As is the case with water supply, analysis of aggregate figures masks some of the subtleties related to the nature of the access. Table 4.12 presents the trends in access to toilet facilities, broken down into access to a flush toilet within the dwelling, a flush toilet on-site, a ventilated pit latrine (VIP) on site, another form of toilet on-site (such as a bucket or an unventilated pit latrine), off-site access only and no access at all. The disaggregated results highlight even further the uneven distribution of high quality access across households. In 1995, almost all white and Indian households had access to a flush toilet in the dwelling, compared to only 40 and 62 per cent of African and coloured households respectively. At the extreme end of poor access (that is, in the category representing no access), only African and coloured households are found.

The results in Table 4.12 suggest that the distribution and nature of access have remained relatively unchanged over the period, with some exceptions.[25] Indian and white households continue to have good access, and African households continue to have poor access, with the proportion of African households reporting a within-dwelling flush toilet perhaps even declining somewhat over the period. Coloured households appear to have had somewhat improved access to within-dwelling flush toilets between 1995 and 2002, however. The decline in within-dwelling access to flush toilets has occurred mainly in urban areas. This is likely to be associated with the rise in the proportion of households living in informal dwellings. There is, however, some evidence of an increase in the proportion of households with access to a flush toilet on site. This can be seen most clearly with regard to urban households and may relate to the nature of service delivery to informal households.

VIPs have traditionally been seen as the second best option when a flush toilet is not an option due to inadequate water supply (DWAF 2003). Access has remained at low levels across all households over the period, however, with the exception of the OHS 1995, which reported far higher access compared to other years. The reason for the difference in 1995 is unclear as the question was asked in a very similar manner across all the years. It is also important to note that among African households the proportion of households with no access to any form of toilet has not fallen, but rather exhibits a slight upward trend. These households are predominantly found in rural areas. Aside from being demeaning, no access to sanitation has been linked to poor health (Pruss et al. 2002).

---

24 Chemical toilets are very uncommon and in the analysis presented in this chapter they are included in the 'other on site' toilet category.

25 Note that the results from the 1997 OHS suggest higher access among African and rural households. While some of the rural variation could be explained by the different definition of the rural/urban variable in 1997 (see note to Table 4.1), the increase in total access cannot be explained as the question in 1997 was asked in a similar manner to the other years.

Table 4.12: The distribution of access to different toilet types

	1995 OHS	1997 OHS	1999 OHS	2000:2 LFS	2001:2 LFS	2002:2 LFS	2002 GHS
All							
Flush in dwelling	40	47	35	35	37	37	36
Flush on-site	14	14	19	22	21	19	19
VIP on-site	7	4	4	4	4	4	4
Other on-site	25	20	23	23	25	26	28
Toilet off-site	6	7	10	6	3	4	3
None	8	8	9	10	10	10	10
	100	100	100	100	100	100	100
African							
Flush in dwelling	22	31	17	20	22	20	20
Flush on-site	18	16	23	27	26	24	23
VIP on-site	10	5	5	4	5	5	6
Other on-site	32	29	31	28	32	34	34
Toilet off-site	7	9	12	8	3	14	4
None	11	10	12	13	12	13	13
	100	100	100	100	100	100	100
Coloured							
Flush in dwelling	62	64	68	69	71	72	70
Flush on-site	15	11	14	16	15	14	14
VIP on-site	2	1	1	1	1	1	2
Other on-site	15	18	8	7	9	8	8
Toilet off-site	3	4	4	4	0	2	2
None	3	2	5	3	4	3	4
	100	100	100	100	100	100	100
Indian							
Flush in dwelling	96	92	92	94	97	95	95
Flush on-site	2	5	4	4	2	3	3
VIP on-site	2	1	1	0	0	0	0
Other on-site	0	1	3	2	1	2	2
Toilet off-site	0	1	0	0	0	0	0
None	0	0	0	0	0	0	0
	100	100	100	100	100	100	100

	1995 OHS	1997 OHS	1999 OHS	2000:2 LFS	2001:2 LFS	2002:2 LFS	2002 GHS
White							
Flush in dwelling	98	92	98	98	99	99	99
Flush on-site	1	6	2	1	1	1	1
VIP on-site	0	0	0	0	0	0	0
Other on-site	1	1	0	1	0	0	0
Toilet off-site	0	1	0	0	0	0	0
None	0	0	0	0	0	0	0
	100	100	100	100	100	100	100
Urban							
Flush in dwelling	63	62	54	51	55	56	56
Flush on-site	21	21	27	30	29	28	28
VIP on-site	2	2	2	2	2	2	2
Other on-site	11	9	9	11	9	9	11
Toilet off-site	2	5	6	4	3	3	1
None	1	1	2	2	2	2	2
	100	100	100	100	100	100	100
Rural							
Flush in dwelling	9	22	7	8	7	8	8
Flush on-site	4	3	7	8	8	6	6
VIP on-site	15	8	6	6	8	8	8
Other on-site	44	38	43	46	50	52	51
Toilet off-site	9	12	16	9	4	4	4
None	19	17	21	23	23	22	23
	100	100	100	100	100	100	100

Source: Own calculations using the Census, OHSs, LFSs and GHS

Conclusion

In this chapter, attempts have been made to draw together the information available from census and household survey data to provide a picture of households' changing access to resources in post-apartheid South Africa. The data available clearly do not allow us to provide a definitive answer to whether or not the economic well-being of households has improved on average over this period. However, the evidence provided does not present a very optimistic outlook, especially with regard to African, and particularly rural, households.

Income from employment, most households' main source of income, has been declining on average between 1995 and 2003 – driven by rising unemployment and falling average wages among the employed. What limited information there is on other sources of income suggests that the proportion of households receiving social grants (the pension and child support grants in particular) has been increasing over the period, while the proportion receiving remittance income has been declining. To what extent the increased provision of state transfers over this period has compensated for the fall in average income from employment and remittances cannot be ascertained using the data currently available, and remains an important area of future research.

Household expenditure data were also analysed, and although these are likely to suffer from reporting errors, they at least provide the opportunity to examine *total* figures. Again, the results do not generate a very positive picture of household welfare levels – the proportion of households falling into the lowest *nominal* expenditure category rose considerably over the period, and particularly among African households.

Given the various problems with collecting information on income and expenditure, the data captured in the household surveys on access to housing and services were also analysed. Disaggregation of the overall figures suggests that, while access has been improving on average, the quality of this access has been less than ideal. Availability of formal housing has increased (although the quality of government-provided housing has been brought into question), but then so has informal housing. Access to piped water has risen but predominantly through the less-desirable method of off-site public taps. In the case of access to toilet facilities, neither the availability to any great extent nor the quality has improved. The realisation of the benefits of increased access to services has also been constrained by economic circumstances. This is evident in the greater number of households with access to electricity, but the stagnant *use* of electricity for cooking and heating.

What has also become clear from the analysis in this chapter is the constraint to research posed by insufficient and inconsistent data. Stats SA now conducts up to three household surveys a year, and yet comprehensive questions aimed at collecting information on all forms of income and expenditure are still not included in any of these surveys. This frustrates attempts to monitor the impact of government policies on household welfare levels.

Perhaps as important as concerns with whether and by how much conditions have improved or deteriorated over time, is that a strikingly large proportion of households *still* report low earnings from income, low expenditure levels, and no access to formal housing, electricity, or good quality water and toilet facilities. Despite the government's laudable attempts to improve households' access to resources in the post-apartheid decade, that such a large number of households are still living in dire conditions, however measured, requires renewed commitment to improving the quality of life among the poor in South Africa.

Acknowledgements

The authors would like to thank Dori Posel, Mattias Lundberg and David Hemson for their useful comments, and Colette Muller for her assistance with the data.

References

BESG (Building Environment Support Group) (2000) Housing consolidation in government subsidised *in situ* upgrading and green field housing projects in Metropolitan Durban, Durban

Bookwalter J & Dalenburg D (2004) Subjective well-being and household factors in South Africa. *Social Indicators Research* 65(3): 333–354

Casale D (2004) What has the feminisation of the labour market 'bought' women in South Africa? Trends in labour force participation, employment and earnings, 1995–2001. *The Journal of Interdisciplinary Economics* 15: 251–275

Casale D, Muller C & Posel D (2004) 'Two million net new jobs': A reconsideration of the rise in employment in South Africa, 1995–2003. *South African Journal of Economics* 72(5): 978–1002

Case A & Deaton A (1998) Large cash transfers to the elderly in South Africa. *Economic Journal* 108: 1330–1361

Checkley W, Gilman R, Black R, Epstein L, Cabrera L, Sterling C & Moulton L (2004) Effect of water sanitation on childhood health in a poor Peruvian peri-urban community. *Lancet* 363 (9403): 112–119

DoSD (Department of Social Development, South Africa) (2003) Fact sheet: Social grant beneficiaries. Press briefing by Minister Zola Skweyiya, Pretoria. Available at www.welfare.gov.za/Documents/2003

DWAF (Department of Water and Forestry, South Africa) (2003) *Strategic framework for water services*. Pretoria: DWAF

Dinkelman T & Pirouz F (2002) Individual, household and regional determinants of labour force attachment in South Africa: Evidence from the 1997 October Household Survey. *The South African Journal of Economics* 70(5): 865–891

Hoogeveen J & Özler B (2004) *Not separate, not equal: Poverty and inequality in post-apartheid South Africa*. Mimeo, World Bank, Washington D.C.

Howard G & Bartram J (2003) *Domestic water quantity, service level and health*. Geneva: World Health Organisation

Klasen S & Woolard I (1998) Unemployment, household formation, poverty and nutrition in South Africa. Unpublished mimeograph, University of Munich and University of Port Elizabeth

Meth C & Dias R (2004) Increases in poverty in South Africa, 1999–2002. *Development Southern Africa* 21(1): 59–85

Muller C (2003) Investigating South Africa's informal sector: Measurement, participation and earnings. Unpublished Master's thesis, University of Natal

Narsoo M (2000) Critical policy issues in the emerging housing debate. Gauteng Department of Housing

Nathan C & Spindler Z (2001) Squatting as a transition problem in South Africa. *Economics of Transition* 9(3): 657–673

Posel D (2003) Moving out of the household and out of the household questionnaire: The coverage of labour migration in national surveys in South Africa (1993–2001). *Development Southern Africa* 20(3): 361–368

Posel D & Casale D (2003) What has been happening to labour migration in South Africa, 1993–1999? *The South African Journal of Economics* 71(3): 455–479

Pruss A, Kay D, Fewtrell L & Bartram J (2002) Estimating the burden of disease from water, sanitation and hygiene at a global level. *Environmental Health Perspectives* 110: 537–542

Ross F, Matzopoulos R & Phillips R (1997) The role of rural electrification in promoting health in South Africa. Cape Town: Energy & Development Research Centre, University of Cape Town

Simkins C (2003) Note written following the HSRC workshop on employment and unemployment statistics, 4 February 2003

Stats SA (Statistics South Africa) (2002) *Earning and spending in South Africa: Selected findings and comparisons from the income and expenditure surveys of October 1995 and October 2000.* Pretoria: Statistics South Africa

Stats SA (2003) *General household survey, July 2002.* Statistical Release P0318, 15 December 2003. Pretoria: Statistics South Africa

Todes A (2001) South African urbanisation dynamics and the normalisation thesis. *Urban Forum* 12(1): 1–26

Tomlinson M (1999) From rejection to resignation: Beneficiaries' views on the South African government's new housing subsidy system. *Urban Studies* 36: 1349–1359

UNDP (United Nations Development Programme) (2003) *South Africa human development report 2003. The challenge of sustainable development: Unlocking people's creativity.* New York: Oxford University Press

Wittenberg M (1999) *Job search and household structure in an era of mass unemployment: A semi-parametric analysis of the South African labour market.* South African Network for Economic Research Working Paper No. 22, Potchefstroom

Woolard I & Leibbrandt M (2001) Measuring poverty in South Africa. In H Bhorat, M Leibbrandt, M Maziya, S van der Berg & I Woolard *Fighting poverty labour markets and inequality in South Africa.* Cape Town: UCT Press

CHAPTER 5

Family formation and dissolution patterns

Ishmael Kalule-Sabiti, Martin Palamuleni, Monde Makiwane &
Acheampong Yaw Amoateng

Introduction

The rates at which marriages are formed and/or dissolved in any society affect the
levels of fertility and hence the birth rate in the broader population. Since, generally,
the bulk of childbearing takes place within the context of marriage (Caldwell 1976), in
the absence of widespread HIV infection and effective use of contraception including
condoms, higher marriage rates mean higher levels of fertility. Available evidence
(see for instance Gregson et al. 1997) suggests association between HIV infection
and reduced fertility in sub-Saharan countries. Thus, nuptiality patterns are of great
importance to the institution of the family.

Labour migration and mobility, in particular – one of the primary legacies of
apartheid – has radically undermined the traditional family (especially the extended
family) and the institution of marriage. First, it has facilitated the capitalist penetration
since that portion of a migrant labourer's earnings that are repatriated 'stand for'
services that he would have rendered in kind had he been there to do so. Such,
however, cannot fulfil the sum total of his multiplex social relationships, the most
obvious being sex and emotional responsibilities. Second, it has increased the
vulnerability to HIV and AIDS both for those who migrate or are mobile and for
their partners (or wives) back home. It has been shown for instance (Godiak &
Keely 1998) that in many countries, regions reporting higher seasonal and long-term
mobility also have higher rates of HIV infection, and higher rates of infection can
also be found along transport routes and in border regions. South Africa has a well-
developed transport system and its ports and borders provide gateways to many parts
of southern Africa (DoSD 2001).

Like most societies, the institution of marriage has always played a central role
in shaping the family in South African society. Notwithstanding variations in the
traditions, customs and norms, particularly among the various African groups, the
centrality of the institution of marriage in pre-colonial Africa was evidenced by the
existence of marriage alliances between lineages, which provided an important basis
of the power of patriarchal lineage heads. In South Africa, key to the process of
marriage was lobola, an age-old African custom that entailed a gift in the form of
cattle from the bridegroom's family to the bride's family symbolising the commitment
of the two families to the marriage, a fact that ensured longevity of marriage in
societies. It was also a symbol of appreciation by the bridegroom's family for having
nurtured their son's future wife.

In recent years, however, this custom has been commercialised to the extent where families with potential husbands are increasingly asked to pay large sums of money in lieu of cattle. In fact, it is alleged that some families negotiate lobola on the basis of their daughters' educational qualifications. This has forced many young couples into living together as married, as they cannot afford to pay the exorbitant amounts required in order to be married formally. But to understand the changes that have taken place in the institution of marriage in rural Africa, one needs to understand its place in the 'traditional' political economy, and the status of women (Kuper 1982). Women were afforded protection in rural African communities by being perceived as extremely valuable property, initially 'owned' by their fathers and brothers, and later by their husbands and in-laws. They were thus protected and dependent for life. A substantial bride wealth (usually roughly equivalent to the entire cattle holding of the *umzi* or homestead unit) underlined their value. But no matter how many beasts were given, nothing could equal a woman who produced sons for the lineage of her husband in the patrilineal kinship systems.

The economic system was characterised by the production and consumption unit being co-terminous, and land being held effectively in trust by the present generation for the next. The so-called 'communal land tenure' meant that a man could sell his property, although it would revert to the chief or a kinsman without compensation. However, a combination of influx control during the apartheid regime and urban unemployment in recent years has discouraged a man from totally abandoning what may be his retirement home (if he still has such a claim) (Kuper 1982).

Thus, although the marriage institution has remained homogenous to an extent, the past one hundred years or so have seen considerable and increasing change in its form and function. There has been a recognisable trend in respect to improvement in women's status through modernisation (for example, education, urbanisation, the introduction of money economy) and the opening up of employment opportunities outside the home. The change over the years through modernisation has not only affected women. It has affected men in a similar manner or for the same reason except with the additional factor of labour migration. Certainly the changes of the last hundred years or so have affected attitudes towards marriage, patterns of marriage, parenting, divorce, dissolution of marriage, casual unions and so on (Acsadi & Hamman 1976).

This chapter makes no attempt to deal with the complex issues of HIV and AIDS and their impact on marriage and the family institution as a whole. Rather it is intended to analyse the patterns of nuptiality in South Africa especially with regards to the prevalence, incidence, timing and stability of unions.

The conceptual framework

The examination of nuptiality in the African context, is riddled with such problems as defining marriage and measuring marriage rates. Radcliffe-Brown and Forde (1960) describe marriage in the African context as a developing process with several stages between preliminary rites and the full recognition of the couple as a social unit.

There are therefore many different types of units with each possibly having to go through stages before it is completed. For instance, marriage in Africa assumes diverse forms, a fact that explains the difficulty of demographic studies of marriage in most African societies (Amoateng & Kalule-Sabiti 1995). Adegboyega (1994) observed that the form of marriage in any given African society could range from a legal marriage, which is a union that conforms to a country's legal requirements, and could be civil, religious, or customary, or a combination of all these; a common-law marriage or consensual union or cohabitation, which is a marital union which does not meet legal requirements but nonetheless is counted as marriage in the collection of statistics on marriages; to a visiting union, which is a type of union whereby the persons do not live together but have a marital relationship which may involve the procreation of children. According to the United Nations:

> Marriage is the legal union of persons of opposite sex. The legality of the union may be established by civil, religious or other means as recognised by the laws of each country; and irrespective of the type of marriage each should be reported for vital statistics purposes. (UN 1955: 60)

Marriage in South Africa, like most sub-Saharan African societies, is a process involving a series of negotiations over several years and is not a single event. It is this dynamic nature of marriage in traditional African society that makes it difficult to determine the exact date of marriage in censuses and surveys and to define precisely the concept of marriage, with obvious implications for the quality of data on family events (Adegboyega 1994).

Statistics South Africa (Stats SA 2001) defined marriage to include all those that had gone through civil or religious ceremony, all those married by customary law and all those living together permanently. The above definition however poses a problem when determining the exact beginning of married life. Faced with such practical difficulty, it is worth bearing in mind that data on marriage should be interpreted with caution since reporting of marital statuses, current age and age at first entry into union are subject to considerable reporting errors, particularly in communities with low levels of literacy. Such reporting errors include, inter alia: transfer of women across age groups because of misstatement of date of birth or because the data was supplied by the enumerator; misreporting of current age or date of birth — in many traditional communities exact age, in the western sense, has had little cultural significance in the African setting and hence many respondents cannot recollect their ages or dates of birth accurately (Kpedekpo & Serunjogi 1974); misstatement of date of marriage or age at first marriage. There is expectation that reporting errors would increase for events that occurred further in the past; older persons often experience memory problems and therefore tend to either overstate or understate their ages at first marriage – thus producing spurious rather than genuine patterns and trends, especially for older age groups (35 years and older); and variations in the completeness of registration, which may be attributed to lack of uniformity and universality in national legislation. Past legislation on the registration of marriages and divorces in South Africa resulted in customary and some religious marriages and divorces being excluded from the civil registration system.

With the enactment of the Recognition of Customary Marriages Act (No. 12 of 1998) and its subsequent implementation on 15 November 2000, the civil registration system now recognises and records those marriages solemnised under customary rites. However, some religious marriages (mainly Muslim and Hindu) are still not recognised (Budlender et al. 2004). The former is still being discussed (see South African Law Commission 2002). Moreover, these statistics would only get included in the official statistics for the year 2000 and beyond. According to the 1996 census, traditional marriages comprised 32 per cent of all marriages and 46.5 per cent of all African marriages (Stats SA 1996). Finally, cultural attitudes about marital status are also known to constitute a problem in the analysis and interpretation of results of marital patterns. For instance, Udjo (2003) points to the existence of social stigma attached to divorce in many African cultures including in South Africa. As a result many census or survey-based estimates may underestimate the extent to which divorce has occurred as some divorcees may report that they have never been married at the time of census or survey (Udjo 2003).

Similarly, divorce as a concept is faced with practical difficulties. Divorce or separation does not only cover an array of situations – ranging from protracted grass-widowhood to divorce by court decision – but where divorce or separation are followed by rapid remarriage, individuals involved may often record their statuses as only 'currently married' and/or 'never married' when some of them were divorced at the time of censuses or surveys. In addition, many with failed marriages may tend to report themselves as 'never married' in order to increase their marriageability in society. It is this lack of formal procedures to mark marriage dissolution in many societies in sub-Saharan Africa and segments of the population in South Africa, in addition to other factors, that may facilitate underestimation of divorce rates.

These problems notwithstanding, the Statistical Commission of the United Nations defines divorce as 'a final legal dissolution of marriage, that is, the separation of husband and wife by a judicial decree which confers on the parties the right to civil and/or religious remarriage, according to the laws of each country' (UN 1955: 62). However, in contemporary surveys and censuses the distinction between 'divorce' and 'separation' can be very fuzzy, as dissolution of marriage in most African societies does not lead to formal procedures to mark such events. In such cases it may lead to an undercount of divorces as they may be mistaken for separations. In order to overcome this problem, the analysis in this chapter grouped together 'separation' and 'divorce' categories as 'divorce'. Data on widowhood are equally beset with problems. In sub-Saharan Africa, the death of a spouse does not often sever ties between the two families or kinship groups involved, and in circumstances where inheritance of widows or widowers by the siblings of the deceased is common practice, widowhood status may often never be recorded in censuses and surveys.

Socio-economic differentials in nuptiality

Demographic events that influence the number of people who marry in a given society are those related to the timing of entry into union during their life cycle, the rate of marital dissolution and the incidence of remarriage (Singh & Samara 1996).

Demographic factors affect nuptiality patterns directly. For instance, age at first marriage is affected by the deficit of persons of the opposite sex in the marriageable ages, sometimes referred to as the 'marriage market'. This may result directly from the practice of polygyny and age-sex selective mortality and migration as well as conscription for military services (Sivamurthy & Seetheram 1976).

Although Singh and Samara (1996) have observed that marital status in the African context has been less responsive to socio-economic factors compared to countries elsewhere due to the fact that marriage in Africa is generally universal, early and characterised by low divorce rates, there has, however, been a recognisable change in the marriage pattern and trend, particularly among women, due to an improvement in their social standing in society through modernising forces like education, urbanisation, employment, and so on.

But, while modernisation may affect marriage rates, there is no consensus in the literature on its effect on the stability of unions. On the one hand, as Goode (1993) has observed, historically social science has treated modernisation as the root cause of divorce in society. On the other, it has also been seen to have some stabilising effect on marriage since it breaks some of the practices in traditional society, which are assumed to be negatively impacting on the stability of family life. A case in point here is the practice of arranged marriages, which are generally perceived in the west to be conducive to marital instability (Goode 1993).

Education is of overriding importance as a modernising factor with regard to nuptiality since it is selective of such socio-economic factors as rural–urban residence, employment, religious affiliation, occupation, and so on. In the absence of contraception, the longer women spend at school the shorter the time of their exposure to marriage. Formal education is also known to narrow women's range of potential marriage partners since women are generally expected to marry men either with the same or a higher level of education. Education of women in particular plays an important role in transforming attitudes towards marriage and childbearing. Delayed marriage, stability of unions, low levels of mortality and better communication between couples are particularly associated with better educational achievement. Also, individuals with high educational qualifications are most likely to be urban and metropolitan residents and to be in high status employment and occupations.

However, it can also be argued that in countries experiencing strong urban-oriented development, such as South Africa, rural–urban residence becomes the overriding factor in defining the effect on nuptiality of all other socio-economic factors. In other words, where one resides determines the quality of education one gets, and influences not only opportunities for formal employment but the quality of lifestyle in general. For instance, urbanisation is generally associated with moving away from kinship obligations and less societal control. Women living in urban or metropolitan centres are therefore more likely to be exposed to better quality education, which will lead to formal employment, compared to their counterparts in rural areas. They are also less likely to experience family pressures to be in marital unions – hence they experience lower marriage rates. All in all, therefore, urbanisation, education and formal employment collectively have the net effect of transforming old traditional values into new aspirations and modern outlook and provide an alternative to marriage for women in particular.

One of the recent international comparative studies of the socio-economic antecedents of nuptiality comes from Singh and Samara (1996). They observed that urbanisation, education and formal work differentials were considerable in Latin America and less so in Africa in general. In Latin America, for instance, rural women younger than 20 years of age were found to be 25 per cent more likely to be married than their urban counterparts. Similarly, in Asian and North American countries, young rural women were two-thirds more likely to be married compared to their peers in the urban areas. Such findings were not unexpected, however, as informal employment based on rural subsistence is more likely to encourage women to marry and to do so at early ages. Subsistence farming by its nature is labour-intensive and necessitates women to seek family alliances in the form of marital relationships.

As far as employment away from home goes, it is one of the main socio-economic factors influencing nuptiality patterns. Work experience, especially in the formal sector, exposes women to ideas and norms that discourage marriage, while their access to cash income gives them the independence that makes it possible to go on in life without marriage. Related to paid employment is the issue of power and autonomy of women, which has been regarded as a mechanism that destabilises marriage bonds, resulting in high divorce rates. Increased labour market participation of women in particular is thought to reduce marriage returns, resulting in unstable marriages. But it is not only labour force participation of women that destabilises marriages; the type of jobs available to women is an important factor. In countries where many women have ascended to high-ranking jobs in society, marriage stability has been negatively affected (Makiwane 1996). While studies that have examined socio-economic differentials in nuptiality are generally scarce in South Africa, available evidence suggests that women's entry into the labour force generally has a depressing effect on marriage rates (Maconachie 1989). Unemployment and general loss of income are likely to force young people to delay marriage or to stay away from it completely.

Data sources and methods of analysis

The analysis in this chapter utilises data from three sources, namely, the 1996 and 2001 Population Censuses (Stats SA 1996, 2001) and the 1998 South African Demographic and Health Survey (DoH 1998). Both of the censuses collected information on the marital status of each member of the household. The 1996 census collected data on six categories of marital status: never married, married (civil/religious), married (traditional/customary), living together (with partner), widower/widow, and divorced/separated. However, it provided no standard definition of marriage during data collection. The 2001 census expanded the marital status categories to eight – providing separate categories for 'divorced' and 'separated' plus an additional category for polygamous marriages.

The 1998 South African Demographic and Health Survey (SADHS) administered three questionnaires: the household, individual and adult questionnaires. The purpose of the household schedule in the SADHS was basically to identify women eligible for the individual questionnaire. The household schedule did not collect information on the marital status of each member of the household. Instead, such information, plus data on age at first marriage, were collected in the individual questionnaire, which was administered to all women in the reproductive age group 15–49 years. Two approaches have been used to analyse the patterns in ages at first marriage, namely indirectly, from marital status data from the 1996 and 2001 censuses using singulate mean ages at marriage (SMAM), and directly, from the individual data in the SADHS 1998. In the former, SMAM were computed from the classification of the population by marital status, age and sex based on the 1996 and 2001 census data.

This indirect method of calculating ages at first marriage was first devised by Hajnal (1953) and estimates the average number of years lived by a cohort of persons before their first union (SMAM). The computational procedure is explained in detail elsewhere (Shryock et al. 1976). The method assumes a synthetic cohort (an untenable assumption) in circumstances where the proportions marrying are experiencing changes. The procedure is also very sensitive to biases in age-reporting. Thus two types of errors in the data could cause differences in the SMAM: errors in the classification of marital status and errors in-age reporting. Both of these are rampant in the African context where illiteracy levels are high and consensual unions are prevalent, as in South Africa.

In the second approach, age at first marriage is treated as an intermediate fertility variable and also considered a duration variable. It is measured in terms of the time elapsed before the event occurred. It is thus recorded as the time elapsed between the date of birth of an individual woman and the date of first marriage. However, since for some individual women the time elapsed to the day of the interview may not have been sufficient for the event to have occurred, the information on age at first union is unknown and is therefore censored by the date of the interview. In such a situation, the analytical technique commonly used is the life-table method. Since in the survey, detailed information in the individual questionnaire was collected for all women in the childbearing ages 15–49, no adjustment to the data was necessary.

Age at first marriage

Following the onset of ovulation, for childbearing to take place a woman must engage in sexual relations. In societies where premarital births are uncommon (and/or premarital sex not encouraged), having a sexual partner is approximated by marriage as most sexual intercourse occurs within marriage (Mpiti & Kalule-Sabiti 1985). In that context, therefore, age at first marriage defines the onset of exposure to sexual intercourse. Thus the ages at which women first marry, the proportion of all women who ever marry, the proportion who remain single, the forms that marriages take, the prevalence of multiple marriages, marital disruptions through divorce/separation, the prevalence of HIV infection as well as level of condom use to prevent infection all combine to influence the overall number of children ever born. To evaluate the timing of first marriage in South Africa, a comparative classification proposed by Bogue (1969) is used. Using data from a number of countries, Bogue proposed a typology of the timing of first marriage for females as follows:

- child marriage (median age at first marriage <18 years);
- early marriage (median age at first marriage 18 or 19 years);
- marriage at maturity (median age at first marriage 20 or 21 years); and
- late marriage (median age at first marriage 22 years or over).

Table 5.1 presents the SMAM for both males and females according to province and race estimated indirectly from the 1996 and 2001 censuses. The data confirm that South Africa is typified by a late marriage pattern. A similar pattern was noted by Adegboyega (1993) in his review of the timing of marriage in African countries. He observed very high SMAM in southern Africa, that is, in the region of 26 years for females and 29 years for males, with no significant changes in SMAM for males in the two periods under study (1970–79 and 1980–90).

Table 5.1: Singulate mean age at first marriage by province and race, 1996 and 2001

	Census 1996		Census 2001	
	M	F	M	F
South Africa	31.0	28.7	30.5	27.7
*Province**				
EC	32.9	29.1	32.1	28.2
FS	28.6	26.8	29.2	26.7
G	30.1	27.7	29.8	26.3
KZN	33.0	31.0	32.0	29.7
M	31.0	28.8	30.4	27.2
NC	30.3	28.6	30.8	27.8
L	30.7	27.4	29.7	27.3
NW	31.7	29.5	31.3	28.4
WC	29.5	27.9	29.3	27.0
Race				
African	32.0	29.6	31.2	28.1
Coloured	28.9	27.9	28.7	27.0
Indian	26.9	23.9	27.3	24.5
White	27.0	24.5	27.2	24.8

Source: Compiled by the authors using data from censuses 1996 and 2001 (Stats SA 1996, 2001)

Note:
* Eastern Cape – EC; Free State – FS; Gauteng – G; KwaZulu-Natal – KZN; Mpumpalanga – M; Northern Cape – NC; Limpopo – L; North West – NW; Western Cape – WC

Table 5.2 presents data on age at first marriage derived directly from the 1998 SADHS. The results in Table 5.2 are presented both in medians and in a series of quantiles, Tx. The latter are defined as the time elapsed before x per cent of the persons concerned have experienced the given event. Thus, T10, T25, T50 and T75 are given as time elapsed before 10, 25, 50 and 75 per cent of all women respondents in the individual survey aged 15–49 married. Quartile estimates by age are only shown for older women aged 25 and over. This has to do with the issue of censoring. Very few of the younger women were actually married at the time of the interview, so that over 95 and 76 per cent of them in the age groups 15–19 and 20–24 years respectively were censored. Consequently it was not possible to estimate the T10 and T25 quantiles for those two age groups. The trimeans presented are given as a weighted average of the quantiles (Tx).

These results generally confirm the fact that a combination of historical, cultural, economic and political factors ensure that women marry late in South Africa; the median age at first marriage for all women is 25 years, while the the trimean for the whole country is about 27 years. By ages 18, 20 and 36, 10 per cent, 25 per cent and 75 per cent of the women are married respectively. Except for the 50 per cent quantile of older cohort of women aged 35 and over, the distribution by current age in the 10 and 25 per cent quantiles shows remarkable consistency and conveys the impression that age at first marriage has remained unchanged even in the recent past. However, for the 50 per cent quantile, there is a clear indication that age at first marriage has changed in the past 20 years or so, due perhaps to such modernising factors as rapid urbanisation, increased education and employment as well as political and economic emancipation, particularly of women.

Older women married earlier, on average at 23 years, compared to their younger counterparts aged less than 35 at the time of the survey. Women in the age group 30–34 married midway between ages 24 and 25 whereas those in the age group 25–29 married slightly under age 27. However, considering that the marriages the older women reported at the time of the survey occurred in the past 20 to 25 years or so, it is possible that their ages at first marriage were underestimated. The racial differentials in age at first marriage between, on the one hand, African people and coloured people and, on the other, Asian people and white people, are marked. While 50 per cent of Africans and coloured women were married by, on average, around age 26, their Asian and white counterparts were married at earlier ages (21 and 22 respectively.) The trimean for Africans was about 28, for coloureds 27 and for both Asians and whites 22. The highest median ages at marriage were recorded for women from North West and KwaZulu-Natal provinces (26.9 and 26.5 respectively), while Limpopo and Free State had the lowest at 21.5 and 23.1 respectively. The rest of the provinces had their medians between the two extremes but in line with the national average of 25.

Table 5.2: Age at first marriage by selected background variables, all women 1998

Selected variables	Quantiles				Trimean	N
	T10	T25	T50	T75		
Age						
25–29	17.7	20.9	26.8			1 811
30–34	16.9	19.8	24.6	–	–	1 616
35–39	16.6	19.2	23.0	32.1	24.3	1 628
40–44	16.8	19.2	22.7	30.1	23.6	1 255
Usual place of residence						
Rural	16.8	19.3	23.9	35.0	25.5	5 217
Urban	18.3	21.2	25.8	36.6	27.3	6 518
Educational level						
None	15.0	17.4	21.3	29.4	22.4	810
Primary	16.6	18.7	23.0	33.3	24.5	3 134
Secondary	18.4	21.2	26.1	38.5	28.0	6 929
Higher	20.3	22.8	25.8	33.7	27.0	862
Race						
African	17.3	20.3	25.8	39.4	27.8	8 993
Asian	17.0	18.8	21.4	25.8	21.9	393
Coloured	18.7	21.6	25.6	35.4	27.0	1 533
White	18.0	19.7	21.8	24.4	21.9	755
Region of usual residence						
WC	18.6	21.3	24.8	35.7	26.7	919
EC	17.4	20.2	25.2	41.5	28.0	2 756
NC	18.6	21.2	25.4	36.3	27.1	1 041
FS	17.5	19.7	23.1	29.0	23.7	936
KZN	18.0	21.0	26.5	36.3	27.6	1 826
NW	17.9	21.3	26.9	37.3	28.2	931
G	18.2	20.7	25.2	32.9	26.0	1 057
M	16.8	20.0	25.4	6.8	26.9	1 131
L	15.8	17.9	21.5	32.1	23.3	1 138
SA	17.6	20.4	25.1	36.1	26.7	11 735

Source: Compiled by the authors using data from the 1998 SADHS (DoH 1998)

Table 5.3 presents percentage distribution of the timing of first birth in relation to first marriage by race. About 44 per cent of all women had a first birth before first marriage, while only about 26 per cent followed a normative pattern of waiting to get married before starting a family, and another 26 per cent reported no birth and no marriage. The data in the table also show that childbearing before marriage in South Africa is more prevalent among African and coloured people (48 and 52 per cent respectively) than among their Asian and white counterparts (10 and 4.5 per cent respectively). Conversely, the normative trend of starting a family after marriage is more common among Asian (57 per cent) and white people (63 per cent) compared to African (23 per cent) and coloured people (19 per cent).

Table 5.3: Percentage distribution of timing of first birth in relation to first marriage by race of respondent, all women 1998

| Race | First marriage in relation to first birth | | | | | |
	Married, 1st birth	1st birth before 1st marriage	1st birth, not married	No birth, not married	No birth, married	Total no. of women
African	22.7	21.6	26.0	27.0	20.8	
	(2 038)	(1 943)	(2 338)	(2 425)	(249)	8 993
Coloured	18.7	29.9	22.2	24.8	4.3	
	(287)	(459)	(340)	(381)	(66)	1 533
Asian	56.7	8.4	1.8	28.2	4.8	
	(223)	(33)	(7)	(111)	(19)	393
White	62.8	4.0	0.5	23.7	9.0	
	(474)	(30)	(4)	(179)	(68)	755
All	25.9	21.1	23.0	26.5	3.4	100
Women	3 022	2 465	2 689	3 096	402	11 674

Source: Compiled by the authors using data from the 1998 SADHS (DoH 1998)

Thus, although many studies have observed a declining total fertility rate among all race groups (see, for example, Moultrie & Timaeus 2003; Udjo 2003), this study shows that childbearing is still popular among South Africans. Moreover, as Table 5.3 shows, as first birth often precedes first marriage, the effect of nuptiality on fertility (especially on the African and coloured population groups) is much weaker than in other parts of the world.

Prevalence of marriage and stability of unions

Although it is generally believed that marriage in Africa is a universal institution, in South Africa the aggregated figures show that it is not universal as evidenced by the data in Table 5.4. Disaggregation of the data, however, indicates that this is because of the low marriage rates of the African and coloured population groups. Table 5.4 shows a classification of the total population of South Africa in terms of marital status as at the time of the 2001 census. This represents a combined effect of age at first marriage, marriage prevalence, dissolution and remarriage.

Overall, almost half (49 per cent) of the total population 15 years and older were recorded never married with married people accounting for approximately 42 per cent; widowed and divorced/separated about 6 and 3 per cent respectively (total figures not shown). Approximately 52 and 46 per cent of males and females aged 15 and over respectively were recorded as never married. At the oldest age of 50+, around 10 per cent of males and 12 per cent of females had never been married. The data for the oldest group across provinces show modest variations for both sexes, with North West and KwaZulu-Natal provinces recording the highest percentages of single old females (15 and 14 per cent respectively) (see Tables 5.5a and 5.5b).

The percentage married at the time of the 2001 census was approximately 44 and 41 for males and females respectively (Table 5.4). These percentages reach high levels of 78 and 64 per cent for the age groups 45–49 and 40–44 for males and females respectively. The percentage drops to 47 for females in the quinquennial age group. There is however substantial gender differences by age, with more males aged 35 and over reporting themselves married compared to their female counterparts. The situation is, however, reversed in the younger age groups (20–34 years), with more females reporting married at the time of the census. Marriages are generally delayed for both sexes so that almost 70 and 56 per cent of males and females respectively were still 'never married' by ages 25–29.

A more detailed analysis of the universality of marriage in South Africa than that provided by inspection of data on current marital status at the time of Census 2001 is revealed in Figures 5.1, 5.2, 5.3 and 5.4, which present a classification of the population by race, gender and current age. Keeping in mind the possible problems inherent in census and survey data in the African context discussed in the introduction, what emerges from these figures is that marriage is a fairly universal institution among the white and Asian population groups but less so among the coloured and African population groups. The proportions of males never married drop sharply among white and Asian people after age 24, so that by age 35 approximately 70 per cent are already married.

Table 5.4: Percentage distribution of the population by current age and marital status, South Africa 2001

Current age	Males						Females					
	Never married	Currently married	Divorced	Widowed	Total	No. of males	Never married	Currently married	Divorced	Widowed	Total	No. of females
15–19	98.7	1.1	0.1	0.1	100	2 453 067	95.6	4.1	0.2	0.1	100	2 528 642
20–24	91.9	7.7	0.3	0.1	100	2 099 305	79.0	20.3	0.5	0.2	100	2 195 230
25–29	69.9	29.2	0.7	0.2	100	1 899 135	56.0	42.0	1.4	0.6	100	2 035 814
30–34	45.2	52.7	1.7	0.4	100	1 594 497	39.0	56.0	3.3	1.7	100	1 746 412
35–39	29.3	69.1	3.0	1.6	100	1 441 496	29.0	62.3	5.3	3.4	100	1 630 263
40–44	20.5	74.1	4.2	1.2	100	1 233 627	23.2	63.6	7.2	6.0	100	1 385 833
45–49	15.4	78.0	4.9	1.7	100	967 600	19.4	62.9	8.0	9.7	100	1 119 776
50+	9.7	78.5	4.2	7.6	100	2 576 813	12.5	46.9	5.4	35.2	100	3 546 971
Total	52.4	43.7	2.1	1.8	100	14 264 540	45.8	41.1	3.5	9.6	100	16 188 941

Source: Compiled by the authors using data from census 2001 (Stats SA 2001)

Table 5.5a: Percentage single males by age group and province, South Africa 2001

Age group	WC	EC	NC	KZN	NW	G	M	L	FS	SA
15–19	98.4	98.8	98.4	98.6	99.1	98.4	98.9	98.8	98.4	98.6
20–24	89.6	95.0	89.1	93.7	94.0	90.5	91.9	90.7	88.9	91.9
25–29	61.5	78.8	65.0	77.5	76.1	64.9	71.6	69.0	61.5	69.9
30–34	35.8	56.5	4.4	56.4	51.3	39.0	46.7	43.7	34.4	45.2
35–39	23.0	39.1	29.6	39.0	32.9	24.1	29.0	25.8	20.1	29.3
40–44	16.2	27.9	22.7	26.9	23.6	16.5	19.4	17.6	14.0	20.5
45–49	12.2	20.7	17.3	19.8	18.4	12.2	14.7	12.5	10.6	15.4
50+	8.4	10.5	12.5	11.9	12.4	8.3	10.4	7.2	7.0	9.7
Total	44.8	58.1	48.3	59.4	53.3	46.5	54.3	56.6	46.3	52.4

Source: Compiled by the authors using data from census 2001 (Stats SA 2001)

Table 5.5b: Percentage single females by age group and province, South Africa 2001

Age group	WC	EC	NC	KZN	NW	G	M	L	FS	SA
15–19	95.8	96.4	95.3	96.7	96.8	94.4	95.1	94.4	94.5	95.6
20–24	77.3	83.2	77.7	85.5	83.2	72.7	78.7	75.0	74.5	79.0
25–29	49.7	59.8	53.0	67.5	61.1	48.5	56.9	52.2	47.7	55.8
30–34	32.9	41.6	36.9	49.4	41.8	34.1	39.8	34.3	29.9	38.7
35–39	24.1	31.4	27.9	36.6	30.8	27.1	29.4	24.1	20.9	29.0
40–44	19.0	25.5	22.0	28.4	25.2	22.6	23.6	18.2	16.8	23.2
45–49	15.9	21.7	18.6	22.7	21.4	19.6	19.5	15.0	13.8	19.4
50+	10.7	13.7	13.4	14.5	15.0	12.0	12.6	9.6	9.6	12.5
Total	40.7	47.6	59.7	52.4	48.5	41.4	48.3	44.6	40.4	62.4

Source: Compiled by the authors using data from census 2001 (Stats SA 2001)

Figure 5.1: Percentage of males never married by population group, South Africa 2001

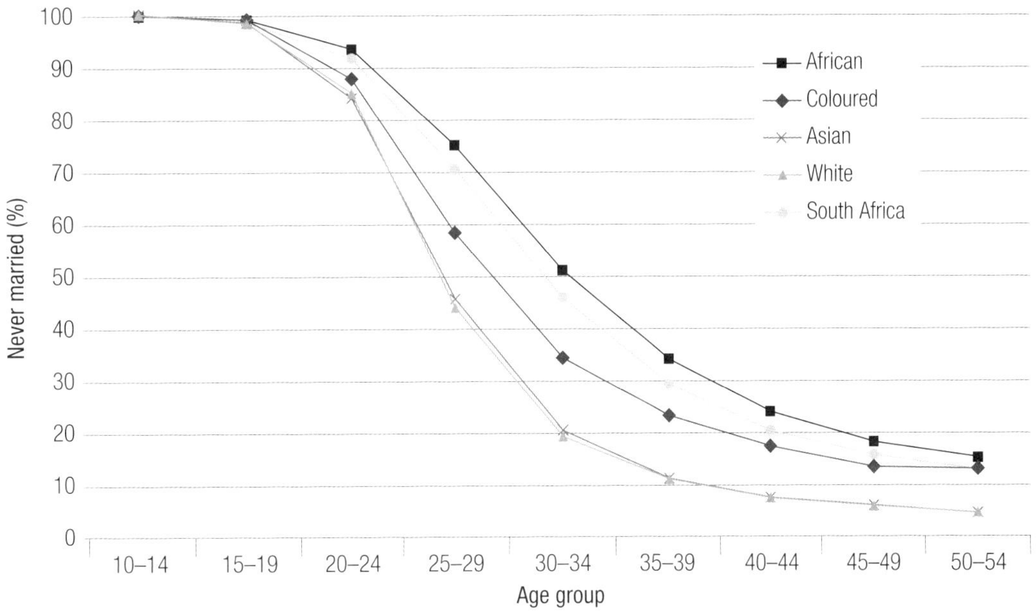

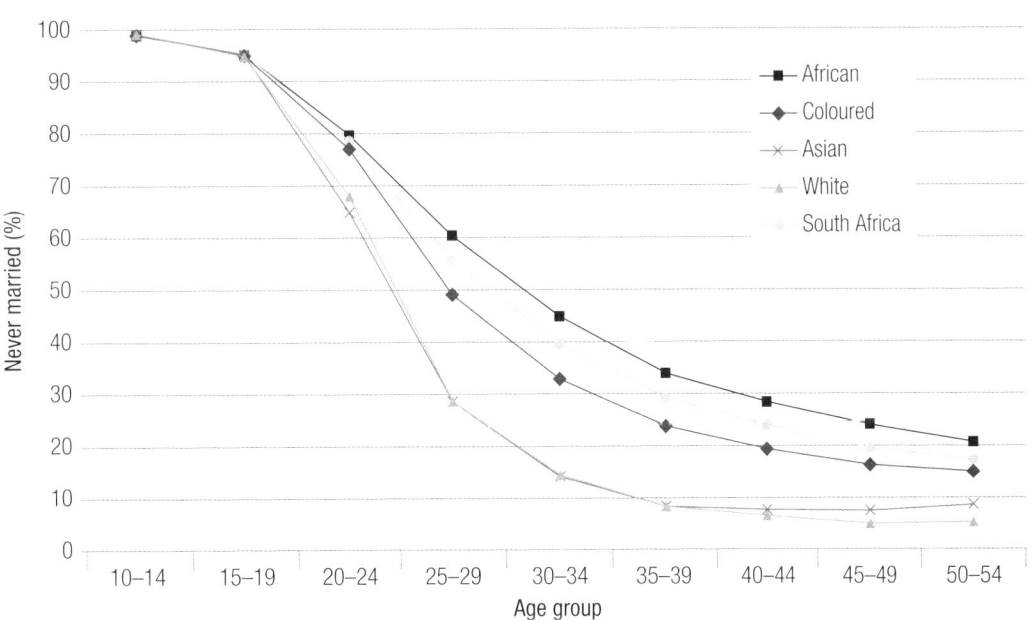

Source: Compiled by the authors using data from census 2001 (Stats SA 2001)

Figure 5.2: Percentage of females never married by population group, South Africa 2001

Source: Compiled by the authors using data from census 2001 (Stats SA 2001)

Figure 5.3: Percentage of males married, by population group, South Africa 2001

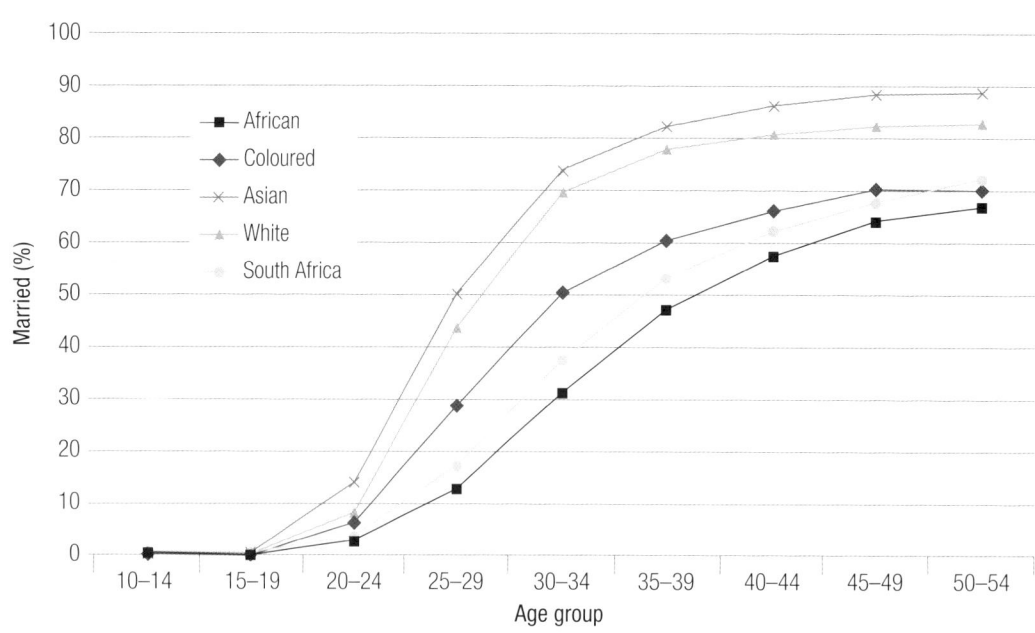

Source: Compiled by the authors using data from census 2001 (Stats SA 2001)

Figure 5.4: Percentage of females married, by population group, South Africa 2001

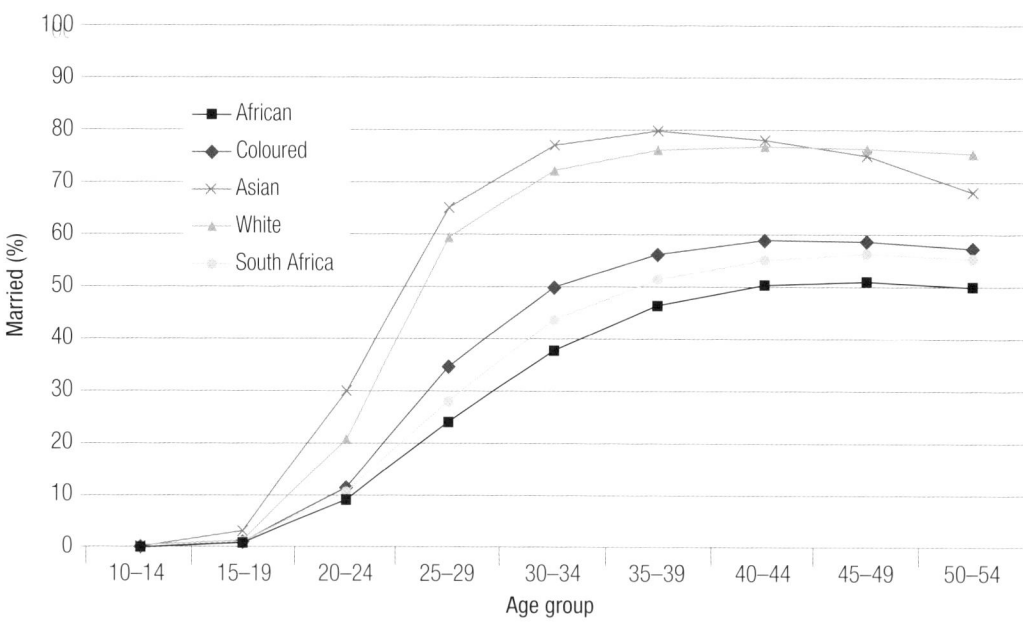

Source: Compiled by the authors using data from census 2001 (Stats SA 2001)

In contrast, the highest percentages for 'never married' were recorded for the African and coloured population groups. Similarly among females, fewer Asian and coloured females reported themselves as never married while more Asian and white females reported themselves married compared to their African and coloured counterparts. While the racial differentials in the marriage patterns project a genuine picture of the dynamics among the white and Asian population groups in South Africa, the patterns among the African and coloured population groups may be subject to scrutiny. For one thing, these two racial groups represent the disadvantaged communities in the country, and as such they experience not only high levels of illiteracy, a factor that probably complicates definitional and classification problems, but poverty and unemployment are also rampant. These factors, coupled with increasing marriages terminated by the death of husbands, the effect of the economic migration that replaced the labour migratory system after 1994 and so on, all affect the quality of reporting of marital status. Focusing on the marriage patterns among the oldest age group (50 years and over), about 85 and 82 per cent of the Asian and white males respectively were married compared to approximately 50 and 58 per cent of the Asian and white females respectively. Female proportions for the coloured population group in this oldest age group were around the national average of 44 per cent while the African proportions were well below the national average (Table 5.6).

Table 5.6: Proportions married within each five-year age group by race

	15–19	20–24	25–29	30–34	35–39	40–44	45–49	15+	50+
Male									
African	0.8	3.0	12.5	30.7	47.4	57.5	63.7	30.2	68.9
Coloured	0.8	5.9	28.4	50.1	60.5	66.2	69.6	49.9	67.8
Asian	1.1	13.2	50.2	73.9	82.2	86.1	88.1	59.1	85.0
White	1.0	8.1	43.6	69.0	77.3	80.3	82.1	61.2	82.1
Total	0.8	3.8	17.4	37.8	53.2	62.4	67.8	35.6	72.1
Female									
African	1.9	9.4	23.8	38.2	46.6	50.0	51.1	29.0	40.0
Coloured	1.5	12.0	35.1	50.1	55.8	58.6	59.0	37.6	44.4
Asian	3.8	30.4	65.5	77.0	79.3	77.5	74.6	54.9	50.5
White	2.0	21.1	59.1	72.7	76.0	76.4	76.0	56.1	57.6
Total	1.9	10.8	28.5	44.0	51.7	55.1	56.1	33.5	43.9

Source: Compiled by authors using data from census 2001 (Stats SA 2001)

Analysis of the results from the SADHS 1998 showing race differences in marriage rates are shown in Figure 5.5 and the accompanying regression analysis in Table 5.7. In general the results show that marriage rates in the country have declined by about 3 per cent per year, are lower among younger women, more educated women, and women in urban areas, and are lower for African and coloured people than for white and Asian people.

Figure 5.5: Race differences in marriage

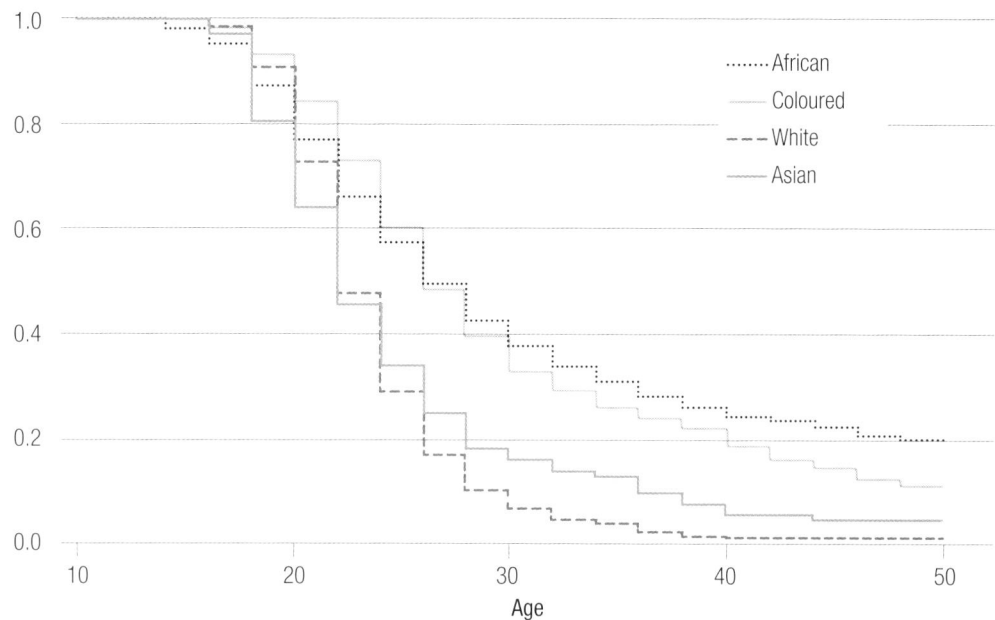

Source: Compiled by authors using data from SADHS (DoH 1998)

Table 5.7: Logistic regression analysis of marriage patterns

	B	SE	Wald	df	Sig.	Exp(B)
Year of birth	−.030	.002	327.910	1	.000	.970
Education	−.216	.019	135.791	1	.000	.806
Urban	−.303	.028	113.337	1	.000	.738
Coloured	.032	.039	.686	1	.408	1.033
White	.895	.049	336.327	1	.000	2.447
Asian	.756	.064	138.447	1	.000	2.129

Source: Compiled by the authors using data from SADHS (DoH 1998)

* Note: Abbreviations used: B=Beta; SE = Standard Error; Wald = Computed values which show the strength of association between dependent and independent variables; df = degree of freedom; sig. = level of significance; Exp(B) = Odds ratio

Marital dissolution

Marital dissolution may occur as a result of either divorce or widowhood. It may impact indirectly on the marital fertility of a population through shortening the fertile periods of women. This, however, depends on the age at which women enter the divorce or widowhood state and how long it lasts. The situation can otherwise be reversed when the women remarry and resume their normal sexual life (Sivarmurthy 1979). Since generally South African society is relatively tolerant of cohabitation and childbirth before and outside of marriage, and divorce and remarriage of both divorced and widowed women, the effect of marriage dissolution on fertility in South Africa may not be as substantial as the data on divorce and widowhood as shown in for example, Table 5.4. Some marriages are also dissolved at early ages, probably indicating the impact on marriages of migration, particularly of young men and women to urban centres, poverty or lack of employment and the possibility that some women are married to husbands much older than themselves.

Examination of the data on marital dissolution through divorce and or separation reveals surprisingly low levels with only approximately 2 and 3.5 per cent of males and females reporting themselves divorced or separated respectively. Furthermore, about 2 and 10 per cent reported themselves widowed, the level of widowhood naturally increasing with age to reach a maximum of approximately 8 and 35 per cent in the age group 50 years and over for males and females respectively.[1] The results of the regression analysis of the SADHS 1998 (not shown) revealed that divorce rates are highest for white people, while Asian people have the lowest rates. But the difference between white and African people is not statistically significant. The data further show that divorce is more likely as people get older, in urban areas, among the least educated and in all groups except Asians.

Polygyny

In most traditional African cultures social, economic, political and cultural life largely revolved around the institution of the family as defined by marriage and childbearing. The family, therefore, was the most important resource over which political, economic and social power converged (Kabwegyere & Mbula 1979; Molnos 1973). As several scholars have noted, it was within this context of the importance of family life that the practice of polygyny in several African societies must be understood (see for example, Kabwegyere & Mbula 1979; Mbiti 1966, 1969; Molnos 1973). According to this argument, a large and extended family provided a strong economic base for the family and community through the provision of labour to ensure firm control of land, continued supply of revenue and food.

Although some studies (for example, Goody 1973) have suggested that the reasons for the practice of polygyny were mainly sexual and reproductive rather than economic, others like Fortes (1978) argue that this holds equally for other marital arrangements. According to Fortes, polygyny was associated with social status and prestige in such societies. Moreover, sexual abstinence by wives/women, which encouraged child spacing while breastfeeding, was observed in several cultures in Africa; a man with several wives would continue to have sexual intercourse with his other wives while others observed abstinence.[2]

Polygyny, moreover, provided social justice for all women since every woman had to marry, while at the same time it ensured a place for the barren or the childless. The practice of inheriting widows in some cultures by brothers or close relatives of the deceased often led to polygyny, and the children born by the inherited wives/

---

1 This may well be due to high male adult mortality in the older age groups.
2 It is even suggested that some monogamously married wives often encouraged their husbands to take on other wives to allow child spacing and to lighten the workload in the family.

widows could in some cases be counted as children of the deceased to ensure the line of continuity among the living. Furthermore, given a situation where diseases, sickness and famine were widespread and reduction of male numbers through wars, brutal raids and so on was very common, it is possible that women outnumbered males in many societies and therefore polygyny was one sure way women could obtain social security and self-dignity.

Finally, the sex of the child was another important issue in the family, which has often been mentioned in the literature. A man's status, wealth and security of the family depended on the number of sons, although daughters too were important in their contribution to domestic work and in agriculture. The bride wealth from the daughters could be used to pay for sons' marriages (Molnos 1973). In short, men often took on additional wives in search of a particular combination of sons and daughters, although it must be noted that not all men could afford to be polygynous; only those who offered wealth, comfort and social status were able to acquire additional or several wives. The young unmarried and poor men found it difficult to compete in the marriage market.

In contemporary South Africa, the trend is clearly towards monogamy and polygyny is generally on the decline. For example, in an analysis of a recent social attitudes survey by the Human Sciences Research Council, Amoateng (2006) found near universal support for marital monogamy, with an average of 87 per cent of all race groups supporting marriage to one partner throughout a person's life, even though there were significant racial and other differences in the support for monogamy, with African people being somewhat more likely to endorse polygamy. The literature on polygyny, particularly in the South African context, is relatively scanty. The question on polygyny in the SADHS 1998 was only asked of women who were currently in a union at the time of the survey. The prevalence of polygyny was measured by the number of wives in a union or the number of co-wives a wife said she had. In all, below 7.0 per cent of all current marriages among women in the childbearing ages 15–49 were polygynous.

Further analysis of the data showed that polygyny was more common among older women aged over 30 (6.5 per cent), among the less educated women with primary and no education (9.6 per cent), among rural women (8.3 per cent) and among African women (7.6 per cent). As far as provinces go, polygyny is more prevalent in Limpopo (14.0 per cent), Mpumalanga (12.0 per cent) and KwaZulu-Natal (9.0 per cent). It is lowest in the Western Cape and Free State provinces (1.7 per cent).

Conclusion

The nuptiality trend in South Africa points to both late and low marriage by both males and females. Thus, the almost universal marriage pattern that characterises most sub-Saharan African countries is certainly not the case in South Africa, especially, among the African and coloured population groups; marriage is more popular among whites and Asians. Observed singulate mean ages at marriage

(SMAM) are very high – averaging 28 years for females and 30 years for males. Although these are in line with those estimated for other African countries (Adegboyega 1993; UN 2003), they may well be the result of irregularities in the marriage data in African censuses. The median and trimean figures computed directly from the individual data from the SADHS 1998, on the other hand, are lower than the SMAM, with half of all the women marrying at age 25; the average trimean is about age 27. Among the factors that are making marriage less compelling for women may be the emancipation of women as a result of expansion of educational opportunities, increased urbanisation and increased participation in the labour force. All of these factors would reduce women's economic dependency on the marriage institution.

However, the low marriage rates, among, especially, the majority African population group, can also be attributed to such other factors as the long-lasting effect of colonisation and the apartheid system with its associated migratory labour system. This accounted for the frequent and often prolonged absence of able-bodied males and/or husbands from the rural, mostly bantustan areas, as well as from neighbouring countries. Many of these young migratory labourers often never returned home; some died in mining accidents, while others entered new relationships – thus deserting their fiancés or the newly wed young wives they had left behind (Mpiti & Kalule-Sabiti 1985). Moreover, the relatively low marriage rate could be due to the increasing popularity of non-marital cohabitation and the gradual but steady increase in the divorce rate.

Thus, in conclusion, even though several studies have found that African societies are invariably characterised by a universal marriage pattern due to early entry into marriage and lower divorce rates, the present study has documented a rather unique nuptuality regime in South Africa. Specifically, the study has shown that due to a combination of historical, cultural, economic and political factors, women generally marry late in South Africa. However, unlike marriage, childbearing is still popular among South Africans as a family formation event, although the fertility rate has been declining among all ethnic groups in the population. Moreover, because first birth often precedes first marriage, the effects of nuptiality on fertility – especially in the African and coloured racial groups – is much weaker than in other parts of the world. A young African woman in South Africa gains adult status by becoming a mother rather than becoming a wife or a cohabitant.

Acknowledgement

We express our sincere appreciation to Professor Richard Madsen of the Department of Statistics, University of Missouri for statistical and programming assistance and Dr David Lucas (ANU) for his preliminary comments.

References

Acsadi GT & Hammam NM (1976) Marriage and family among selected female health personnel in Cairo. In SA Huzayyin & GT Acsadi (Eds) *Family and marriage in some African and Asiatic countries*. Research Monograph Series, No. 6, Cairo Demographic Centre, Cairo

Adegboyega O (1993) Structure and dynamics of family formation in Africa. Unpublished manuscript

Adegboyega O (1994) The situation of families in East and Southern Africa. Unpublished manuscript

Amoateng AY (2006) On marrying, mixing and everything else: The changing face of family life in South Africa. *HSRC Review* 4(2): 4–5

Amoateng AY & Kalule-Sabiti I (1995) Family life Among the Batswana of the North West Province of South Africa. In *Family Perspective*, Centre for Studies of the Family, College of Family, Home, and Social Sciences, Brigham Young University, 29(4): 405–422

Bogue DJ (1969) Marriage and marriage dissolution. In DJ Bogue *Principles of Demography*. New York: John Wiley & Sons

Budlender D, Chobokoane N & Simelane S (2004) Marriage patterns in South Africa: Methodological and substantive issues. *Southern African Journal of Demography* 9(11): 1–26

Caldwell JC (1976) Marriage, the family and fertility in sub-Saharan Africa with special reference to research programmes in Ghana and Nigeria. In SA Huzayyin & GT Acsadi (Eds) *Family and marriage in some African and Asiatic countries*. Research Monograph Series, No. 6, Cairo Demographic Centre, Cairo

DoH (Department of Health, South Africa) (1998) *South African Demographic and Health Survey (SADHS) 1998*. Pretoria: DoH

DoSD (Department of Social Development, South Africa) (2001) *Planning in the new millennium: A primary HIV/AIDS capacity development course for government planners. Facilitators Handbook*. Pretoria: DoSD

Fortes M (1978) Family, marriage and fertility in West Africa. In C Oppong, C Adaba, M Bekombo-Priso & J Mogey (Eds) *Marriage, fertility and parenthood in West Africa*. Changing African Family Monograph Series, No. 4, Vol. 1, Australian National University, Canberra

Godiak EM & Keely CB (Eds) (1998) Migration and AIDS. *International Migration*. 36(4). Washington DC: Blackwell Publishing

Goode W (1993) *World changes in divorce patterns*. New Haven: Yale University Press

Goody J (1973) Polygny, economy and the role of women. In J Goody (Ed.) *The character of kinship*. Cambridge: Cambridge University Press

Gregson S, Zhuwau T, Anderson M & Cahndiwana SK (1997) HIV and fertility change in rural Zimbabwe. *Health Transition Review* 7 (Supplement 2): 89–112

Hajnal J (1953) Age at marriage and proportions marrying. *Population Studies* 7: 111– 132

Kabwegyere T & Mbula J (1979) *A case of the Akamba of Eastern Kenya*. Changing African Family Monograph Series, No. 5, Australian National University, Canberra

Kpedekpo GMK & Serunjogi MS (1974) The population of Uganda. Unpublished manuscript

Kuper A (1982) *Wives for cattle: Bride wealth and marriage in Southern Africa*. London: Routledge and Kegan Paul

Maconachie M (1989) Dual-earner couples: Factors influencing whether and when white married women join the labour force in South Africa. *South African Journal of Sociology* 20(3): 143–151

Makiwane M (1996) Fertility in rural South Africa. Unpublished PhD thesis, University of Witwatersrand

Mbiti JS (1966) *Akamba stories*. Oxford: Oxford University Press

Mbiti JS (1969) *African religion and philosophy*. London and Nairobi: Heinemann

Mpiti AM & Kalule-Sabiti I (1985) *The proximate determinants of fertility in Lesotho*. WFS Scientific Reports, No. 78, International Statistical Institute, Voorburg, Netherlands

Molnos A (1973) *Cultural source materials for population planning in East Africa: Beliefs and practices*. Institute of African Studies, No.11, University of Nairobi

Moultrie TA & Timaeus IM (2003) The South African Fertility decline: Evidence from two censuses and a demographic and health survey. *Population Studies* 57: 265–283

Radcliffe-Brown AR & Forde D (1960) *African systems of kinship and marriage*. London: Oxford University Press

Seetharam KS & Duza MB (1976) Nuptiality and fertility in selected areas of four Arab and African cities. In SA Huzayyin & GT Acsadi (Eds) *Family and marriage in some African and Asiatic countries*. Research Monograph Series, No. 6, Cairo Demographic Centre, Cairo

Shryock HS & Siegel JS (1976) *The methods and materials of demography*. New York: Academic Press

Singh S & Samara R (1996) Early marriage among women in developing countries. *International Family Perspectives* 22: 148–157, 175

Sivamurthy M (1979) Nuptiality and fertility: Some comparative features in two capital cities. Seminar on Population Change and Development in some African and Asiatic Countries, 15–22 December, UN-A.R.E., Cairo Demographic Centre, Doc.coc 3579/22, Cairo: 31 (Draft unpublished)

Sivamurthy M & Seetharam KS (1976) Age at marriage in selected areas of four Arab and African cities. In SA Huzayyin & GT Acsadi (Eds) *Family and marriage in some African and Asiatic countries*. Research Monograph Series, No. 6, Cairo Demographic Centre, Cairo

Stats SA (Statistics South Africa) (1996) *Population census 1996: Community Profile databases*. Pretoria: Stats SA

Stats SA (2001) *Population census 2001: Community profile databases*. Pretoria: Stats SA

Stats SA (2002a) *Marriages and divorces 1999*. Pretoria: Stats SA

Stats SA (2002b) *Census of death in South Africa 1997–2001*. Pretoria: Stats SA

Udjo E (2003) Marital patterns and fertility in South Africa: Evidence from the 1996 Population Census. Statistics South Africa. Unpublished

UN (United Nations) (1955) *Handbook of vital statistics methods. Studies in methods.* Series F, No. 7. Statistical Office. New York: UN

UN (1973) *The determinants and consequences of population trends.* T/5OA/SER.A/50, Vol. 1. New York: UN

UN (2003) *Marriage patterns.* POP/1/DB/2000/3. New York: UN

CHAPTER 6

Fertility and childbearing in South Africa

Martin Palamuleni, Ishmael Kalule-Sabiti & Monde Makiwane

Introduction

One remarkable demographic achievement in South Africa has been the decline in fertility in the past four decades (Caldwell & Caldwell 1993, 2003; DoH 1998). Currently South Africa has one of the lowest fertility levels on the continent (Caldwell & Caldwell 2003; Anderson 2003). Although past estimates were based largely on unreliable and often fragmented data, many studies confirm the decline in fertility in South Africa (Caldwell & Caldwell 2003; Sibanda & Zuberi 1999; Udjo 2003). Fertility in South Africa declined from an average of 6 to 7 children per woman in the 1950s to an average of 4 to 5 children in the 1980s and about 3.3 children per woman in the mid 1990s (Chimere-Dan 1993, 1999; Moultrie & Timaeus 2003; Sibanda & Zuberi 1999; Udjo 1998, 2003).

The observed decline in fertility in South Africa varies by population group. The white population group experienced sustained fertility decline from the end of the nineteenth century until 1989, when they reached below replacement level with a total fertility rate (TFR) of 1.9 children per woman (Department of Population and Social Development 1998). Since then the TFR for the white population has remained unchanged. The nature and pattern of fertility transition for the white population in South Africa resembles the European fertility transition (Oosthuizen 2000).

The Asian population group witnessed fertility decline from around the 1950s. TFR declined from about 6 in the 1950s to 2.7 in the late 1980s and 2.5 in the mid 1990s. Fertility for the coloured population group, however, showed a rising trend in the mid 1940s up to early 1960 and thereafter showed a downward trend. TFR declined from 6.5 in the late 1960s to about 3 by the 1980s and 2.5 by the mid 1990s. As for the African population group, who constitute more than 75 per cent of the country's population, fertility decline commenced in the early 1960s and continued to the present (DoH 1998). TFR for this group declined from 6.6 in 1960 to 4.5 in 1980s and down to 3.3 in the 1990s. The pace of fertility decline appears to be slower among the African population than among the coloured population (Department of Population and Social Development 1998).

The observed fertility decline has not been uniform in this 'rainbow' nation, which prior to 1994 was dominated by a minority political regime committed to racialisation, classification and ethnification of society. Thus the observed differentials in fertility are largely a reflection of the socio-economic and general imbalances of the past in terms of standards of living. For instance, apartheid policies favoured the white population and this in return led to white people attaining better living conditions and access to various health facilities while other racial groups suffered. The relationship between levels, trends and differentials in fertility in South Africa and apartheid ideology and policies is complex and not fully understood (Burgard 2004). One thing that is clear, though, is that demographic concerns were central to many apartheid policies (Camlin et al. 2004). While official population policies sought to reduce African fertility (driven by white South Africans' fear of being 'swamped'), other policies ensured that African people were systematically denied access to education, healthcare and urban residence – factors that were important in determining the pace of fertility decline in a variety of settings in both the developing and developed world (Camlin et al. 2004).

This chapter is therefore intended to examine the determinants of South African fertility using data from the 1998 South African Demographic and Health Survey (SADHS) and from the 1996 South African population census (DoH 1998; Stats SA 1999). More specifically, the analytical objective is to identify the differentials in fertility among sub-groups of populations in South Africa. The study will reveal whether the recent expansion of modernisation factors such as education, health, urbanisation and housing reform programmes have affected childbearing patterns in South Africa.

The findings of the analysis are provided in two parts. Part one deals with differentials on cumulative fertility by selected socio-economic and cultural factors (also known as the indirect determinants of fertility). Part two analyses the proximate determinants (also referred to as intermediate variables or direct determinants) using Bongaarts' model (Bongaarts 1978, 1985).

Determinants of fertility

The level of fertility of any given population is known to be influenced by both indirect and direct determinants or factors. The former refers to socio-economic and cultural systems and includes factors such as education, rural–urban residence, religion, technology, housing, health, social security and so on. The latter are also referred to as proximate determinants or intermediate fertility variables and include the proportion of women in the total population who marry, effective contraceptive use, induced abortion, length of amenorrhea, and so on. These proximate determinants are of interest because of their direct impact on fertility, and consist of a set of biological and behavioural factors through which social, economic and cultural conditions can affect fertility. As noted by Freedman, 'the proximate variables stand between fertility and all other preceding variables. They immediately determine fertility, and all other variables act through combinations of them' (1986: 773).

The analytical framework of the proximate determinants (intermediate variables or direct determinants) first introduced by Davis and Blake (1956) and later modified by Bongaarts (1978, 1985), provided an opportunity for demographers to have a deeper understanding of how socio-economic, cultural and environmental, and biological factors affect fertility. Thus knowledge has been instrumental in deciding the various means and ways best suited to achieving fertility reduction – more particularly in developing societies. This linkage between the socio-economic, cultural and environmental factors is demonstrated in Figure 6.1.

Figure 6.1: Linkages between fertility and the socio-economic and cultural system through biosocial and proximate determinates

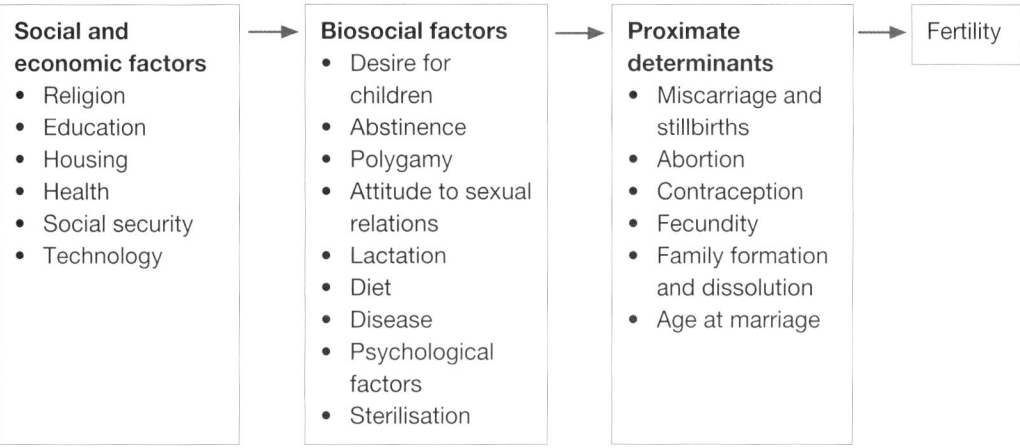

Socioeconomic and cultural determinants

In part one of the analysis, the relationship between selected socio-economic and cultural variables and fertility is discussed. The variables examined include education, type of place of childhood residence, region of usual residence, race or population group and a woman's work status for pay.

Education and fertility
The spread of education and literacy among women is believed to be fundamental to changes in reproductive behaviour. The effect of women's education on fertility in less developed countries is found to be curvilinear; that is, fertility tends to rise first with education and then decreases sharply once a certain level of education is attained (Cochrane 1979). The argument is that education is positively associated with improved health and hygiene standards, which translate into lower chances of spontaneous abortion or foetal loss, lower levels of infertility, abandonment of traditional constraints upon sexual behaviour and the practice of breastfeeding, all of which are known to raise fertility levels. As the educational level increases, marriage tends to be postponed which causes a negative effect on fertility and counteracts the initial effect of fertility increase. Moreover, educated women desire relatively fewer children. They have high contraceptive prevalence and a high chance of working outside their homes. All of these factors are known to lower fertility levels (Cochrane 1979). However, there is also a possibility of the reverse causation that is less documented: that is, the initiation of childbearing causing the termination of education (Cochrane 1979). While analysing the relationship between fertility and the level of education in sub-Saharan Africa, Cohen (1993) has shown that fertility

is either curvilinear or negatively related with education but does not appear very responsive to few years of education.

According to the 1998 SADHS, fertility is highest among those with no education, followed by those with primary education, then those with secondary education, and lowest amongst those with tertiary education.

Type of place of childhood residence and fertility
Generally speaking, fertility is higher for women whose childhood place of residence up to age 12 was in rural areas compared to those who grew up in urban areas. A study by Cohen (1993) demonstrated that rural fertility is substantially higher than urban fertility in every African country included in the analysis. The 1998 SADHS indicated that TFR in urban areas was 2.3 compared to 3.9 in rural areas (DoH 1998). Higher levels of education, occupation, a more modern environment and aspirations for higher levels of living are among the factors that can cause fertility among urban women to be lower than among rural women. Also, it is assumed that urban women have a better knowledge of and access to modern contraception than women in rural areas (Cohen 1993).

Region of usual residence and race or population group and fertility
Variations in fertility have been observed in different regions or provinces and different race/population groups of the same countries. Such variations are, however, a reflection of differences or imbalances in social, economic and cultural development, which express themselves in the different levels (and quality) of education, urbanisation, industrialisation, employment, and access to health facilities and family planning services including abortion services and so on.

The role played by industrialisation and access to health facilities needs particular mention here. The influence of increasing industrialisation on the family, and on the role of the different members in the family, makes it a factor in fertility change. Abu-Gamrah (1977) identified such indicators as land area per tractor, use of fertilisers, steel consumption, energy consumption, production of manufactured goods, consumption of cement and number of commercial vehicles as among those used to measure the level of industrialisation.

Generally, it is expected that fertility is very low in those societies that have achieved radical changes in the level of industrialisation and therefore the mode of production. Likewise it can be argued that fertility transition will be completed much faster in those high-fertility societies experiencing rapid industrialisation.

As far as access to health facilities is concerned, societies with advanced health provision have also managed to bring their mortality to very low levels. Since high mortality, especially infant mortality, has been associated with high fertility, couples tend to respond to high infant loss with continued childbearing. A sharp decline in infant mortality, therefore, creates a favourable environment for family limitation.

Work status of women and fertility

Many studies have found working women to experience lower fertility than their counterparts who are not working. For instance, the 1998 SADHS indicated that TFR for women who are working is 2.2 children per woman whereas TFR for women who are not working is 3.3 children per woman. 'Role conflict' theory is often advanced as the basis for the differences in fertility of women who are in the workforce and those who are not. Working women, especially those engaged in non-domestic enterprises, have a conflict between work and reproduction. They find the care of children more difficult than those women who are not working and hence tend to have fewer children than the latter group. Even among the employed group there are substantial differentials by occupational groups. From the experience of contemporary rich nations, women engaged in agricultural pursuits tend to have higher fertility than those engaged in non-farm enterprise.

Data source

This study utilises data extracted from the 1998 SADHS, which was conducted on behalf of the government of South Africa by the Medical Research Council (MRC) of South Africa in collaboration with Macro International (DoH 1998). The 1998 SADHS involved the use of three basic questionnaires. The first questionnaire on households recorded information on all household members. The second questionnaire recorded detailed information on eligible women who were identified from the household questionnaires. A total of 11 735 women were interviewed using the individual questionnaire. This questionnaire collected information on the respondent's background characteristics, reproductive history, knowledge and practice of family planning, breastfeeding practices, marriage, fertility preferences and so on, as well as information about her husband's background characteristics. The third questionnaire was administered to adults in every second household and a total of 8 156 women and 5 735 men were interviewed using this questionnaire. The analyses in this chapter will use data from the individual questionnaire only.

Methods of analysis

Estimates of fertility

There are a number of measures of fertility and these include crude birth rate (CBR), age-specific fertility rates (ASFR), TFR, gross reproduction rate (GRR), net reproduction rate (NRR) and lifetime fertility measures such as the average number of children ever born. In this study, usage is made of lifetime fertility measures.

The analysis of cumulative fertility differentials in part one of the chapter is based on all women, using the index of children ever born. The data were standardised for age at first marriage and for never married women to avoid the intervening effect on fertility of those variables analysed. This helped to clarify the relationship between those variables of interest and fertility. Standardisation for age at first marriage and the proportion never married was done based on the distribution of each entire age group according to the age at marriage (for more detailed discussion on the standardisation procedure see Pullum 1978). The initial data consist of the unstandardised means of children ever born for each combination of age at marriage and selected socio-economic variables. The first step involved multiplying the proportions of women in the entire age group for each category of age at marriage by the unstandardised means in each combination of age at marriage and background variable. The numbers generated are then added across all categories of age at marriage. The result is the standardised means of children ever born for each age category of, for instance, type of place of residence in that age group.

Age at first marriage and never married women, together with current age, were the major demographic control variables in world fertility surveys. As Pullum (1978) observed, women who belong to the same birth cohort share many cultural and socialising experiences. They will have been exposed to a similar background of some norms and behaviour patterns. Women who marry at about the same historical time constitute a marriage cohort. When there is little premarital sexual activity and less marital separation and disruption, marital duration will tend to classify women in the same way as age. This will tend to go through similar changes in the introduction of modern contraception and attitudes towards induced abortion. It should be noted, however, that marriage is not such a good control for fertility because a lot of births occur before and outside marriage (Pullum 1978). In other words, childbearing is not confined to marriage. South Africa is no exception in this respect.

Methods of analysis of the proximate determinants

Part two of this chapter aims to quantify the proximate determinants of South African fertility and to find out whether fertility levels can be accounted for by the intermediate fertility variables using the model first developed by Davis and Blake (1956) and later modified by Bongaarts (1978, 1985). The model was developed to facilitate the understanding of the mechanism through which socio-economic and biosocial factors (the indirect determinants) affect fertility through biological and behavioural variables, otherwise known as the direct determinants of fertility.

In the initial model, Davis and Blake (1956) proposed 11 variables through which the various socio-economic and biosocial factors operate to affect fertility. Following this pioneering work, Bongaarts modified this model and introduced his own model based on seven intermediate variables, namely (1) proportion married among females; (2) prevalence of induced abortion; (3) contraceptive use and effectiveness; (4) duration of postpartum amenorrhoea; (5) fecundability (that is, probability of conception), normally assumed to reflect frequency of intercourse; (6) spontaneous intrauterine mortality rate; and (7) prevalence of permanent sterility. While the first four variables are known to exert strong influence on fertility, the remaining three are assumed to vary little between populations (Kalule-Sabiti 1984). In fact, proportion married, contraceptive use and effectiveness, induced abortion and postpartum infecundity are the most important variables in explaining fertility variation, accounting for up to 96 per cent of fertility change in some populations (Bongaarts 1985, 1978). Based on this finding, Bongaarts (1985) developed the following four indices:

- Index of proportion married (denoted as C_m): this captures the proportion of the population that marry or remain never married. Bongaarts defines marriage to include consensual unions. This variable measures the extent to which women are exposed to regular intercourse.

- Index of contraception (denoted as C_c): this measures the prevalence of effective contraceptive use. These two variables measure the prevalence of deliberate marital fertility control. C_c equals 1 if no form of contraception is used and 0 if all fecund exposed women use modern methods that are 100 per cent effective.

- The index of postpartum infecundity (denoted as C_i): this index measures the natural marital fertility factors such as the length of period of non-susceptibility to conception after birth, frequency of intercourse, extent of involuntary sterility, extent of spontaneous intrauterine mortality and duration of viability of ova and sperm. These factors together determine the amount of postpartum infecundity. Postpartum infecundity refers to the period between childbirth and the time when the normal menstrual cycle resumes. Its length is induced by the intensity of uninterrupted breastfeeding. In the absence of contraception, intense and fulltime breastfeeding delays conception, thereby giving rise to longer non-susceptible period. It is therefore referred to as the period of infecundity or sterility. Like the other remaining three less important variables it is determined by the level of natural fertility.

- The index of induced abortion (C_a): this index measures the extent of use and non-use of induced abortion. Even though it is said that the practice of abortion, like prostitution, is as old as civilisation itself, requisite data to allow a detailed investigation on the impact of abortion are not readily available. As such, although abortion is one of the components of the Bongaarts model, few studies have incorporated it fully. The role of abortion is in effect assumed, but it is rarely quantified due to the lack of available data on the subject. Abortion was legalised in South Africa in 1996. In this application C_a is assumed to be 1.

The fertility-inhibiting effects of the most important determinants are quantified in Bongaarts' model by these four indices, each of which assumes a value between 0 and 1. When the index is close to 1, the proximate determinant will have a negligible inhibiting effect on fertility, whereas when it takes a value of 0, it will have a large inhibiting effect.

The main equation of the model is: TFR = $C_m * C_c * C_a * C_i *$TF, where TFR is the total fertility rate and TF is the total fecundity.

The four indices are calculated using the following relationships:

C_m = TFR/TMFR

where TMFR is the total marital fertility rate and TFR is the total fertility rate. To calculate total marital fertility rates two approaches were considered. First, births in the last 36 months were cross-tabulated by marital status data. Using births occurring to married women only, age-specific marital fertility rates (ASMFRs) were calculated. From the calculated ASMFRs, total marital fertility rate (TMFR) was calculated as the sum of ASFMRs multiplied by 5. Second, using the distribution of women by marital status, the proportion married was calculated. ASFMR was obtained by dividing the age-specific fertility rate (ASFR) by the proportion married, assuming that all births took place to married women.

$C_c = 1 - 1.08 * u * e$

where u is the proportion currently using contraception among married women of reproductive age, and e is the average use-effectiveness of contraception and 1.08 is the sterility correction factor. The method-specific use-effectiveness level (e_i) is adopted from Bongaarts and Potter (1983). The weights are, in effect, equal to the proportion of women using a given method (u_i). The weights used are presented in Table 6.1.

Table 6.1: Use-effectiveness of different contraceptive methods

Contraceptive method	Use-effectiveness
Pill	0.90
IUD	0.95
Injection	0.99
Sterilisation	1.00
Others	0.70

Source: Bongaarts & Potter 1983

$C_i = 20/ 18.5 + i$

where i is the average duration (in months) of postpartum infecundity caused by breastfeeding or postpartum abstinence. According to Bongaarts, 20 is the average birth interval (in months in absence of breastfeeding and postpartum abstinence), while 18.5 is the sum of 7.5 months of waiting time to conception, 2 months of time added by spontaneous intrauterine mortality and 9 months of full-term gestation. In absence of breastfeeding, the average duration of postpartum infecundity is assumed to be 1.5 months. In order to estimate the average duration (in months) of postpartum infecundity (i) the following equation was used:

$I = 1.753 * e^{0.1396 * B - 0.001872 * B * B}$

where B = mean or median duration of breastfeeding in months.

$C_a = TFR/(TFR+(b*TA))$

where TA is the total abortion rate equal to the average number of induced abortions per woman at the end of the reproductive period if induced abortion rates remain at prevailing levels throughout the reproductive period. B is the number of births averted per induced abortion which may be approximated by the equation b = 0.4 (1+u).

The above framework has therefore two components: (1) the equations that express the effect on fertility of the first four determinants (which Bongaarts considered to exert a strong effect on fertility) in the model; (2) the assumption that the remaining proximate determinants vary little between populations. Evidence was produced that foetal loss, sterility and fecundability do not vary sufficiently between most populations to account in any appreciable way for differences in fertility levels.

Figure 6.2 represents the suppressing effects of the four intermediate variables named above. When the influence of all four are present, as in the real world, fertility will be observed at a level of TFR. When the suppressing effect of non-marriage on fertility is removed, that is, when all women enter marriage at age 15 and marriages are stable, fertility will rise to a level of total marital fertility rate (TMFR). Eliminating further the suppressing impact of contraception and induced abortion, that is, they are not practised in a population, fertility will rise further to a level of total natural fertility rate (TN). And removing the effect of postpartum infecundity, fertility reaches the maximum level of total fecundity rate (TF) (Kalule-Sabiti 1983).

Figure 6.2: Impact of proximate determinants on fertility

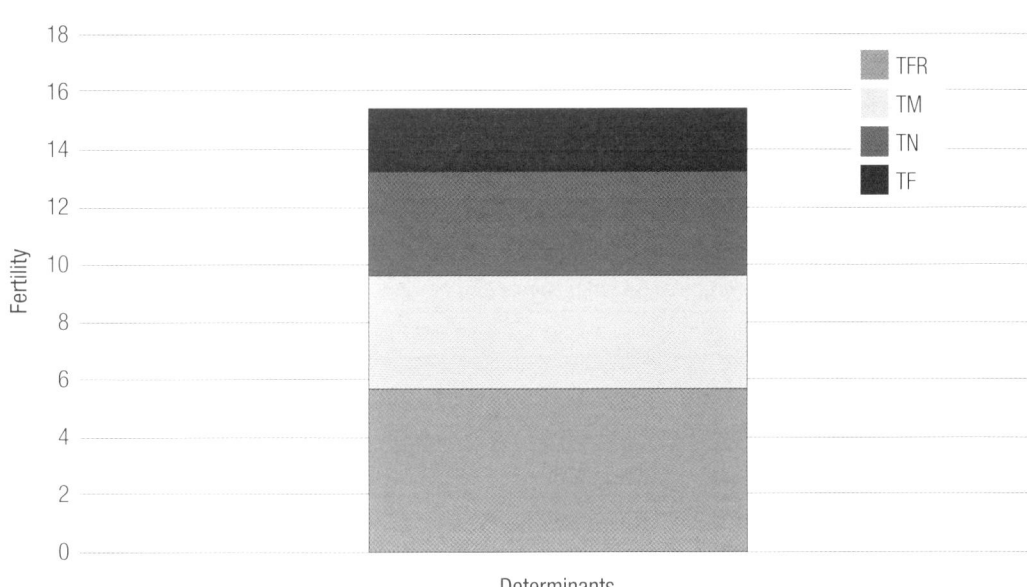

The basic assumption made by Bongaarts in developing the model was that in the absence of lactation and contraception there is an average birth interval of about 20 months, of which about 7 months represent the interval of exposure (the menstruating interval); and in the absence of all determinants, the model is based on the premise that potential fertility of populations would vary within a narrow range of 13.5 to 17.5 births per woman with an average of 15.3 (Kalule-Sabiti 1984). The model has been validated on a number of populations (see Bongaarts 1985; Ferry & Page 1984; Kalule-Sabiti 1984).

The model was applied to the South African data sets using the following four steps:
- estimation of the intermediation fertility variables;
- estimation of the indices;
- estimation of total fertility rates;
- a comparison of the model estimates of the total fertility rates with the observed total fertility rates.

Results and discussion

Table 6.2 presents estimates of fertility for selected socio-economic factors. In general the estimates confirm the findings from other countries. Differentials in fertility have been noted by education, childhood place of residence, province of residence, population group and working status of women. According to Table 6.2, fertility is highest among African people, closely followed by coloured then Asian people and lowest for white people. Mean number of children ever born is higher among females whose childhood place of residence is rural areas. Fertility is also affected by the level of education of women, with a mean number of children ever born of 3.39 children for women aged 45 years and over with no education compared to 2.54 children for women aged 45 years and over with tertiary education.

Table 6.2: Mean number of children ever born to women by age and selected socio-economic factors, South Africa, 1998

Selected socio-economic factors	All ever married	Never married	15–24		25–34		35–44		45+	
			Unst.	St.	Unst.	St.	Unst.	St.	Unst.	St.
Education										
None	2.12	0.77	1.09	1.16	3.08	2.70	4.33	4.22	5.38	5.39
Primary	1.40	0.43	0.63	0.58	2.61	2.50	3.92	3.92	4.52	4.54
Secondary	1.00	0.33	0.41	0.42	1.79	1.83	2.88	2.94	3.14	3.13
Tertiary	1.10	0.22	0.29	0.36	1.26	1.37	2.33	2.43	2.62	2.54
Childhood place of residence										
City	0.93	0.26	0.33	0.37	1.57	1.60	2.60	2.67	3.02	3.05
Town	0.99	0.28	0.35	0.39	1.73	1.74	2.83	2.91	3.20	3.28
Rural/farm	1.21	0.40	0.54	0.52	2.32	2.25	3.93	3.93	4.72	4.69
Province of residence										
WC	0.88	0.28	0.35	0.36	1.63	1.70	2.75	2.74	3.07	3.26
EC	1.16	0.33	0.42	0.44	2.27	2.27	3.68	3.72	4.34	4.38
NC	1.02	0.36	0.46	0.45	1.86	1.91	2.91	3.00	4.31	4.28
FS	1.02	0.24	0.35	0.36	1.76	1.62	3.20	3.01	3.83	3.62
KZN	1.26	0.41	0.50	0.53	2.16	2.18	3.58	3.64	4.17	4.21
NW	1.31	0.37	0.45	0.51	1.83	1.90	3.30	3.36	4.15	4.06
G	1.04	0.29	0.40	0.40	1.82	1.77	2.85	2.89	3.29	3.32
M	1.27	0.45	0.54	0.57	2.24	2.19	3.81	3.80	5.09	4.92
L	1.15	0.33	0.55	0.44	2.48	2.29	4.45	4.09	5.26	5.19

Selected socio-economic factors	All ever married	Never married	15–24		25–34		35–44		45+	
			Unst.	St.	Unst.	St.	Unst.	St.	Unst.	St.
Race/population group										
African	1.16	0.37	0.48	0.49	2.11	2.10	3.62	3.67	4.46	4.45
Coloured	1.09	0.36	0.45	0.47	1.69	1.75	2.83	2.86	3.42	3.61
Asian	0.59	0.01	0.08	0.10	1.61	1.11	2.22	1.90	2.59	2.30
White	1.12	0.01	0.24	0.17	1.80	1.27	2.67	2.38	2.84	2.80
Work status										
Working	1.18	0.33	0.44	0.45	2.15	4.11	3.74	3.76	4.38	4.38
Not working	0.91	0.42	0.53	0.49	1.79	1.79	2.96	3.02	3.63	3.64

Source: SADHS (DoH 1998)

Variations in fertility are also observed at provincial level. Mean number of children ever born for women aged 45 years and older indicate that fertility is highest in Limpopo, Mpumalanga, Eastern Cape, Northern Cape, KwaZulu-Natal and North West provinces and is lowest in Western Cape, Gauteng and Free State provinces. According to these estimates provinces that are less developed also experience higher fertility rates (Limpopo and Eastern Cape) while those that are developed experience lower fertility rates (Gauteng, Western Cape and Free State). Furthermore, differentials in fertility by province are a reflection of the racial composition and the different levels of education, urbanisation and access to health and family planning services as created by the apartheid regime (Moultrie & Timeaus 2002).

Other things being equal, fertility is higher in provinces that have a high proportion of the African population group and is lowest in provinces with a high proportion of the white and coloured population groups. Provinces that are highly urbanised, such as Gauteng, Western Cape and Free State, have lower fertility as compared to the least urbanised provinces of Limpopo, Eastern Cape and North West.

The indices of marriage, contraceptive use and postpartum infecundity and the TFR and TF as obtained using Bongaarts' model for the year 1998 are presented in Table 6.3 and Figure 6.3.

Table 6.3: Indices of proximate determinants of fertility by population group, South Africa 1998

	African	Coloured	Asian	White	Total
Reported TFR	3.30	2.60	1.70	1.40	3.10
TMFR	8.80	5.50	23.70	11.20	8.70
u	0.49	0.54	0.58	0.56	0.50
e	0.38	0.45	0.54	0.52	0.40
i	13.30	10.30	2.50	4.80	12.20
C_m	0.38	0.46	0.07	0.13	0.35
C_c	0.59	0.52	0.42	0.44	0.57
C_a	1.00	1.00	1.00	1.00	1.00
C_i	0.63	0.69	0.95	0.86	0.65
$C_i C_a C_c C_m$	0.14	0.17	0.03	0.05	0.13
TF	15.30	15.30	15.30	15.30	15.30
TN	9.60	10.60	14.60	13.10	10.00
TMFR	5.70	5.50	6.10	5.80	5.60
Estimated TFR	2.20	2.50	0.40	0.70	2.00

Source: Calculated by authors

The model indices show that the most important index in explaining the level of fertility in South Africa is the index of marriage (or non-marriage) followed by indices of contraception and of postpartum infecundity. Furthermore, the results indicate that the effect of proximate determinants on fertility differs by population group. Post-partum infecundity (PPI) is most important for Africans followed by coloured then white people and least important for Asians. Contraceptive use is most important for the white population group, followed by the coloured and the Asian and least important among the African population group. The effect of marriage is almost the same in all population groups in that marriage accounts for nearly 25 per cent of the fertility.

Owing to unavailability of requisite information on induced abortion, we assume that the overall total induced abortion rate is zero. However, the effect of this variable will be automatically subsumed in the estimation of the total fecundity.

Figure 6.3: Proximate determinants of fertility in South Africa by population group

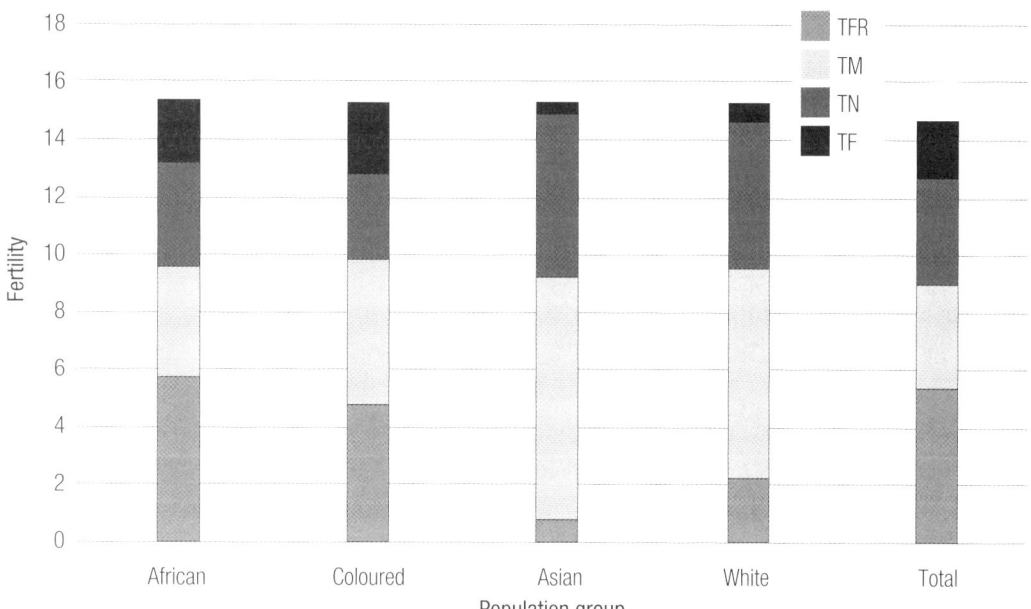

Marriage

The importance of marriage in determining the overall level of fertility in South Africa is consistent with the changes that are taking place with the institution of marriage in the country. In most societies, marriage not only signals the onset of a woman's exposure to the risk of childbearing, but also determines the length and pace of reproductive activity. Therefore, marriage is considered one of the four main proximate determinants of fertility (Bongaarts & Potter 1983).

In most African countries marriage takes place at an early age and is universal. In the absence of contraception, early and universal marriage practice leads to, among other consequences, higher fertility. Women who marry late will have on average shorter exposure to the chance of becoming pregnant, implying late age at childbearing and lower fertility for a society.

This is not the case with South Africa where, although motherhood begins early, marriage takes place later in life. Available statistics indicate that adolescent fertility is very high in South Africa. According to the 1998 SADHS, one-sixth of the more than 26 000 children born to African women in the 36 months preceding the survey were to women younger than 20 years at the time of birth (DoH 1998). In the past most African societies considered virginity to be essential for the first marriage and premarital pregnancy was a social embarrassment among most ethnic groups in Africa. Today, however, this is being accepted as an inevitable consequence of the modernisation process, even among the most conservative communities. In the olden days, a girl who became pregnant before marriage was required to confess, and the man responsible was forced to marry her. Today the man responsible is only required to accept supporting the child financially.

Data on marital status presented in Chapter 5 indicate that the proportion of never-married women has increased for all age groups with the exception of those aged 15–19 where it has decreased slightly. Overall for women of reproductive age group the proportion of never married has increased slightly from 54 per cent in 1996 to 55 per cent in 2001. These figures indicate that more than half of women in childbearing are single.

In addition, the proportion of married women has decreased for all age groups in the childbearing period. Overall for women of reproductive age group, the proportion married has decreased from 35 per cent in 1996 to 31 per cent in 2001. Assuming that marriage was once universal in South Africa, and that almost all women were expected to marry, these figures indicate that nowadays only about a third of women marry.

Available data indicate that the proportion of women living together has increased for all age groups in the childbearing period. Overall for women of reproductive age group, the proportion of women living together has increased from 6 per cent in 1996 to 9 per cent in 2001.

Another important variable that contributes to fertility levels in a society is marital disruption arising from separation, divorce or widowhood. The analysis in Chapter 5 has shown that the proportion of women divorced and separated has decreased for all age groups in the childbearing period. Overall for women of reproductive age group, the proportion married has decreased from 3.2 per cent in 1996 to 3.0 per cent in 2001. At the same time the proportion of women widowed has increased slightly for all age groups in the childbearing period, with the exception of age groups 20–24 and 25–29, where it has remained constant. The highest increase was observed in the age group 45–49. Overall for women of reproductive age group, the proportion widowed has increased from 2.1 per cent in 1996 to 2.4 per cent in 2001. The slight increase in the number of widowed women may be due to the increase in mortality among adults probably arising from HIV/AIDS.

Recent decades have witnessed a dramatic increase in the proportion of all births that occur out of wedlock, from 5 per cent in 1960 to 27 per cent in 1989 (Mostert 1991). This change has paralleled delays in the age of first marriage and increases in female labour force participation.

It was also noted in Chapter 5 that a significant percentage of all women in the reproductive age group are unmarried. The large prevalence of unmarried women led to society accepting that many of these women will, during their lifetime, give birth to children, hence a universal fertility among women, irrespective of their marital status. In the past childbearing was limited to married couples only. These days any woman, married or not, can have children. As a result of this some studies have found little difference in fertility rates between married and unmarried women in South Africa (Chimere-Dan 1999). This observation has led to the saying that 'marriage has lost its value as a determinant of fertility' (Department of Population and Social Development 2000).

Nevertheless, unmarried women are less constrained in the choice of number of children by husbands and in-laws, making them more susceptible to reducing fertility in response to socio-economic advancement. Thus, unmarried women have a considerably lower fertility rate than married women, resulting in lower overall fertility.

The net effect of changes observed in marital status on fertility depends on the combined effect of the variables described here. On the one hand, variables such as the high age at first marriage, increased proportion of never married, increased widowhood, and reduced proportion married have a negative impact on fertility. On the other hand, the increased proportion of living together and reduction in the proportion divorced/separated at all ages increases the proportion married, and is likely to enhance fertility. This means that the combined effect of all the changes in marital variables is to depress fertility.

Contraception

Contraceptive use has also contributed to the level of fertility in South Africa. One of the reasons for low fertility in South Africa is the relatively high contraceptive knowledge and use. Knowledge about family planning methods is now almost universal. The 1988 and 1998 SADHS collected data about knowledge and use of family planning methods. The 1998 DHS indicated that 97 per cent of all women interviewed had heard at least of one modern method of family planning (DoH 1998). This high level of knowledge is a result not only of the long history of the national family planning programme but also of the general improvement of social and economic conditions as measured by adult literacy levels.

Current use of contraception is expressed as the proportion of currently married women who report they are using a method at the time of the interview (in a survey). The level of modern contraceptive use in South Africa has increased gradually in the last two decades. The contraceptive prevalence rate (CPR) in South Africa increased from 55 per cent in 1990 to 60 per cent in 1994 (DoH 1998). Furthermore, the 1998 SADHS indicated that CPR is highest for Asian women (80 per cent), followed by white women (76 per cent) then coloured women (69 per cent) and lowest among African women (59 per cent). The high contraceptive use for Asians is surprising and may be related to sampling fluctuation or the methodological problem arising from small sample size.

Contraceptive use has increased in all provinces. Contraceptive prevalence ranged from 74 per cent in Western Cape, 70 per cent in North West, 68 per cent in Free State, 66 per cent in Northern Cape, 62 per cent in Gauteng, 60 per cent in Eastern Cape, 57 per cent in KwaZulu-Natal and 53 per cent in Mpumalanga and Limpopo (DoH 1998). This variance can be complemented with the socio-economic divisions along racial and urban–rural lines (Department of Population and Social Development 2000). The statistics presented here suggest that although CPR is high throughout the country, there is need to intensify the family planning programme in the poorer provinces to bring them in line with the rest of the country.

Another important aspect of contraceptive use in South Africa is the heavy reliance on reliable, long-term and permanent methods such as injectables, pills and female sterilisation. Two things can be said about this issue. First, this may be an indication that women are now using contraception to limit rather than space births. Second, the methods indicate that contraceptive use in South Africa is clinic-based. This suggests that the South African model of family planning delivery is expensive and raises doubts as to whether it can be replicated in other African countries that are still struggling to increase contraceptive use and reduce fertility (Caldwell & Caldwell 2003).

The high contraceptive knowledge and use in South Africa was partly achieved as a result of the apartheid government's funding of the private and public family planning services and the provision of free contraception from as early as 1963. In addition, available data suggest that South Africa is one of the first nations on the continent to disseminate information about family planning. Although designed for the white population, family planning programmes were introduced in the early 1930s (Kaufman 1997, 1998; Klausen 1999). One consequence of the introduction of family planning among the white population was to create awareness among the other racial groups (African, Asian and coloured) about the existence of methods to prevent pregnancy.

In 1974, at the time when developing countries rejected family planning programmes at the Bucharest Conference by proclaiming that 'development is the best contraceptive', the South African government launched a relatively well-funded National Family Planning Programme.

Breastfeeding

Breastfeeding is another important proximate determinant of fertility. The fertility-reducing effect of breastfeeding arises from its role in lengthening the period of postpartum amenorrhea and consequently in extending the birth interval. Lengthy and intense breastfeeding lengthens the duration of postpartum amenorrhea. The duration of postpartum amenorrhea is much shorter among women who partially breastfeed their infants. Breastfeeding is also known to delay the return of ovulation following a birth, thereby contributing to longer birth intervals than would otherwise occur in absence of lactation. Both breastfeeding and postpartum abstinence delay the return of the menstrual flow and therefore the period during which the woman is exposed to the risk of getting pregnant. Thus the net effect of breastfeeding on fertility is to delay the return of menstrual periods after birth (postpartum amenorrhea), leading to longer birth intervals.

Breastfeeding is a common practice in South Africa. According to the 1998 SADHS about 87 per cent of the babies are breastfed for at least some time (DoH 1998). Rural, non-literate and older women are more likely to breastfeed for longer periods than their urban, educated and younger counterparts. On average South African women breastfeed their children for 16 months. The median duration of breastfeeding ranges from 5 months for Asian women, 0.6 months for white women, and 11 months for coloured women to 17 months for African women (DoH 1998).

The 1998 SADHS also showed that the median birth interval in South Africa was 47 months (DoH 1998). The median birth interval varies by population group. The median birth interval is 58 months for coloured women, 47 months for African women, 35 months for white women and 34 months for Asian women (DoH 1998).

The median duration of postpartum amenorrhea was estimated to be 2.4 months in 1998 (DoH 1998). It is lowest amongst coloured women (0.7 months), then Asian women (2.1 months) followed by African women (2.4 months), and highest among white women (3.4 months).

The median duration of postpartum abstinence was estimated to be 4.9 months. The variations by population group were such that it was lowest among Asian women (0.4 months), followed by white women (2.2) then African women (5.2 months) and highest among coloured women (5.5 months).

Conclusion

In this study, an attempt has been made to estimate the fertility-inhibiting effect of the three most important proximate determinants: marriage, contraception and lactational infecundity. Although abortion is legal in South Africa, data on induced abortion are not readily available and its effect therefore remains essentially immeasurable. The analysis shows that the fertility level of South Africa is low; TFR is estimated at around three births per woman.

The study has also shown that the strongest reduction in fertility has been caused by the index of marriage. In South Africa today, other things being equal, marriage is no longer universal and is characterised by late age at marriage, high rate of divorce and remarriage and a high rate of single parenthood. These factors are associated with lower levels of fertility.

The second factor contributing to the level of fertility is high contraceptive use. There is no doubt that the previous minority government in South Africa paid great attention to increasing both the availability and utilisation of contraception, especially among African women. Many studies indicate that during the apartheid regime the government policy was such that fertility of white people was encouraged whereas that of African people was discouraged (Moultrie 2001).

Given that some provinces still exhibit high fertility levels, there is a need to manipulate the proximate determinants of fertility in these provinces in order to have further decline in fertility in South Africa. Much can be done to increase the contribution of contraception and induced abortion, especially in areas that still have high fertility. In these areas governmental policies can concentrate on efficiently increasing contraceptive utilisation and effectiveness, particularly of condoms, and on encouraging breastfeeding and raising the age at first marriage.

Whether the established fertility transition will be sustained remains to be seen. Future fertility trends are likely to be influenced by the HIV/AIDS epidemic. There has been much apprehension about the effect of HIV/AIDS on fertility in South Africa (Anderson 2003). There is evidence that being HIV-positive lowers fecundity. There are also arguments that behavioural changes among those who are HIV-positive could lead to either lower or higher fertility. It is possible that young unmarried people will postpone entry into sexual union (preferably marriage) leading to further increase in age at first marriage or that couples may avoid having sex for fear of becoming infected with the HIV virus or of worsening the progression from HIV to AIDS if they are already infected. Studies indicate that HIV seropositive women tend to have lower fertility, possibly because they know that pregnancy may lead to early progression to AIDS and early death.

Based on a variety of studies in Africa, being HIV-positive seems to lower fertility from 25 to 40 per cent in comparison with HIV-negative women (UN 2002; Zaba & Gregson 1998). The United Nations (UN 2002) further argues that a 25 per cent national adult prevalence of HIV/AIDS translates into a 10 per cent decline in the total fertility rate, mainly through biological mechanisms.

A recent review of the literature on the relationship between HIV/AIDS and fertility based on studies conducted in Zaire and Uganda revealed that fertility was reduced by approximately 20 per cent among HIV-positive women after controlling for factors such as exposure and contraception (Camlin et al. 2004). Stover (2002) made a similar conclusion based on studies conducted in Uganda and Zimbabwe. In his projection model of the demographic impact of HIV/AIDS, Stover recommended a 20 per cent reduction of fertility among HIV-positive women aged 20–49 years, and a 50 per cent reduction of fertility among HIV-positive women aged 15–19 years.

The following policy implications relating to the achievement of further fertility decline can be drawn from this study. There is a need to:
- Campaign for a further increase in the age at marriage of women, especially in rural areas and poor provinces where early marriages are still common;
- Strengthen the existing national family planning programme in order to increase the quality and the quantity of contraceptive use and achieve higher use-effectiveness that will lead to a greater contribution to fertility decline, especially in areas where fertility is still high;
- Provide a method mix that meets the varied needs of couples and individuals. In this regard, condoms that provide dual protection need to be promoted;
- Ensure the commitment of additional resources to maintain current programme momentum; and

- Provide more information to women about the low cost and much greater benefits of longer duration breastfeeding in order to encourage full and intensive breastfeeding.

References

Abu-Gamrah H (1977) *Analytical framework for studies of socio-economic determinants of fertility.* Technical Papers, R/55, The American University in Cairo

Anderson BA (2003) Fertility, poverty and gender. In Department of Social Development (2003) *Fertility: Current South African issues of poverty, HIV/AIDS and youth – Seminar Proceedings.* Pretoria: Human Sciences Research Council

Bongaarts J (1978) A framework for analyzing the proximate determinants of fertility. *Population and Development Review* 4(1): 105–132

Bongaarts J (1983) The proximate determinants of natural marital fertility. In RA Bulatao & RD Lee (Eds) *Determinants of fertility in developing countries.* New York: Academic Press

Bongaarts J (1985) The fertility-inhibiting effects of the intermediate fertility variables. In WBrass & AG Hill (Eds) *The analysis of maternity histories.* Liege: Orderia for IUSSP

Bongaarts J (1987) The proximate determinants of exceptionally high fertility. *Population and Development Review* 13(1): 133–139

Bongaarts J & Potter RG (1983) *Fertility, biology and behavior: An analysis of the proximate determinants.* New York: Academic Press

Burgard S (2004) Factors associated with contraceptive use in late- and post-apartheid South Africa. *Studies in Family Planning* 35(2): 91–104

Caldwell JC & Caldwell P (1993) The South African fertility decline. *Population and Development Review* 19(2): 225–262

Caldwell JC & Caldwell P (2003) The fertility transition in sub-Saharan Africa. In Department of Social Development *Fertility: Current South African issues of poverty, HIV/AIDS and youth – Seminar proceedings.* Pretoria: HRSC

Camlin CS, Garenne M & Moultrie TA (2004) Fertility trend and pattern in a rural area of South Africa in the context of HIV/AIDS. *African Journal of Reproductive Health* 8(2): 39–54

Chimere-Dan O (1993) Population policy in South Africa. *Studies in Family Planning* 24(1): 31–39

Chimere-Dan O (1996) Contraceptive prevalence in rural South Africa. *International Family Planning Perspectives* 22(1): 4–9

Chimere-Dan O (1999) Marriage and the fertility transition in South Africa. Paper presented at the African Population Conference, Durban, South Africa, 6–10 December

Cochrane SH (1979) *Fertility and education: What do we really know?* World Bank Staff Occasional Papers, No. 26

Cohen B (1993) Fertility levels, differentials, and trends. In KA Foote, KH Hill & LG Martin (Eds) *Demographic change in sub-Saharan Africa.* Washington DC: National Academy Press

Davis K & Blake J (1956) Social structure and fertility: An analytical framework. *Economic Development and Cultural Change* 4(4): 211–235

Department of Population and Social Development (1998) *White Paper on Population Policy.* Government Gazette, Vol. 399, No. 19230. Pretoria: Government Printer

Department of Population and Social Development (2000) *The state of South Africa's Population Report.* Pretoria: National Population Unit

DoH (Department of Health, South Africa) (1998) *South African Demographic and Health Survey: Preliminary report.* Pretoria: DoH

DoH (2002) *An evaluation of the implementation of the Choice on Termination of Pregnancy Act South Africa 2000.* Pretoria: DoH

Dickson KE, Brown H, Rees H & Muvuya L (2003) Abortion service provision in South Africa three years after liberalization of the law. *Studies In Family Planning* 34(4): 277–284

Ferry B & Page HJ (1984) *The proximate determinants of fertility and their effect on fertility patterns: An illustration analysis applied to Kenya.* WFS Scientific Reports No. 71

Freedman R (1986) Fertility determinants. In Cleland & Scott (Eds) *World fertility survey: An assessment of its contribution.* London: Oxford University Press

Kalule-Sabiti I (1983) Patterns and differentials in nuptiality and fertility in Kenya. Doctoral Thesis, Faculty of Social Sciences, University of Durham, England

Kalule-Sabiti I (1984) Bongaarts' proximate determinants of fertility applied to group data from the Kenya Fertility Survey 1977/78. *Journal of Biosocial Science*

Kaufman CE (1997) *Reproductive control in South Africa.* Policy Research Division Working Papers No.97, Rockefeller Foundation

Kaufman CE (1998) Contraceptive use in South Africa under apartheid. *Demography* 35(4): 421–434

Kaufman C, de Wet T & Stadler J (2001) Adolescent pregnancy and parenthood in South Africa. *Studies In Family Planning* 32(2): 147–160

Klausen SM (1999) The formation of a national birth-control movement and the establishment of contraceptive services in South Africa, 1930–1939. PhD thesis, Department of History, Queen's University, Kingston, Ontario, Canada

Mfono Z (1998) Teenage contraceptive needs in urban South Africa: A case study. *International Family Planning Perspective* 24(4): 180–190

Mostert W (1991) Recent fertility trends in South Africa. In W Mostert & J Lotter (Eds) *South Africa's demographic future.* Pretoria: Human Sciences Research Council

Moultrie TA (2001) Racism and reproduction: The institutional effects of apartheid on the South African fertility decline. Paper presented at the XXIV IUSSP General Population Conference, Salvador, Brazil, 18–24 August

Moultrie TA & Timaeus IM (2002) *Trends in South African fertility between1970 and 1998: An analysis of the 1996 Census and 1998 Demographic and Health Survey.* Technical Report, Burden of Disease Research Unit, Medical Research Council

Moultrie TA & Timaeus IM (2003) The South African fertility decline: Evidence from two censuses and a Demographic and Health Survey. *Population Studies* 57(3): 265–283

Oosthuizen K (2000) Demographic changes and sustainable land use in South Africa. *Genus* 56(3–4): 81–107

Pullum TW (1978) *Standardisation*. Technical Bulletins, No.3 Tech. 597, World Fertility Survey

Sibanda A & Zuberi T (1999) Contemporary fertility levels and trends in South Africa: Evidence from reconstructed census birth histories. Paper presented at the Third African Population Conference, Durban, South Africa, 6–10 December

Stats SA (Statistics South Africa) (1999) *Census in Brief*. Pretoria: Stats SA

Stover J (2002) *SPECTRUM/AIM: A computer program for making HIV/AIDS projections and examining the social and economic impact of AIDS*. Washington DC: The Futures Group International

Udjo EO (1998) *Additional evidence regarding fertility and mortality trends in South Africa and implications for population projections*. Pretoria: Statistics South Africa

Udjo EO (2003) A re-examination of levels and differential in fertility in South Africa from recent evidence. *Journal of Biosocial Science* 35(1): 413–431

UN (United Nations) (2002) *HIV/AIDS and fertility in sub-Saharan Africa: A review of the research literature*. New York: United Nations

Zaba B & Gregson S (1998) Measuring the impact of HIV on fertility in Africa. *AIDS* 12 (S1): s41–s50

Children's household work as a contribution to the well-being of the family and household

Sharmla Rama & Linda M Richter

Introduction

In the social science domain, notions about children and childhood are predominantly represented in the study of child development and socialisation (Alanen 2000), with the former having primary roots in psychology and the latter in sociology. In psychology, innate as well as proximal (family) and distal (institution and community) influences are the key theoretical frameworks in studies on children and childhood; and in sociology, it is socialisation, familialisation and institutionalisation (Alanen 1988, 2000; Edwards & Alldred 2000). In both disciplines, emphasis is placed on children being the responsibility of their parents with the assumption that children's upbringing and home life shape their behaviour and attitudes (Edwards & Alldred 2000). Within these notions, the principal social function of the family is to care for children until they can support themselves (Bongaarts 2001). The ability of the family to perform this function, and its access to relevant resources, is key in determining the well-being and development of children (Seaberg 1990; Vogel 2003) and, by and large, the theoretical orientation focuses on the forces acting on the child.

In this chapter, we adopt a different approach to the subject matter of children and their families and households in post-apartheid South Africa. We introduce the idea of a child-centred perspective to the analysis of the data on children's activities. In this emergent paradigm, *the child* rather than the family, household or school is the centre of theory and analysis. This approach to theorising about children and childhood first emerged in Europe and is still relatively fluid, with ongoing debate and empirical engagement (James & Prout 1990).

Concurrently, there has been growth in the development of indicators for monitoring children's health and well-being. This approach uses as its conceptual framework the United Nations Convention on the Rights of the Child (CRC), but is not limited to this document. In addition, the *child well-being approach* aims to identify internationally comparable indicators that extend beyond those cited by the UN and in the CRC (Brown 1999). Well-being goes beyond children's physical health and also encompasses emotional and psychological health (Montgomery et al. 2003).

In this chapter we stress the importance of presenting positive attributes of children and childhood (Pollard & Lee 2003). Robson, for example, in reviewing key and current issues of concerns in youth and childhood in Africa, highlights this point: 'by focusing on them as victims [or actors] in a discourse of crisis, ordinary young people in Africa who are not "in crisis" are neglected' (2004: 192). In the choice and analysis of data from the first national South Africa Time Use Survey (TUS), we emphasise the importance of understanding children's daily activities and the valuable (albeit often overlooked) contribution they make to the livelihood and functioning of the family and household. Included in the discussions are the issue of child labour and possible differences between child 'work' and child 'labour'. We begin this chapter by discussing some of the key characteristics of this emergent child-centred and child well-being approach, followed by a brief overview of time use surveys, and a discussion and review of studies on children's time use and daily activities.

Key conceptual ideas

The status, well-being and development of children are usually contextualised within the family, the school, and the relationship between family (home) and school. Alanen (1988: 54) remarks, 'The triangularity of childhood, the family and socialisation proves to be as if moulded into one piece that cannot be broken into parts for separate consideration.' This notion is not only present within normative family policies but also in economic domain of children and families. With regard to economic analysis, the role of the household and residential family is also central to the analysis because these units are usually the locus of joint decisions regarding consumption, production, labour force participation, savings, and capital formation of the household (Bongaarts 2001). Children are therefore viewed as being economically dependent on their families, or as Qvortrup (cited in Edwards & Alldred 2000: 435) notes, the conceptualisation of children and childhood is often in terms of their familial dependency status (Boyden & Levinson 2000; Qvortrup 1994).

The above conceptualisation of children is indicative not only of the 'theoretical' positioning of children but of children's position in society as a whole. Children are assigned a subordinate role in a hierarchic structure, and this prescription is done on the basis of culture, generation and gender (Boyden & Levinson 2000; Brembeck et al. 1999). In this structure, children (everywhere) are in a subordinate position to adults (Boyden & Levinson 2000). Children are ascribed the status of minors or dependents, with boys generally having more autonomy than girls (Boyden & Levinson 2000). Generalisations about children, and their lives, their needs and concerns, are thereby determined or based on adult conceptualisation, even their idealisation, of children and childhood.

Alanen (1998) describes the shift in thinking about children and childhood as having emerged from a discontent with the existing state of childhood knowledge, combined with an interest in bringing to the study of childhood a range of perspectives already applied in other, more established fields of social science. Alanen (1998) identifies three different methodologies utilised in researching children and childhood, particularly by sociologists. While the perspectives have different methodological roots, Alanen (1998) notes that in all three there is a shared view on the agency of children. Children are not theorised as being the passive subjects of social structures and processes. Instead, in this reconceptualising of childhood, the relations between children, and between children and adults, indicates a renegotiation of how childhood is understood and lived (Brembeck et al. 1999).

In the first strand, which Alanen (1998) terms the 'sociology of children', children are seen to act in the social world, and to participate in ongoing social life, and are centrally involved in the construction of their own childhoods through their negotiations with the adult world and among themselves. Children's actions and experiences are the immediate focus. The second strand focuses on a socially constructed notion of childhood (Alanen 1998). The point is that perceptions and understanding of childhood and children vary between one culture and another, and from one point in history to another (Woodhead & Montgomery 2003). Differences in culture, history, politics, and economic and social aspects need to be taken into account when trying to understand the variety of contexts faced by children. The third perspective (referred to by Alanen [1998] as the 'sociology of childhood') is a more macro-level elaboration of the first strand. It presents childhood as a relatively permanent element in the life of modern societies even though, for individual children, 'childhood' is a temporary period. In this view, childhood is a structural category, comparable and parallel to the proto-sociological issues of ethnicity, race, class and gender. In this approach childhood is also conceptualised and analysed as a socially constructed category.

It is also important to note that social and cultural notions of childhood vary. Under African customary law, for example, the distinction between a child and adult lies not in chronological age but in various life stages. In this context, initiations, ritual or rites of passage, as well as marriage and childbearing, may be the criteria of adulthood, rather than chronological age (Boyden & Levinson 2000; Qvortrup 1994). On the other hand, legal and political notions of what a 'child' and 'childhood' are, are bound by rules, laws, regulations and policies of a state and are age-specific. What is noted from the above is that legal and cultural criteria are used, particularly in countries outside the industrialised world (Boyden & Levison 2000), in determining the point of transition from childhood to adulthood.

The advent of the international treaty, the CRC, and the African Charter on the Rights and Welfare of the Child, created a benchmark for childhood and the rights to which all children are entitled. Both these and other charters promote the importance of a child-centred focus. In both documents, a child is defined as any person below 18 years of age. However, despite this definition, children are not a homogenous group, and therefore any analysis has to take into consideration diversity, especially in terms of age, ethnicity, race (population group), gender and social class (James & Prout 1990). For the purposes of this study, the definition of a child (or children) is based on the legal definition provided in Section 28 of the South African Constitution; that is, as someone under the age of 18 years.

Children as a unit of observation and analysis

Boyden and Levinson (2000) observe that most economic analyses, in particular of poverty-related issues, take the household or the family as the unit of observation. In this approach, children are at risk simply because they belong to particular adults or live in certain households, but the adults are the focus of attention, and the material and social conditions of children as a category are obscured.[1] This familialisation of children is not confined to economic analysis. Ben-Arieh and Goerge (2001), in reviewing recent international publications in which the focus is on measuring and monitoring children's well-being or status, note that in most of the data collection efforts, the unit of observation is the family and, in the case of some reports, orientation is towards the programme or service provided and not towards the child.

Similarly, Qvortrup (1990) draws attention to this conceptual and numerical marginalisation of children in reports about children in national statistics. Data about children in public statistics are characterised by the following emphases: the production of children (vital statistics), expenses incurred on behalf of children, and system efficiencies such as educational attainment or throughput. In most instances, the child is not the unit of observation. The idea of giving children a perspective, voice or status equal to other groups in society goes against conventional thinking. Nonetheless, it is an important approach to describing and understanding children's life situations. On this point, Ben-Arieh and Goerge (2001) point out that there is a shift, albeit a very slow one, towards the use of the concept of the child as the unit of observation, including in official statistics on the status or well-being of children (Saporiti 1994).

In discussing the numerous methodological challenges to analysis in which the child is the unit of observation, Saporiti (1985), illustrates the use of children (or the child) and childhood as a unit of observation by re-examining and tabulating statistics from the UK and Italy on children, their families and life situations. As an example from Saporiti's work, we use information on children and derived monthly household income from the South Africa 1996 census data. As a point of illustration we focus, in the analysis, on households that report they have no monthly income.

In Table 7.1, the first two columns show the household as the unit of observation, more specifically households with children whose ages range between 0 and 17 years. The first section shows that 14.2 per cent (n=801 938) of households with children aged 0–17 years report that they have no monthly income. In contrast, the second two columns show that 15.2 per cent (n=2 483 083) of all children, whose ages range between 0 and 17 years, live in households that report that they have no monthly income. While there seems to be very little difference in the percentage points, when using the child (or children), rather than the household, as the unit of analysis, we note that in 1996 just over 2.4 million children lived in households that reported that they had no monthly income compared to 801 938 households with

---

1 Categories of children who are at risk or vulnerable, that is homeless children or child (orphan)- headed households, cannot be dealt with in this approach.

children aged between 0–17 years who reported that they had no monthly income. The analysis of children who are at risk or made vulnerable by lack of income, in this illustration, moves away from household to child-centred analysis.

Table 7.1: Derived household income by households with children, and children by derived income of household

Derived household income (monthly)	Households with children 0–17 years		Children 0–17years	
	Number	Percentage	Number	Percentage
None	801 938	14.2	2 483 083	15.2
R1–R200	475 326	8.4	1 499 940	9.2
R201–R500	894 278	15.8	2 817 644	17.2
R501–R1000	787 240	14	2 456 723	15
R1 001–R1 500	559 600	9.9	1 623 290	9.9
R1 501–R2 500	537 940	9.5	1 530 719	9.4
R2 501–R3 500	301 969	5.4	801 757	4.9
R3 501–R4 500	211 384	3.7	534 331	3.3
R4 501–R6 000	227 152	4	543 815	3.3
R6 001–R8 000	156 125	2.8	358 710	2.2
R8 001–R11 000	161 465	2.9	353 147	2.2
R11 001–R16 000	96 541	1.7	203 758	1.2
R16 001–R30 000	67 023	1.2	143 644	0.9
R30 001 or more	19 791	0.4	49 072	0.3
Unspecified	344 986	6.1	947 763	5.8
Total	5 642 760	100	16 347 397	100

Source: Own calculations from Stats SA 1999

When we begin to conceptualise the material and social conditions of children in a child-centred manner, we can also factor into the analysis and theorising aspects relating to gender lines, class divisions, population group and other proto-sociological categories. In doing this, childhood can be constructed beyond the notion of a single and universal phenomenon, to recognition that childhoods vary. This also raises the issue of children's development trajectories, and the relevance of age or sub-group disaggregation of information; for example, statistics on infants and toddlers, preschoolers, children in school care, those not in school and adolescents. Ben-Arieh and Ofir (2002) note that in studies where the specific focus area is children's daily activities and time use, there is an increasing engagement with conceptual ideas from studies of childhood, especially the child-centred perspective.

In the following section we review the literature on time use studies, particularly relating to children's patterns of time use within the household, children's household work, both unpaid and paid (in cash or kind) domestic work, and the issues of exploitative child labour practices.

Review of literature on children's time use and household work

Time use surveys emerged prior to the Second World War as a statistical tool for social research and the development of social indicators (Fleming & Spellerberg 1999). Traditionally, time use survey data has been used to study national and cross-national trends in life styles, quality of life and well-being. Over the years, time use or time budget surveys have gained increasing recognition and importance in economic analyses. In particular, the increased awareness of unpaid labour activities has, on the one hand, challenged conventional approaches to economic analysis and, on the other hand, contributed to the gender discourse.

Drawing on this debate, Floro (1995) explains that a significant aspect of economic life takes place in an area of production largely ignored in standard macroeconomic analysis, namely, the household production of non-marketed goods and services. These household-produced goods and services are vital for social reproduction and human development. A large amount of unpaid work also takes place in the community, ranging from transport provision for ill, dependent and vulnerable people, to the administration of schools and social organisations such as clubs (Fleming & Spellerberg 1999). The invisibility in economic analysis, and the growing importance, especially within the feminist discourse, of women's economic contribution through unpaid labour such as household work and care-giving (Fleming & Spellerberg 1999), prompted a suggestion for countries to implement parallel accounts to the System of National Accounts (SNA).[2] The 'new household economics' recognises that, in addition to consuming goods and services produced in the market, households also produce and consume goods and services through the unpaid work of their members, especially women, which includes aspects of caring for others and domestic work (Fleming & Spellerberg 1999).

Fleming and Spellerberg (1999) note that while the focus on gender is currently topical, time use data can also be used to describe differences in the lives and work of other groups in the population, differences between ethnic groups, for example, or between people of different ages. The authors also point out that national time use studies do not usually include data on children (Flemming & Speller 1999). The design and purpose of most national time use surveys is to determine variations in men and women's labour participation, both their market and non-market activities. Children in these studies and surveys are generally seen as 'mere consumers of adult time' (Qvortrop 1994: 7). In surveys that do include time use diary information on young people and children (usually for children 10 years and older), the children and young people are often invisible in the statistics or treated as little adults (Burratta & Sabbadini cited in Fleming & Spellerberg 1999). Moreover, children's economic contribution through unpaid labour, such as household work and caregiving, is often overlooked (Robson 2004).

---

2 An international system from which macro-economic indicators such as the gross domestic product is calculated, that is it measures goods and services produced in the labour market, and other activities.

Time use studies of children are, therefore, usually specially designed surveys such that children's own time use is central to the analysis (Fleming & Spellerberg 1999). Two thematic concerns emerge in such studies. The one examines whether factors such as age, gender, social class, family composition, family size, position in the family and so on, have an impact on the types of activities in which children engage, as well as the amount of time children spend on these activities. For example, Bianchi & Robinson's (1997) study of Californian children aged 3 to 11 years examines correlations between the amount of time children spend on four activities presumed to affect their cognitive and social development – reading or being read to, watching television, studying and doing household work – and parental education, maternal employment, number of parents in the household and family size (Bianchi & Robinson 1997).

The other thematic concern focuses on the types of household and non-household activities in which children engage. The 1998–99 India Time Use Survey, for example, was designed to determine the prevalence and extent of child labour and child workers (Hirway 2001). Time use activity information on children aged 6–14 years was collected, and coded to distinguish between SNA[3] and non-SNA work. The analysis summarised children's engagement in activities across gender and age. The study showed that children participate in both economic and non-economic activities, and that both contribute to family and household welfare. In addition, girls engage in more household activities such as child-care and household maintenance than boys.

Gender and, to some extent, age differences are evident in such studies, especially in household work and children's patterns of time use. Boyden and Levinson (2000) note that gender is one of the most striking and enduring examples of power differences within childhood, with consequences for survival, well-being, competencies and susceptibilities. In most societies, the authors note, children's jobs are gendered, especially after age 6 or so, and that the gendering of childhood jobs is context-specific. Gender roles in one society or community may be reversed in another society or community. Moreover, childhood gender roles are not necessarily fixed, but can be susceptible to birth order and the sex composition of the sibling group. Istat (Italian National Institute of Statistics), for example, noted from the analysis of data of children's time use from their previous surveys that gender roles emerge at a very young age, develop through adolescence and young adulthood, and gradually become consolidated during adult life (Comporeses & Romano 2003).

Goodnow (1988), in her review on the nature and functions of children's household work, observes that work is generally understood to mean an activity paid for in money, and suggests that two concerns underlie the interest in children's household labour. On the one hand, children's participation in household work is viewed as a benefit to the household and to children themselves. On a psychological level, this analysis delves into issues of childrearing practices, and whether the allocation of household tasks according to gender, age and position in the family predicts a

---

3 See previous footnote for the definition of SNA.

child's later behaviour, such as responsibility and future achievement in the labour market. Based on her empirical studies, Goodnow (cited in Larson 2001) found little evidence to support the idea that household work fosters these aspects of children's development. Rather, household work assists children to gain specific activity skills, such as cooking, but the mundane and repetitive nature of these tasks, Goodnow (cited in Larson 2001) suggests, does little to stimulate children's development.

The shift in interest toward analyses and theorising of children's household work, Goodnow (1988) explains, stems from the usefulness of the topic for exploring a variety of issues namely, the development of pro-social or co-operative behaviour, the fostering of responsibility, the nature of parental control or adult-guided learning, the acquisition of gender roles and the relation of children's household work to family socio-economic status, a mother's paid work outside the home, and changes in the concept of childhood and child labour. The other aspect deals with social problems, in particular, arguments for and against the legitimacy, appropriateness and desirability of work by children in the household. These concerns centre on the impact of a mother's employment status on the well-being and development of children, the socialisation of girls and boys in terms of the gendering of tasks allocated, and the reduction of children's time for education and for socialising with others. While these concerns dominate social policy and family policy debates, there also exist explicitly exploitative forms of child household work, especially in households headed by someone other than the child's own parents or caregivers. Blagbrough and Glynn (1999), for example, look at the practice in some societies in which children, especially young girls, are given or sold into domestic work. As an example, the authors cite the practice known as *mui tsai* (little sister) in southern China, and *pei nu* (slave girls) in the north, both stemming from its false portrayal of child domestic servitude as a form of adoption (Blagbrough & Glynn 1999: 52). Such practices are seen as normal and unproblematic, in that they are rooted in traditional norms of the society. Blagbrough and Glynn (1999) explain that even child rights activists are often unable to see the parallels between the exploitation of children on the factory floor and the abuse of child domestics in other people's homes, and some even employ children as domestic servants themselves. Blagbrough and Glynn (1999) note that, far from enjoying a protected life in their employers' households, many children are on duty throughout the day and night and face discrimination in the household. What such domestic service entails is the sacrifice of the servant's own childhood for the well-being of the employer. Such children, who are aged from as young as 5 years, are entirely dependent on the employer. These children are often deprived of the chance to play and make friends, and are vulnerable to verbal, physical and sexual abuse.

These practices also exist in Africa (Jacquemin 2004; Turner & Kwakye 1996). In a study of mainly girls' domestic work in Abidjan, Côte D'Ivoire, Jacquemin (2004) reported that the employment of little nieces is an ancient custom practised throughout west Africa; one that is intended to create solid networks (family or other). The little maids represent a kind of category of fostered children and this practice is part of a process of the girl's socialisation and education (Jacquemin 2004).

The customary practice of fostering children is not necessarily restricted to females only (Turner & Kwakye 1996). Jacquemin (2004) notes that the practice of fostering girls has been gradually disappearing and is being replaced with the practice of 'little waged maids'. The result is a blurring between whether these practices constitute employment (paid labour) or work (defined as everything needed to run a household). The type of domestic work in which the girls engage varies in terms of the method of payment (cash or kind), relationship to the household members or head (that is the household in which they work in) and the way in which the girl came into the job. Nonetheless, the study found that the girls work extremely long hours, are sometimes treated very badly (physical and verbal abuse) by both related and non-related 'employers', have little or no education and are sometimes 'forced' to pay for their food, medical needs and clothes.

Francavilla and Lyon (2003), as part of the Understanding Children's Work (UCW) project, used survey data sets from six countries – Guatemala, Zambia, Peru, Guinea, Brazil and Kazakhstan – in an attempt to shed light on child household work and the relationship between household work and child health. The authors concluded that a large proportion of children in the six countries spend some time in each week in household production activities, such as collecting firewood, fetching water, food preparation and childcare – and that these activities constitute a major time burden only for a much smaller proportion of children in the six countries studied (Francavilla & Lyon 2003). The authors estimate that around one in ten children in Guatemala, Guinea and Peru, and even fewer in Brazil and Kazakhstan, spend at least 28 hours per week on household chores. They suggest that children's involvement in work may yield a positive income effect. By freeing the time of an adult for productive work, children's household work might contribute to a higher level of household income. Higher income, in turn, might lead to better levels of nutrition and care and, ultimately, to better health. It may also prevent children from engaging in hazardous labour practices as a means to supplement household income. On the other hand, the long periods of time spent on a daily basis on strenuous tasks such as fetching water or collecting firewood, and the impact this has on children's physical development and also on their participation in education and in future labour market activities, needs more in-depth documentation and investigation (Francavilla & Lyon 2003).

Children in South Africa, note Budlender and Bosch (2002), participate in domestic work either for other households in exchange for payment in cash and kind, or within their own households as unpaid domestic workers. Empirical evidence, for example, from the South Africa Survey of Activities of Young People (SAYP) (Stats SA 2000a, 2000b) regarding the reasons children engage in economic activities for pay, profit and economic family gain, show that 58.6 per cent of children report that it is part of their duty to help the family, 14.7 per cent to assist family with money, and 15.7 per cent for pocket money, while proportionately fewer children report that it is to gain experience (2.4 per cent), or to earn money for their schooling (1.9 per cent). Budlender and Bosch (2002) conclude that while a small number of children are reportedly engaged in paid domestic work, this probably represents an undercount as a result of households not disclosing the presence of child domestic workers, and the under-estimation of the extent of unpaid child household work.

Some possible explanations for the undercount or under-estimation of the extent of unpaid household work in time use studies may lie in the methodology and conceptualisation of children's work. Gager et al. (1999), for example, suggest that studies that focus on household-related tasks collect information on activities more appropriate to adults rather than to children and the household work activities they usually engage in, for example baby sitting, caring for pets, ironing, washing clothes, washing dishes, sweeping and so on. The classification of the activities in the TUS data groups together different activities, giving us a general picture of children's contribution to household work; for example, cooking, making drinks, setting and serving tables and washing up is grouped together under a single code rather than as a separate code for each of these activities.

This sort of categorisation, Gager et al. (1999) argue, may lead to conclusions that children's contributions to the household are minimal, especially in comparison to the adult's contribution in the household, and this leads to an under-estimation of children's unpaid household work. The under-estimation of children's household work suggests that more comprehensive child-centred studies into children' time use may be needed.

Another aspect of children's household work that needs to be taken into account is care for adults and other children within and outside of the household. In his review of literature on intra-household allocation of time and tasks, Ilahi (2000: 37) makes reference to the impact that illness of a member or members of the household and unemployment may have on children, especially on girls – 'exogenous shocks that lower household income [and wealth] may adversely affect girl time use and school a lot more than they would boy time use'. Results, for example, from the 2002 Kaiser Foundation's survey of 771 AIDS-affected households in South Africa (Steinberg et al. 2002) show that about 8 per cent of children under the age of 18 years were responsible for caring for a family member sick with AIDS. About 4 per cent of the households surveyed reported that they had to cut school-fee payments as a result of having to care for family member/s who are sick with AIDS. Girls, the study revealed, are more likely than boys to drop out of school, be forced to stay home because of financial limitations or to care for a sick person. Even before children are orphaned the strains of coping with HIV/AIDS cause families to split up. The report highlights the difficult circumstances that households and the children in these households encounter, and the strategies that families adopt in an effort to cope with death or the caring of a household member who is ill.

Data and methodology

In the next section we not only focus on the structure and design of the TUS survey but on some of the challenges that the data presented to the analysis of children's household work. The data used in this study are from South Africa's first national

TUS, conducted by Statistics South Africa[4] in 2000. The main aim and objective of the TUS was to provide information on the division of both paid and unpaid labour between women and men, as well as less-understood productive activities such as subsistence work, casual work and work in the informal sector, and to gendered aspects of time allocation to child-care activities (Budlender et al. 2001).

The sample for the TUS survey covered all nine provinces, and was stratified, within each province, according to settlement type – namely formal urban, informal urban, commercial farms and other rural settlements.[5] The time use study sample was based on the frame prepared for the 1999 Survey of Activities of Young People (SAYP), which, in turn, was based on the 1996 population census enumerated areas (EAs) and the number of households counted in the census. The planned sample size was 900 primary sampling units (PSUs) and 10 800 dwelling units. The fieldwork was conducted in three rounds – February, June and October, so as to compensate for possible seasonal variation in the time use patterns and activities of both men and women. In each tranche, a third of the allocated number of PSUs was enumerated, that is 3 600 dwelling units per tranche. The realised sample was smaller than planned, and consisted of 8 564 households and 14 533 respondents (unweighted figures).

The TUS questionnaire comprises five sections. Section one covers the household details, including a matrix for all household members. Within each household two persons aged 10 years and older were systematically selected and asked what activities they had performed the previous day. The second section comprises the demographic details of one of the two persons (referred to as the first selected person), selected as the respondent for the 24-hour diary, and the third is the 24-hour diary in which the first selected person's activities are recorded from 4am on the day preceding the day of the interview to 4am on the day of the interview. Sections four and five were for the second selected person of the household, and asked the same questions in sections two and three.

The 24-hour diary was divided into half-hour slots. In each slot a maximum of three activities could be recorded. For each recorded activity the questionnaire also included two location codes. The first code consisted of eight broadly defined locations (for example, own dwelling, educational institution) and a code for travel or waiting to travel. The second code, in relation to the first location code, asked whether the activity took place outside or inside of a building, and the different modes of travel (for example, travelling by train, travelling by foot) the respondent may have used to and from the location. The activities recorded in the time diary were post-coded by the fieldworker according to an activity classification system (see Budlender et al. 2001 for details).

---

4 The data and tables in this chapter, unless otherwise stated, are based on the 2000 Time Use Survey data. The survey was conducted by Statistics South Africa (Stats SA), which has also developed the relevant statistical methods, questionnaire design, data collection techniques and initial analysis that have made the chapter possible. Stats SA has given users access to the anonymised time use database.
5 The four types of settlement, used in the survey, are defined as follows: formal urban includes areas with formal houses, flats and other dwellings; informal urban includes areas such as 'squatter' settlements, commercial farming includes rural areas in which commercial landholdings predominate, and other rural areas correspond to previous 'homelands' or 'ex-homeland' areas (Budlender et al. 2001: 10).

An adapted version of the UN trial classification coding system was used to code the activities in the South African TUS diary. Ten sub-categories[6] were created, namely personal care and self-maintenance, employment for establishments, primary production activities not for establishment, services for income and other production of goods not for establishment, household maintenance, management and shopping for own household, care for children, the sick, elderly and disabled for own household, community services and help to other households, learning, social and cultural activities, and mass media use.

The data are available as ASCII files, and there are a total of six data files.[7] The files include weights, which allow the raw data to be weighted to adjust for the responses collected to be representative of the underlying sample frame (Budlender et al. 2001). Budlender et al. note that because of the relatively small size of the sample, the results were weighted to reflect the 25 000-odd individuals aged 10 years and above, expected to be found in the 10 800 dwelling units, rather than the number of people of this age in the South African population This approach was adopted to remind users and readers that the survey is smaller that the usual Stats SA survey and thus slightly less reliable in terms of the extrapolation. The proportions, the authors point out, should, nevertheless, reflect the full population.

Limitations and challenges in the TUS data sets

The analysis of the TUS data for this chapter presented a number of challenges. One relates to classifying of household or family types.[8] Most surveys ask about the household member's relationship to the household head and this information is used to construct family or household types. In the TUS, the question on relationships of the household members to each other was phrased differently. In each household two persons aged 10 years or older were selected to participate in the 24-hour diary – the question on relationships within the household asked about the relationship of the selected persons (referred to as selected person 1 and 2) to each of the other members of the household. The listing of the household members was done according to age – that is, ranking the household members from oldest to youngest, with no indication of which person was the household head. Consequentially the algorithm for determining family types by using relationship to household head, as defined for the broader project on families and households included in this volume, could not be adapted for use here.

6 Based on three broad categories, namely, *SNA production* (employment for establishments, primary production activities for establishments, and services or income and other production of foods for establishments); *non-SNA production* (household maintenance, management and shopping for own household; care for children, the sick, elderly and disabled for own household; and community services and help to other households); and non-productive activities (learning, social and cultural activities, mass media use and personal care and self-maintenance).
7 Four of the files are based on the different sections of the questionnaire, and two are constructed files. The files consisted of one file for the household information (Section 1 of the questionnaire, file name HHOLD), one for the person information (Section 2 and 4 of the questionnaire that contained the demographic information of the two selected respondents, file name PERSON), another file for the diary information (Sections 3 and 5 of the questionnaire, file name DIARY), and another for the information from the household member list (household grid from Section 1 – MEMBER data file). The two constructed files, named ACTIVALL and EPISODE, were constructed from the diary data; the first recorded all the activities, and the second the accumulated similar consecutive activities into a single record.
8 Earlier chapters of this book provide a description and definition of the family/household types utilised in this project.

The other challenge was that the manner in which relationship-related information was collected also made it difficult to establish whether children are living in households headed by their parents, grandparents, relative or non-relative household members. This also meant that analysis by education levels or other characteristics of the head of the household or parents/caregivers, which is included in other chapters in this volume, was not possible for this chapter using the data set available.

An option explored was to use the variables describing various characteristics of the household. One such variable is the household size or the number of people that reside in the household. This information, we hoped, would provide us with data as to whether family size or composition has an influence on the number of household activities or the amount of time children spent on household work.[9] However, a closer examination of the files showed that for some of the households, the two household members selected for the 24-hour diary were not included in the household listing data file, and if they were included, there was a disparity in the ages given in two files. This made it difficult to establish the number and composition of members in the household. It was decided that the variable household size would, therefore, not be utilised in the analysis.

In this chapter, while we emphasise the need to conduct analysis of childhood using proto-sociological categories such as population group or developmental stage of the child, the sample size (weighted and unweighted) for some of these variables is too small to determine if there the statistical relationship is significant. For example we do not do any analysis by population group (race) because the sample sizes (unweighted and weighted) across categories are too small for valid statistical analysis (see Table 7.2).

Analysis of the data

For this analysis, we selected children 10–17 years of age, together with their relevant demographic and household characteristics. We excluded the small number of individuals who reported that they are married or that they have children of their own, because their experiences and daily household responsibilities may not be typical of children in the age range 0–17 years (Woodhead & Montgomery 2003). Of the initial sample of 2 916 children in this age range 10–17 years (unweighted data), we removed the records of the latter group, leaving an analytical sample of 2 855 children (unweighted data). This is about 20 per cent of the total unweighted sample of the full age range of respondents (n=14 306) in the TUS. Table 7.2 shows, for both the weighted and unweighted data, the distribution of children by their background characteristics.

---

9 For this purpose we hoped to utilise the MEMBER file, and from this information derive the household size and so on. The MEMBER file was selected in that according to the TUS metadata notes it is described as containing one record for every household member recorded in the grid in section 1 of the questionnaire (Stats SA 2001 b).

Table 7.2: Distribution of children by background characteristics (weighted and unweighted)

Category		Unweighted		Weighted*	
		Number	Per cent	Number	Per cent
Gender**	Male	1 367	47.9	3 493	50.2
	Female	1 488	52.1	3 470	49.8
	Total	2 855	100	6 963	100
Population group	African	2 305	80.8	5 745	82.6
	Coloured	72	2.5	173	2.5
	Indian	294	10.3	556	8.0
	White	179	6.3	477	6.9
	Other	4	0.1	7	0.1
	Total	2 854	100	6 958	100
Age group	10–14	1 801	63.1	4 546	65.3
	15–17	1 054	36.9	2 417	34.7
	Total	2 855	100	6 963	100
Province	Western Cape	290	10.2	552	7.9
	Eastern Cape	421	14.8	1 320	19.0
	Northern Cape	166	5.8	137	2.0
	Free State	333	11.7	439	6.3
	KwaZulu-Natal	478	16.7	1 505	21.6
	North West	239	8.4	614	8.8
	Gauteng	293	10.3	903	13.0
	Mpumalanga	308	10.8	455	6.5
	Northern Province***	327	11.5	1 036	14.9
	Total	2 855	100	6 963	100
Stratum	Urban formal	1 071	37.5	2 693	38.7
	Urban informal	588	20.6	502	7.2
	Other rural	818	28.7	3 466	49.8
	Commercial agriculture	378	13.2	301	4.3
	Total	2 855	100	6 963	100

Source: Own calculations from Stats SA 1999

Notes:
* The files include weights, which allow the raw data to be weighted so as to adjust the responses collected to be represented of the underlying sample frame. The results were weighted to reflect the 25 000 odd individuals aged 10 years and above whom one would have expected to find in the 10 800 dwelling units rather than the number of people of this age in the full population
** The weighted values for gender yield higher estimates for males than females (see note 1 for possible explanation)
*** Province name has changed to Limpopo

In this chapter we examine whether age, gender and stratum affects the nature, distribution and the extent of the different kinds of household work in which children participate. For this analysis, age is categorised into two groups: 10–14 years and 15–17 years. The categorisation reflects early and later adolescence.

With regard to education, the questionnaire asked about the highest standard/ grade passed but did not ask whether the selected person was still at school. We are, however, able to extract from the diary records details about time spent on education-related activities; where applicable, data about school or non-school attendance for the day is included in the analysis. Cognisance is also taken if activities were reported for a weekday or weekend. The majority of children (unweighted data n=2 495, 87.8%) said that the activities they reported were for a typical day. Analysis of the diary day shows that just over one quarter (unweighted data 25.1 per cent, n=720) of the children provided details of activities in which they engaged over the weekend (Saturday and Sunday), while most (74.1%, n=2 113) of the children reported on activities in a week day. Of the total sample, attendance at school is recorded in the diary as an activity by 65.3 per cent (unweighted data, n=1 865) of the children.

The analyses focus only on those activity codes (categories) that relate to household work. In time use studies, unpaid work usually covers household work, childcare activities, maintenance work, purchase of goods and services, as well as travel connected to these tasks (Kitterøde 2002). For this chapter, the activities of focus include household maintenance; management and shopping; care for children, the sick, elderly and disabled in own household, as well as other households; and primary production activities not for an external establishment/business (for example collection of water and fuel sources). Household work is a multifaceted and complex activity, and any one person can carry out a number of different tasks in a single day or for a particular period in a day. In addition to the descriptive overview of the activities in which children engage, we analyse, where applicable and relevant, the extent and distribution of multiple household work engaged in by children over the 24-hour diary period. Both total time and mean time spent on a particular activity is reported. The mean time is calculated by dividing the total time spent on an activity by the number of people who reported that they participated in the activity.

Descriptive overview of children's household work and patterns of time use

In the following section we focus on the household work activities in which children reportedly engaged during the 24-hour diary-day. These include activities within their own homes and, activities in which they participated in other households. As an introduction to, and illustration of, the descriptive overview of the data on children's household work, we begin this section with the extracted 24-hour day diaries[10] of two female children, both 10 years of age. In Table 7.3 we describe the activities and tasks they engage in, the time spent on these tasks and the household or living

10 Extracted from the DIARY data file

circumstance of the children. Both girls live in rural areas, one in KwaZulu-Natal and the other in the Northern Province. Girl A is in Grade 2 and Girl B in Grade 4.

Table 7.3: Diary of main activities for two girls aged 10, residing in an area categorised as other rural

	Description of main activity (diary day – Monday)	
	10-year-old female, residing in KwaZulu-Natal (in Grade 2)	10-year-old female, residing in Northern Province (in Grade 4)
Time period	Girl A	Girl B
04h00–05h30	Sleep	Sleep
05h30–06h00	Sleep	Personal hygiene and health
06h00–06h30	Sleep	School
06h30–07h00	Personal hygiene and health	School
07h00–07h30	Travel related to learning	School
07h30–08h00	School	School
08h00–08h30	School	School
08h30–09h00	School	School
09h00–09h30	School	School
09h30–10h00	School	School
10h00–10h30	School	Receiving medical and personal care from non-household non-professionals
10h30–11h00	Personal hygiene and health	School
11h00–11h30	School	School
11h30–12h00	School	School
12h00–12h30	School	School
12h30–13h00	Eating and drinking	Eating and drinking
13h00–13h30	School	School
13h30–14h00	School	School
14h00–14h30	School	School
14h30–15h00	Travel related to learning	School
15h00–15h30	Personal hygiene and health	Travel related to learning
15h30–16h00	Eating and drinking	*Cleaning and upkeep of dwelling and surroundings*
16h00–16h30	*Collecting water*	*Cleaning and upkeep of dwelling and surroundings*
16h30–17h00	Games and other pastime activities	Socialising with family
17h00–17h30	Games and other pastime activities	Socialising with family
17h30–18h00	Games and other pastime activities	Socialising with family

	Description of main activity (diary day – Monday)	
	10-year-old female, residing in KwaZulu-Natal (in Grade 2)	10-year-old female, residing in Northern Province (in Grade 4)
Time period	Girl A	Girl B
18h00–18h30	Games and other pastime activities	Socialising with family
18h30–19h00	Homework, studies and course review	*Crop farming and market/kitchen gardening: planting, weeding, harvesting, picking and so on*
19h00–19h30	Homework, studies and course review	Doing nothing, rest and relaxation
19h30–20h00	Eating and drinking	Eating and drinking
20h00–20h30	Listening to music or radio	Socialising with family
20h30–21h00	Sleep	Socialising with family
21h00–04h00	Sleep	Sleep

Source: Own calculations from Stats SA 1999

At first glance, the days of the two girls have a lot in common. They both attended school and spent some time either socialising with family or playing games. These activities are typical of children in their age group. On closer inspection, we note that Girl A spent half an hour collecting water for the household. Girl B, on the other hand, spent up to an hour on the cleaning and upkeep of the household dwelling and surroundings, and up to half an hour on activities coded as crop farming and market/kitchen gardening: planting, weeding, harvesting, picking and so on.

If we delve further into the two girls' household characteristics another layer of the picture emerges. Girl A lives in a dwelling that can be described as a traditional hut made of traditional material. The household has no access to a car, refrigerator, television, stove, or telephone. The household does, however, have access to a radio. The main source of fuel for cooking and heating is wood and for lighting it is candles. The main source of water is from a spring that is about 100 to 200 metres from the household and the women in the household usually collect the water. In terms of access to facilities and services, the household in which Girl A lives has a primary school and bus service that is within a 30-minute (2km) walk from the household. Other services and facilities (shop, hospital and secondary school) are more than 2km away from the dwelling. The main source of income in the household is state grants (that may include disability, old age pension and/or child support) and the estimated monthly income of the household ranges between R400 and R799. Girl B, on the other hand, lives in a dwelling described as a brick house in a separate yard. The household has access to a radio, car, television and refrigerator, but no access to a stove or telephone. The main source of fuel for cooking and lighting is paraffin and for heating it is wood. The household has access to water from a piped tap in the dwelling. The dwelling is within a 30-minute (2km) walk of a primary and secondary school, a hospital, a shop, and most modes of transportation. The main source of income in the household is state grants (that may include disability, old age pension and/or child support), and the estimated monthly income of the household ranges between R400 and R799.

From the diary and household information extracted for the two girls, we can begin to formulate questions about how the locale (geographic location), population group, gender, and age of the child, their socio-economic status (that is the information about the household in which the child lives), and the household composition[11] and relationships affect how children spend their time, the type of activities they engage in or are allocated and the duration or timing (whether they do it before or after school and so on) of the activities. Such questions are necessary to understanding why Girl B, who lives in a more 'modern' household, does more household work than Girl A. Within this context, children's time use and the focus on their economic contribution to the household through unpaid labour such as household work and caring-related activities becomes as important to understand as the time use of men and women (both paid and unpaid work). In the following analyses we delve into some of these issues, beginning with the most common activities in which children engage, followed by activities that can be described as time-consuming and strenuous (for example, the collection of fuel sources and water) when compared to other activities children engage in within the household.

Cooking, cleaning, care of textiles activities

One of the most common household activities children across all categories engage in is household maintenance and management-type activity. Of the 2 855 children (unweighted sample) that completed the 24-hour diary, just over one half of the children (50.2%, n=1 433) report that they engage in cooking-related activities. The total number of minutes spent on the activity is 101 530, with a mean time of 71 minutes. The amount of time spent ranges from 10 minutes to 510 minutes. Table 7.4 shows (for the unweighted data) the distribution of the mean and total time by age and gender of the children that reported participating in cooking activities.

Table 7.4 shows that while more girls engage in cooking-related activities, spending on average more than an hour (81 minutes) per day, a significant number of boys also engage in cooking-related activities. Similar results are obtained in the weighting of this data – girls (n=2 317) spend on average more time (86 minutes) on cooking-related activities compared to boys (n=1 133, mean time of 49 minutes).

The above data suggest that fewer children in the age range 15–17 years engage in cooking-related activities but that, on average, they spend more time on this activity than children aged 10–14 years. However, caution must be exercised in making this generalisation because the (total) sample size for the 10–14-year-olds is slightly higher than that for 15–17-year-olds. The analysis by stratum shows that children residing

11 In looking at the household composition the data was not very reliable. The member data file shows that in Girl A's household there were four members and their ages range from 0–3 years, and for Girl B's household there were five household members whose ages range from 10–44 years. In both cases the girls' details were not included in the member file – the 10 year-old in Girl B's household is male. It was therefore not possible based on this information to look at the division of labour by gender, age, and family size and composition.

in areas categorised as other rural[12] spent, on average, more time on cooking-related activities (84 minutes), compared to children from commercial agriculture areas (65 minutes), or informal (69 minutes) and formal (61 minutes) urban areas.

Table 7.4: Total and mean time children spend on cooking-related activities, by age and gender (unweighted)

Gender	Age categories	Mean time	Number of children	Total time	% of total time
Boys	10–14	45	250	11 270	11.1
	15–17	52	209	10 915	10.8
	Total	48	459	22 185	21.9
Girls	10–14	72	586	42 110	41.5
	15–17	96	388	37 235	36.7
	Total	81	974	79 345	78.1
Total	10–14	64	836	53 380	52.6
	15–17	81	597	48 150	47.4
	Total	71	1 433	101 530	100

Source: Own calculations from Stats SA 1999

Table 7.5 shows the total and mean time children spent on the cleaning and upkeep of the household. Less than half of the children (44.8%, n=1 278) participated in this activity. More girls (n=805) than boys (n=473) engaged in cleaning and upkeep of dwellings and surroundings, with boys spending on average 50 minutes and girls 58 minutes per day.

Table 7.5: Total and mean time children spend on the cleaning and upkeep of the dwelling, by age and gender (unweighted)

Gender	Age categories	Mean time	Number of children	Total time	% of total sum
Boys	10–14	44	246	10 850	15.4
	15–17	57	227	12 945	18.4
	Total	50	473	23 795	33.8
Girls	10–14	53	492	26 250	37.3
	15–17	65	313	20 285	28.8
	Total	58	805	46 535	66.2
Total	10–14	50	738	37 100	52.8
	15–17	62	540	33 230	47.2
	Total	55	1 278	70 330	100

Source: Own calculations from Stats SA 1999

12 Other rural areas correspond to previous 'homelands' or 'ex-homeland' areas (Budlender et al. 2001: 10).

In terms of variation by locale, children residing in areas categorised as other rural, urban formal and urban informal, spent on average, 57, 56 and 54 minutes on the cleaning and upkeep of the dwellings respectively, compared to children who reside in commercial agriculture areas (an average of 49 minutes). Table 7.5 shows similar results for age as reported for cooking. Children 15–17 years of age spend on average more time on the cleaning and upkeep of the household than children aged 10–14 years.

Table 7.6 shows children who report engaging in activities related to the care of textiles (sorting, mending, washing, ironing and ordering clothes and linen). As in the analysis of the cooking and cleaning-related activities, the data show that more girls (unweighted data, n=377 versus n=232) than boys engage in this activity, with girls spending on average more time (54 minutes) than boys (45 minutes). The mean time is 51 minutes, with a range from 10 to 360 minutes (6 hours). The top end of the range indicates that some children are spending the greater part of their day working in the household.

Table 7.6: Total and mean time children spend on the care of textiles, by age and gender (unweighted)

Gender	Age categories	Mean time	Number of children	Total time	% of total sum
Boys	10–14	41	127	5 200	16.9
	15–17	50	105	5 255	17.1
	Total	45	232	10 455	33.9
Girls	10–14	45	222	10 040	32.6
	15–17	67	155	10 315	33.5
	Total	54	377	20 355	66.1
Total	10–14	44	349	15 240	49.5
	15–17	60	260	15 570	50.5
	Total	51	609	30 810	100

Source: Own calculations from Stats SA 1999

Analyses of combined household activities: cooking, cleaning and care of textile-related activities

Table 7.7 shows the total and mean time spent on the combined activities of cooking, cleaning and care of textiles-related activities. This shows that a total of 251 children (unweighted data) reported engaging in all three activities on the day for which activities were recorded. Most of these children are girls (80%), and they spent on average 253 minutes on the activities, versus 166 minutes spent by boys. Similar patterns are observed for the analysis of the weighted data.

Table 7.7: Total and mean time children spend on the combined household activities, by age and gender (unweighted)

Gender	Age categories	Mean time	Number of children	Total time	% of total sum
Boys	10–14	189	17	3 215	5.4
	15–17	152	28	4 265	7.2
	Total	166	45	7 480	12.6
Girls	10–14	217	113	24 505	41.1
	15–17	297	93	27 590	46.3
	Total	253	206	52 095	87.4
Total	10–14	213	130	27 720	46.5
	15–17	263	121	31 855	53.5
	Total	237	251	59 575	100

Source: Own calculations from Stats SA 1999

An analysis of the above combined activities by attendance at an education institution, for the unweighted data, shows that a total of 118 children did not mention in their diary any activities related to school attendance. The analysis by the diary day and typical day shows that 29 children (25 girls and 4 boys) reported that this was a typical day for them, and that they were reporting for activities that had occurred over a weekday. The age range for the 29 children is 11–17 years, with 14 of the children's ages ranging from 11–15 years. The remaining 89 children who did not report school attendance were reporting for an activity they engaged in over a weekend or that the day for which they were reporting on was not a typical day for them – that is, they were either attending a family occasion such as a funeral or a wedding, or that the weather was bad.

An assumption that can be drawn from the above summary is that for the children under 16 years who are working long hours in the household, and for whom this is a typical day, non attendance at school could be problematic for their access to and prospects in the labour-market.

Collection of fuel, firewood and dung

The household section of the TUS questionnaire asked basic information about the household's main sources of fuel for cooking, heating and lighting and, in cases where these sources need to be collected, who in the household (in terms of gender) is usually the main person/s to collect these fuel sources, as well as an approximation of the distance they need to travel to access these resources. While there is variation in the type of energy/fuel sources used by the households in which the children reside (unweighted data, n=2 555),[13] electricity is the main source of

---

13 Counted each household once – took into account the possibility that in a household the ages of the two persons selected for the diary could range between 10–17 years.

energy for cooking (43.4%, n=1 108), lighting (68.3%, n=1 744) and heating (33.8%, n=861). There are, however, households that use wood for heating (24.8%, n=633) and cooking (20.6%, n=526), and those that use dung (n=11 for heating and n=11 for cooking). In the households that use wood or dung, women/girls (71.9%, n=488) usually do the collecting. In 13.5 per cent of the households (n=92), both males and females usually collect the wood or dung. Of the households that use wood and dung, about 38.6 per cent (n=262) report that the wood or dung is a kilometre or more from their dwelling. The gender analysis for the diary data is consistent with the analyses of the household data, in that more than a half of the children that reportedly engage in the collection of fuel, firewood or dung are girls (54.8%, n=57). A similar pattern, by gender, emerges for the weighted data (girls, n=143 versus boys, n=135).

Table 7.8 shows the distribution by total and mean time by gender and age. Children spend a total time of 9 280 minutes on the collection of fuel sources, and the time spent ranged from 10 minutes to 510 minutes.

Table 7.8: Total and mean time children spend on the collection of fuel sources for the household, by age and gender (unweighted)

Gender	Age categories	Mean time	Number of children	Total time	% of total sum
Boys	10–14	80	31	2 470	26.6
	15–17	80	16	1 275	13.7
	Total	80	47	3 745	40.4
Girls	10–14	81	32	2 580	27.8
	15–17	118	25	2 955	31.8
	Total	97	57	5 535	59.6
Total	10–14	80	63	5 050	54.4
	15–17	103	41	4 230	45.6
	Total	89	104	9 280	100

Source: Own calculations from Stats SA 1999

Girls spent on average just over one and a half hours on the collection of fuel, firewood or dung compared to just over an hour spent by boys. While more than half of the children that engage in fuel collection are aged 10–14 years (n=63), children aged 15–17 years spent on average more time (103 minutes) on the collection of fuel sources than children aged 10–14 years. Table 7.9 illustrates the total and mean times children spend on the collection of fuel sources by locale. Children residing in areas categorised as other rural spend considerably more time on this activity than children residing in other locales. Table 7.9 also shows that of the total number of children that reportedly collect fuel sources for use in their household, a small number of the children are from urban formal and informal areas.

Table 7.9: Total and mean time children spend on the collection of fuel sources for the household, by gender and locale (unweighted)

Gender	Locale	Mean time	Number of children	Total time	% of total sum
Boys	Urban formal	60	3	180	1.9
	Urban informal	69	5	345	3.7
	Other rural	90	21	1 885	20.3
	Commercial agriculture	74	18	1 335	14.4
	Total	80	47	3 745	40.4
Girls	Urban formal	75	2	150	1.6
	Urban informal	96	5	480	5.2
	Other rural	100	30	3 000	32.3
	Commercial agriculture	95	20	1 905	20.5
	Total	97	57	5 535	59.6
Total	Urban formal	66	5	330	3.6
	Urban informal	83	10	825	8.9
	Other rural	96	51	4885	52.6
	Commercial agriculture	85	38	3240	34.9
	Total	89	104	9 280	100

Source: Own calculations from Stats SA 1999

Collection of water

An analysis of the data on the location (proximity) of the water source in relation to the child's household shows that for 61.0 per cent (unweighted data, n=1 555) of the children, the main source of water is on the site of their dwelling. For 39.0 per cent (n=993), the main source of water is off-site (28 of these households reportedly *buy*[14] water from a vendor). Of the households whose main source of water is off the site, 337 (again a proportion would be more helpful) report that the water source is less than 100m from the dwelling. For 215 households, the water source is 500m or more from their household. As in the case of wood or dung collection, in most of the households, women or girls (70.8%, n=75) are the ones who usually collect the water.

The 24-hour diaries on children's activities show that, while more girls engage in this activity, boys also engage in the collection of water. More than half (unweighted total, n=386) of the children who reported that they spent their time collecting water are girls (58.3%, n=225), with girls spending on average 55 minutes (versus the 49 minutes spent by boys). The total time spent on the collection of water ranges

---

14 This may refer to the practice of paying persons (usually non-household members) to carry/fetch water for the household.

from 10 minutes to 270 minutes. Table 7.10 shows the total and mean time spent on the collection of water by gender and age.

Table 7.10: Total and mean time children spend on the collection of water for the household, by gender and age (unweighted)

Gender	Age categories	Mean time	Number of children	Total time	% of total sum
Boys	10–14	50	112	5 640	27.6
	15–17	47	49	2 305	11.3
	Total	49	161	7 945	38.9
Girls	10–14	55	160	8 870	43.4
	15–17	56	65	3 630	17.8
	Total	56	225	12 500	61.1
Total	10–14	53	272	14 510	71.0
	15–17	52	114	5 935	29.0
	Total	53	386	20 445	100

Source: Own calculations from Stats SA 1999

As might be expected, a significantly higher proportion of the children who reportedly collect water for the household reside in areas categorised as other rural (55.2%, n=213, total time is 12 230 minutes). An analysis of the weighted data shows similar patterns to that of the unweighted data.

Table 7.11: Total and mean time children spend on the collection of water for the household, by locale (unweighted)

Locale	Mean time	Number of children	Total time	% of total sum
Urban formal	40.4	28	1 130	5.5
Urban informal	51.5	83	4 275	20.9
Other rural	57.4	213	12 230	59.8
Commercial agriculture	45.3	62	2 810	13.7
Total	53	386	20 445	100

Source: Own calculations from Stats SA 1999

Analyses of combined household activities

A small number of the children (unweighted, n=29) engage in both the collection of water and fuel sources for their households on the diary day in question. Of this total number, seven children were reporting for activities on a weekday, and for 24 children this was a typical day for them. In excluding from the analysis children who reported that the activity was for a weekend, and those who said that this was not a typical day for them, the figures show that 22 children were reporting for activities that were typical of their weekday. These children spent an average of 143 minutes per day (nearly two and a half hours) on this activity.

In focusing on the combined activities of collection of water and fuel sources for the household, the data on reporting of attendance at school shows that of the 29 children, 11 children reportedly attended schools, while 14 children, despite it being a weekday and not a public holiday, did not report attendance at school as part of their diary activities. The 14 children reported this to be a typical day for them. While this analysis does not necessarily yield reliable numbers, the important point being raised is that there are children who are engaging in labour-intensive and strenuous household work and that, for some of them, the proportion of time spent on this and other activities for the household may result in the non-attendance or irregular attendance at school.

An analysis of the data for children who spent the day cooking, cleaning, caring for textiles and collecting water and fuel shows that there are four children who engage in all of these activities. Their ages range from 15–17 years. Three of the children reported activities for a weekend, and one for a weekday. The child who reported the activities for the weekday, also reported that s/he attended school – this child reported that this was a typical day (which included about four hours of household work – in this case cooking, cleaning, caring for textiles and collection of water and fuel sources).

Chopping wood

In terms of chopping wood, lighting fires and heating water (not for immediate cooking purposes), more girls (unweighted, 55.5%, n= 442) than boys (unweighted, 44.5%, n=354) reported engaging in this activity. The total time spent on chopping wood is 19 915 (give an average) minutes, and the time ranges from 10 minutes to 330 minutes. Table 7.12 shows the data for chopping wood by gender and age. Similar patterns by age and gender are seen to those of the earlier analyses of the different activities, as well as for the analysis of the above combined activities for the weighted data.

Table 7.12: Total and mean time children spend on chopping wood, lighting fires and heating water* for the household, by gender and age (unweighted)

Gender	Age categories	Mean time	Number of children	Total time	% of total sum
Boys	10–14	26	188	4 850	24.4
	15–17	27	166	4 410	22.1
	Total	26	354	9 260	46.5
Girls	10–14	24	267	6 520	32.7
	15–17	24	175	4 135	20.8
	Total	24	442	10 655	53.5
Total	10–14	25	455	11 370	57.1
	15–17	25	341	8 545	42.9
	Total	25	796	19 915	100

Source: Own calculations from Stats SA 1999

Note: * Coded as a single code in the TUS

Tending animals, fish farming, farming and gardening-related activities

Of the children who reported that they spent time tending animals and fish farming, far more boys (n=111, total time=11 025 minutes) than girls (n=9, total time=330 minutes) reported that they engage in this activity. The analysis of the weighted data yields a similar pattern by gender (boys=435, and girls=19). As anticipated, most of the children who engage in the tending of animals reside in areas categorised as other rural (unweighted, n=90, total time=9 460 minutes) rather than in urban formal (unweighted, n=8, total time=300 minutes), urban informal (unweighted, n=4, total time=140 minutes), or commercial agricultural (unweighted, n=18, total time=1 455 minutes) locales.

Childcare and other caring-related activities

Other activities that we included in the analysis are those of children caring for others within and outside of their own household. Table 7.13 shows the detailed breakdown of different categories of care-related activities, reported in the 24-hour diary, weighted and unweighted.

Table 7.13: Total and mean time spent by children on caring for household and non-household members (unweighted and weighted)

Care-related activity	Unweighted			Weighted		
	Total number	Mean time (mins)	Total time (mins)	Total number	Mean time (mins)	Total time (mins)
Care of children, the sick, elderly and disabled in the household not elsewhere classified	2	53	105	81	3	208
Accompanying children to places: school, sports, lessons, and so on	4	23	90	22	6	139
Teaching, training and instruction of household's children	5	84	420	14	88	1 205
Caring for non-household children and adults	11	34	375	14	30	407
Physical care of the sick, disabled, elderly household members: washing, dressing, feeding, helping	13	84	1 095	19	50	972
Supervising children and adults needing care	26	74	1 935	73	89	6 502
Travel related to care of children, the sick, elderly and disabled in the household	44	38	1 685	79	37	2 950
Physical care of children: washing, dressing, feeding	128	74	9 455	322	76	24 585

Source: Own calculations from Stats SA 1999

Note: Cognisance has to be taken that the relatively small number engaging in care-related activities may have more to do with the sampling size and sampling frame or data entry errors

The findings show that comparatively more children engaged in the physical care of children (washing, dressing, feeding), and sick, disabled, elderly persons within their own households than in other households. For some of the children who engage in childcare or caring activities, this included the supervision of other children and adults needing care and the accompanying of a household member to service centres. An analysis of the data (unweighted) on the physical care of children shows that more girls (n=96) than boys (n=32) spend time on the physical care of children. Only a small number of children reportedly cared for non-household children and adults. Children who spent time on the physical care of children (washing, dressing, and feeding) within their own household spent on average over an hour (74 minutes) on this activity per day.

It is important to note that the relatively small number of children reporting care-related activities, as with the analysis of the other TUS activities in this chapter, may be the result of weighting, sampling size, sampling frame or data entry errors. Literature on children as carers, such as reported in the 2002 Kaiser Foundation's survey of AIDS-affected households in South Africa (Steinberg et al. 2002), suggests that children are spending more time on care of others than was found from the TUS data.

Shopping

Shopping for personal and household goods (unweighted, n=272), as with previously analysed activities, is biased towards girls (50.7%, n=138). However the mean number of minutes spent by boys on shopping (32 minutes) is slightly higher than that spent by girls (27 minutes) (see Table 7.14).

Table 7.14: Total and mean time children spend on shopping for the household, by gender and age (unweighted)

Gender	Age categories	Mean time	Number of children	Total time	% of total sum
Boys	10–14	32	79	2 500	31.5
	15–17	32	55	1 770	22.3
	Total	32	134	4 270	53.8
Girls	10–14	23	85	1 955	24.6
	15–17	32	53	1 715	21.6
	Total	27	138	3 670	46.2
Total	10–14	27	164	4 455	56.1
	15–17	32	108	3 485	43.9
	Total	29	272	7 940	100

Source: Own calculations from Stats SA 1999

As in prior analyses, while more children aged 10–14 years engage in shopping activities, children aged 15–17 years spent more time shopping – on average just over half an hour compared to the 27 minutes for the children aged 10–14 years.

Summary of main findings and discussion

The analysis of the TUS data shows that of the children who reportedly engaged in household work-related activities, proportionately more children participate in household maintenance, management and shopping for own household (in-home) than for other households (out-of-home), with more girls than boys performing these activities. While the analysis of the data shows the expected gendered nature of the allocation and participation in household work, it does however highlight the fact that a considerable number of boys participate in a range of activities traditionally stereotyped as women or children's work, such as the collection of water and fuel sources and childcare and other caring-related activities. These are in addition to the tending of animals, which is usually considered a male activity. The TUS data shows that girls (albeit a very small number) also engage in the tending of animals.

Findings from the TUS are consistent with some of the findings from the 1999 SAYP survey (Stats SA 2000a, 2000b). The SAYP data show that economic activities such as fetching wood and water are the most common activities in which children participate. The study estimates that approximately 4.5 million of the 13.4 million children in South Africa aged 5–17 years spent one hour or more per week on this activity (Stats SA & DoL 2001). The study also showed that, in all age categories, substantially more girls than boys were involved in household chores for at least seven hours per week. Data from the SAYP show that one in eight of the children aged 5–17 years reported spending seven hours per week or more assisting in household chores and family care activities, and this was calculated for households in which at least one parent, grandparent or spouse of the child lived (Stats SA & DoL 2001).

While the literature reviewed in this chapter suggests that there exists an expectation in some households and within families for children to participate in household work, an aspect of household work that needs to be considered is that of strenuous and time-consuming activities. Findings from the TUS show that only a small number of children spend time on combined tasks on a given day; nonetheless, these children spend long hours on these activities. In particular, the combined activities in which a child could participate in during the course of a day show that while a minority of children are engaged in time-consuming and, in some cases, strenuous activities, the nature of its impact on children's physical development and well-being, their childhood, their participation in education and in their future labour market activities, is in urgent need of documentation and investigation.

As an illustration, we extracted a 24-hour diary of a child who reportedly engaged in a range of activities that includes collecting water and fuel sources, cleaning-related activities and cooking. The diary below documents the activities of a 13-year-old girl from the Eastern Cape, residing in an area categorised as other rural. The girl completed Grade 5. The diary data show that for the reported day (indicated in the data as a Tuesday), the girl did not attend school. In addition, the girl reported that the information she provided for the diary was for a typical day in her life.

Table 7.15: Activities engaged in by one 13-year-old girl for the diary day, Tuesday

Timeslot	Time period	Main activity (and code)	Other activities (and codes)	Activities done at same time?
1 to 5	4h00–6h30	10 Sleep		No
6	06h30–07h00	420 Cleaning of the dwelling		No
7	07h00–07h30	220 Tending animals and fish farming		No

Timeslot	Time period	Main activity (and code)		Other activities (and codes)		Activities done at same time?
8	07h30–08h00	260	Purchase of goods			No
9	08h00–08h30	250	Collecting water			No
10	08h30–09h00	250	Collecting water			No
11	09h00–09h30	420	Cleaning	831	Socialising with family	Yes
12	09h30–10h00	410	Cooking etc.	930	Listening to music/ radio	Yes
13	10h00–10h30	410	Cooking etc.	831	Socialising with family	No
14	10h30–11h00	410	Cooking etc.	20	Eating and drinking	No
15	11h00–11h30	410	Cooking etc.			No
16	11h30–12h00	491	Chopping wood, lighting fire and heating water	930	Listening to music/ radio	Yes
17	12h00–12h30	30	Personal hygiene and health			No
18	12h30–13h00	30	Personal hygiene and health	930	Listening to music/ radio	Yes
19	13h00–13h30	410	Cooking etc.			No
20	13h30–14h00	410	Cooking etc.			No
21	14h00–14h30	236	Collecting fuel, firewood/dung	832	Socialising with non-family members	Yes
22	14h30–15h00	236	Collecting fuel, firewood/dung	832	Socialising with non-family members	Yes
23	15h00–15h30	236	Collecting fuel, firewood/dung	832	Socialising with non-family members	Yes
24	15h30–16h00	410	Cooking etc.			No
25	16h00–16h30	860	Games and other pastimes			No
26	16h30–17h00	860	Games and other pastimes			No
27	17h00–17h30	410	Cooking etc.			No
28	17h30–18h00	410	Cooking etc.	20	Eating and drinking	No
29	18h00–18h30	20	Eating and drinking			No
30	18h30–19h00	410	Cooking etc.	831	Socialising with family	Yes
31	19h00–19h30	930	Listening to music or radio			No
32 to 48	19h30–04h00	10	Sleep			No

Source: Own calculations from Stats SA 1999

The diary data show that the girl spent a considerable length of time engaged in household-related work, and that time spent on socialising was spent in the course of participating in household work. About one hour was spent on the collection of water, which, according to the household information, is a communal borehole more than 1 km away from the household. The girl reportedly spent one and a half hours on the collection of fuel sources, which are also more than 1 km away from the household. Wood is used by this household for cooking and heating, and candles for lighting. The activity that took up most of the girl's time was cooking; a total of five hours was spent on this activity. The girl spent up to half an hour on the tending of animals, an activity traditionally the domain of males/boys in the household.[15]

The SAYP survey estimates that approximately 667 000 of the 13.4 million children in South Africa engage in labour activities for at least three hours a week, and are not attending school. Of this number, approximately 9 000[16] children give their reason for not attending school as needing to help with household chores (Stats SA 2000b: Tables 7.16–7.19).

Conclusion

The main aim of this chapter was to look at the ways in which children make a meaningful contribution to the family and household, in particular the household chores and work they perform. A review of studies on children's (girls and boys) household work, both paid and unpaid, shows that while children's presence and even assistance in household work can be beneficial for their well-being and that of the household, this is dependent on the nature of the work, its circumstances and the length of time in which children are engaged in this work.

The available studies indicate that more investigation is needed to determine the impact that long periods of time spent on a daily basis on strenuous tasks has on children's physical development, their participation in education and, in future, labour-market activities. In providing a comprehensive picture of the situation of children who engage in time-consuming and strenuous labour, as illustrated in the diary data, we need to think also about the family and household. What support mechanisms need to be put in place that would reduce the burden of household work on children in these situations, as well as improve or maintain the well-being of the family and household?

The literature review and case studies cited in the paper highlight the challenge in 'differentiating' between the customary practices and survival (coping) strategies of poor households and exploitative and hazardous child labour practices. While international treaties exist for enshrining children's rights – such as the African Charter, the CRC and the International Labour Organisation's (ILO) Declaration of

---

15 In looking at the household composition the data were not very reliable. The member data file shows that the information for only two members of the household was recorded. The information was for two females, aged 1 and 8 years respectively. It was therefore not possible based on this information to look at the division of labour by gender, age, and family size.
16 The report notes that the sample size may be too small to be reliable.

Fundamental Principles of Rights at Work and the ILO's Worst Forms of Child Labour Convention – defining or providing benchmarks/indicators of exploitative (hazardous) child labour practices or children who are at risk or made vulnerable, especially within impoverished communities, is not an easy task (see Ennew et al. 2003).

Time use studies such as the South African TUS have limitations in the degree to which they can contribute to understanding the intra-household division of labour among children in the same household, as well as the range of activities that can be characterised as children's work. Time use studies are, however, extremely valuable. The analysis of the South African TUS was useful in determining the total time and mean time children spent on an activity or on a range of activities. The TUS data, in terms of it being weighted, based on the SAYP sample frame rather than the full 1996 census population, does present some problems in terms of estimating the extent of the problems of child labour or children who are at risk or made vulnerable by strenuous work. The SAYP data, however, are able to provide estimates for such analyses, and some analyses of child work/labour in South Africa have been published using both the TUS and SAYP data sets.

In concluding, it is important to note that time use surveys contribute to an understanding and analysis of children's social lives and well-being by providing a description of the activities children engage in and the patterns of their time use. Child-centred approaches to studies on children could contribute to determining which types of household work have negative impacts on children and what sort of negative impacts they may have on the development and well-being of children. On a more positive side, it also provides an account of the contribution children make to the daily upkeep and maintenance of the family and household, as individuals and as a group (Ben-Arieh & Ofir 2002). This gives significance to children's economic contribution through unpaid labour such as household work and caregiving.

Acknowledgement

The authors would like to thank Debbie Budlender, Jill Kruger and the reviewers for their valuable and insightful comments on the chapter.

References

Alanen L (1988) Rethinking childhood. *Acta Sociologica* 31(1): 53–67

Alanen L (1998) Childhood as generational condition: Towards a relational theory of childhood. Paper presented at the 14th ISA (International Sociological Association) World Congress, Montreal, Canada, 26 July –1 August

Alanen L (2000) Review essay: Visions of a social theory of childhood. *Childhood* 7(4): 493–505

Ben-Arieh A & Goerge R (2001) Beyond the numbers: How do we monitor the state of our children? *Children and Youth Services Review* 23(8): 603–631

Ben-Arieh A & Ofir A (2002) Opinion, dialogue, review: Time for (more) time use studies studying the daily activities of children. *Childhood* 9(2): 225–248

Bianchi SM & Robinson JC (1997) What did you do today? Children's use of time, family composition, and the acquisition of social capital. *Journal of Marriage and Family* 59: 332–344

Blagbrough J & Glynn E (1999) Child domestic workers: Characteristics of the modern slave and approaches to ending such exploitation. *Childhood* 6(1): 51–56

Bongaarts J (2001) *Household size and composition in the developing world.* Policy Research Division Working Paper No. 144, Population Council, New York. Available at http://www.popcouncil.org/publications/wp/prd/144.html

Boyden J & Levinson D (2000) *Children as economic and social actors in the development process.* Expert Group on Development Issues Working Paper 2001:1, Ministry for Foreign Affairs, Stockholm, Sweden. Available at http://www.egdi.gov.se/publications/htm#working

Brembeck H, Johanesson B, Torrel VB & Falkström M (1999) Renegotiations of today's childhood. A paper presented at an international conference on 'Research in Childhood: Sociology, culture and history', Child, Youth and Culture, University of South Denmark-Odense, 28–31 October

Brown B (1999) Youth well-being: What we can learn together about our children. Articles for the Child Research Network (CRC) Advisory Board Members. Available at http://www.childresearch.net/cybrary/mabm.index.html

Budlender D & Bosch D (2002) South Africa child domestic workers: A national report. Report submitted to the International Labour Organisation (ILO) International Programme for the Elimination of Child Labour (IPEC), Geneva, May

Budlender D, Chobokoane N & Mpetsheni Y (2001) *A survey of time use: How South African women and men spend their time.* A report prepared for Statistics South Africa. Pretoria: Stats SA. Available at http://www.statssa.gov.za

Comporeses R & Ramano MC (2003) Children's time. Paper prepared for the 25th IATUR (International Association for Time Use Research) Conference on Comparing Time, Bruxelles, 17–19 September

Edwards R & Alldred P (2000) A typology of parental involvement in education centring on children and young people: Negotiating familialisation, institutionalisation and individualisation. *British Journal of Sociology of Education* 21(3): 435–455

Ennew J, Myers WE & Plateau DP (2003) The meaning, nature and scope of child labour. Draft version of document for the Colloquium on Combating Abusive Child Labor, Iowa, July

Fleming R & Spellerberg A (1999) Using time use data: A history of time use surveys and uses of time use data. Report prepared for Statistics New Zealand, Te Tari Tatau, Wellington

Floro MS (1995) Economic restructuring, gender and the allocation of time. *World Development* 23(11): 1913–1929

Francavilla F & Lyon S (2003) Household chores and child health: Preliminary evidence from six counties. Draft report prepared for the Understanding Children's Work Project (UCW), an Inter-Agency Research Project (UNICEF, ILO and World Bank)

Gager CT, Cooney TM & Call KT (1999) The effects of family characteristics and time use on teenagers' household labour. *Journal of Marriage and Family* 61: 982–994

167

Goodnow JJ (1988) Children's household work: Its nature and functions. *Psychological Bulletin* 103(1): 5–26

Hirway I (2001) Understanding children's work in India: An analysis of their time use. Paper presented at a Consultative Workshop on Food insecurity and child work in rural India, 15–17 March. Available at http://hdrc.undp.org.in

Ilahi N (2000) *The intra-household allocation of time and tasks: What have we learnt from the empirical literature?* Policy Research Report on Gender and Development, Working Paper Series No. 13, The World Bank Development Research Group/Poverty Reduction and Economic Management Network. Available at http://www.worldbank.org/gender

Jacquemin MY (2004) Children's domestic work in Abidjan, Côte D'Ivoire: The petites bonnes have the floor. *Childhood* 11(3): 383–397

James A & Prout A (1990) Re-representing childhood: Time and transition in the study of childhood. In A James & A Prout (Eds) (1990) *Constructing and reconstructing childhood: Contemporary issues in the sociological study of childhood.* London: Falmer Press

Kitterode RH (2002) Mothers' housework and childcare: Growing similarities or stable inequalities. *Acta Sociologica* 45: 127–180

Larson R (2001) How US children and adolescents spend time: What it does (and doesn't) tell us about their development. *Current Directions in Psychological Sciences* 10(5): 160–164

Montgomery H, Burr R & Woodhead M (2003) *Changing childhoods: Local and global.* UK: John Wiley and Sons in association with the Open University

Pollard EI & Lee PD (2003) Child well-being: A systematic review of the literature. *Social Indicators Research* 61: 59–78

Qvortrup J (1990) A voice for children in statistical and social accounting: A plea for children's rights to be heard. In A James & A Prout (Eds) (1990) *Constructing and reconstructing childhood: Contemporary issues in the sociological study of childhood.* London: Falmer Press

Qvortrup J (1994) Childhood matters: An introduction. In J Qvortrup, M Bardy, G Sgritta & H Wintersberger (Eds) (1994) *Childhood matters: Social theory, practice and politics.* Volume 13, Public Policy and Social Welfare Series of the Vienna Eurpean Centre. Aldershot: Avebury

Robson E (2004) Children at work in rural northern Nigeria: Patterns of age, space and gender. *Journal of Rural Studies* 20(2): 193–210

Saporiti A (1985) Statistics and childhood. In E Verhellen (Ed.) *Understanding children's rights.* Gent: University of Gent

Saporiti A (1994) A methodology for making children count. In J Qvortrup, M Bardy, G Sgritta & H Wintersberger (Eds) (1994) *Childhood matters: Social theory, practice and politics.* Volume 13, Public Policy and Social Welfare Series of the Vienna Eurpean Centre. Aldershot: Avebury

Seaberg JR (1990) Child well-being: A feasible concept? *Social Work* May: 267–272

Stats SA (Statistics South Africa) (1999) *10% Sample of census data (SuperStar).* Pretoria: Stats SA

Stats SA (2000a) *Survey of activities of young people. Presentation of key findings.* Pretoria: Stats SA

Stats SA (2000b) *Survey of activities of young people, 1999.* Pretoria: Stats SA

Stats SA (2001a) *Time use data – ASCII.* Pretoria: Stats SA

Stats SA (2001b) *Time use 2000: Meta data.* Pretoria: Stats SA

Stats SA & DoL (Department of Labour, South Africa) (2001) Survey of activities of young people 1999: Country report on children's work related activities. Pretoria: Stats SA and DoL

Steinberg M, Johnson S, Schierhout G, Ndegwa D, Hall K, Russel B & Morgan J (2002) *Hitting home: How households cope with the impact of the HIV/AIDS epidemic – a survey of households affected by HIV/AIDS in South Africa.* A report commissioned and published by the Henry J. Kaiser Family Foundation

Turner J & Kwakye E (1996) Transport and survival strategies in a developing economy: Case evidence from Accra, Ghana. *Journal of Transport Geography* 4(3): 161–168

Vogel J (2003) The family. *Social Indicators Research* 64: 393–435

Woodhead M & Montgomery H (2003) *Understanding childhood: An interdisciplinary approach.* UK: John Wiley and Sons in association with the Open University

CHAPTER 8

The family context for racial differences in child mortality in South Africa

Tim B Heaton & Acheampong Yaw Amoateng

Introduction

Our aim in this chapter is to examine racial differences in child and infant survival in South Africa, drawing mainly on data from the 1998 South African Demographic and Health Survey (SADHS).[1] We focus on child mortality in the first five years of life. Even though we look at child mortality from the point of view of the broader social structure of the society, we focus on the family context as our main organising principle to show the importance of racial differences in family conditions for racial differences in child survival. To the extent that healthy populations are seen as having a greater potential for engaging in productive economic activity and, thereby directly contributing to efforts designed to reduce poverty (see for example, HST 1998), infant and child survival takes on a special importance for families, communities and countries (Romani & Anderson 2002). We focus particularly on the impact of family structure, resources, caregiving, reproduction and their interactions on infant survival and child health.

One outstanding characteristic of the South African social structure is its inequality. Because of the racial policy of apartheid the different racial and cultural groups have had differential access to the society's resources, with white people having the greatest advantage in such areas as education, health, housing, and employment. Since family patterns vary across cultures, we examine child survival across the major race and ethnic groups in South Africa, and socio-economic conditions such as education and rural urban residence.

International and national trends in child mortality

To put the discussion of the importance of the family environment for infant and child survival in its proper context, we examine the international and national trends in infant mortality rates in this section. Infant mortality rates (IMRs) vary considerably from country to country due to differences in environmental conditions. Generally, the more affluent or modernised a country is, the lower its IMR and vice versa, with estimates ranging from Finland's 6.5 per 1 000 live births to over 200 in some African countries (Population Reference Bureau, 1980, 1984). As far as South Africa

1 Data contained in tables and figures in this chapter are drawn from the SADHS (DoH 1999).

is concerned, estimates by the United Nations (1999, 2001) show declines in IMR from the late 1980s through the 1990s (UN 1999, 2001). For example, the overall UN estimate for 1982 and 1997 was 67 and 58 respectively, while Yach (1994) put it at 51. These estimates are similar to those based on the SADHS, which show a similar decline from the mid-1980s to the early 1990s, but an increase by the mid-1990s (DoH 1999). Specifically, SADHS estimates were 50, 40 and 45 for 1986, 1991 and 1996 respectively.

There is overwhelming consensus on the differentials in the IMR among the various population groups in South Africa (Anderson et al. 2002; Romani & Anderson 2002). For example, the 1998 SADHS estimated that in 1996 the IMR for Africans was 47, for coloured people 19, and 11 for white people. The estimates by Yach (1994) are very similar to this pattern with 51 for Africans, 38 for coloured people, 7 for white people and 8 for Asians. Many researchers interpret racial difference in mortality as a manifestation of differential access to health care and socio-economic resources. We agree, but add that these differences are manifest within families.

Family influences and child mortality

Because the family is usually the basic unit of interaction for men, women and children, family structures and dynamics impact child outcomes immensely. The family process literature describes the family as a unit that makes decisions and allocates resources in order to achieve goals. Family processes such as flexibility, caring, communication and supervision are important factors influencing the functioning of families and the well-being of individual members (Day et al. 2001). The organisation of family work is important to family and child well-being (Thornton 2001). The bulk of this literature, however, is based on research from developed countries. In applying this model to ethnic groups in South Africa, we argue that in addition to family processes or patterns of interaction and communication, the resources available to families are also essential to child health.

Data and methods

We examine data from the 1998 Demographic and Health Surveys for South Africa (SADHS). The Demographic and Health Surveys focus on fertility, contraceptive use, and health practices in developing countries. Detailed information is reported on children born in the last five years. The reasons for drawing largely from data from the SADHS are twofold. Firstly, since this data set enables us to link a child's information to that of his or her mother, we are able to examine several variables that measure the mother's family circumstances such as fertility, contraceptive use and health practices. Secondly, it is the most recent national data set that contains detailed information on such measures of child health, nutritional status, immunisation, breastfeeding and so on. The 1998 SADHS collected detailed information reported on children born in the previous five years.

Model specifications

Educational resources are measured by an education variable ranging from 1 for no education to 5 for post-secondary education. Media exposure is measured by an index for reading the newspaper, listening to the radio and watching TV, factors which are proxies for exposure to modern lifestyles. Socio-economic status has often been based on measures of consumption and income. In developing countries, however, income may not be the most reliable measure of socio-economic status since many people work in agricultural or informal sectors and do not receive cash payment for their work (Macro International 2002). Demographic and Health Surveys rely on an index of wealth to classify populations according to socio-economic level. Ownership of assets is an accurate proxy for consumption (Macro International 2002), allowing the DHS wealth index to indirectly measure the long-term economic status of a household.

In our analysis, socio-economic resources are measured by a possessions index calculated as the percentage of household items (such as TV, electricity, refrigerator, car and so on) present in the home. Living conditions are also measured by dichotomous variables indicating access to piped water, well-open water, a flush toilet, a latrine, and whether the household has a dirt floor. Family structure and household size indicate whether or not the household is female-headed and the total number of persons living in the household. In addition, residence is included as dichotomous measures contrasting rural areas to towns, small cities and large cities.

The breastfeeding variable attempts to measure breastfeeding for at least six months. It is coded 1 for children who were breastfed for at least six months, who are under six months and still breastfeeding, or who died before six months, but were breastfed until the month of death. It is coded 2 for children breastfed for longer than six months. Reproductive behaviours are measured by whether the child was a first or higher order birth, and duration of the preceding birth interval is coded 0 for less than nine months, up to 7 for more than four years. First births are coded 7 – the mean – on the preceding birth interval variable. The sex of the child is also included as a dichotomous measure and an indicator is included if the child is a twin or higher order birth.

Husband-wife decision-making is also based on a percentage variable because the questions asked vary across countries. Couples were coded 1 if they had discussed family planning, if the couple agreed on how many children they wanted to have and if the wife controlled income from her earnings; the sum of these values was divided by the number of questions to which the woman responded. A dichotomous variable is also included to measure whether the wife has ever used birth control. The major race categories coded include white, Asian, coloured and African. African groups are also classified by language group. There is some variation in rates of child mortality across language groups that would be lost if all Africans were included in one category, yet there are enough similarities among groups that inclusion of a category for each language would yield more detail than necessary to show major differences. Thus, Africans were classified into two groups. Pedi, Tsonga and Ndebele language groups have lower rates of child mortality than other African groups and so they are classified as the advantaged African group and all other African groups are included in the second group.

One obvious shortcoming is our failure to consider the impact of HIV/AIDS on child mortality. The survey does include a few questions on sources of information about AIDS, reasons for not using condoms, and a few other attitudes. Adequate direct measures of exposure were not included. Racial group differences in exposure to HIV/AIDS and consequences for children's survival should be a high priority in future data collection efforts.

Analysis and results

Figure 8.1 shows rates of child survival by race group. As the figure shows, white children clearly have the highest rates of survival with 90 per cent of children surviving to their fifth birthday. Asian, coloured, and a relatively small group of advantaged African children have moderate rates of child survival with three-fourths of children surviving to their fifth birthday. Only 61 per cent of the larger group of African children survives until their fifth birthday. Thus, there are substantial differences in the fate of children across groups. In the subsequent sections of this chapter, we identify some family characteristics that are associated with child survival probabilities in the population.

Figure 8.1: Child survival by race group

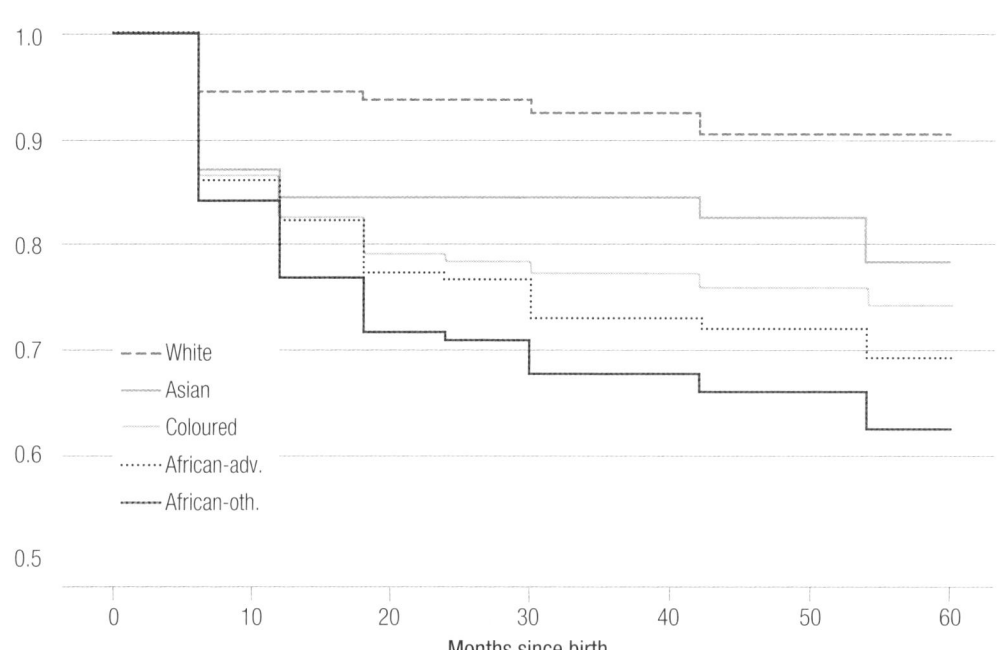

As Figure 8.1 has clearly shown, child mortality rates vary across racial and ethnic groups in South Africa because of differences in life chances. We attempt to understand these differences in terms of the structure and operation of family units;

most children are cared for by their parents, hence most efforts to improve child health involve family units. Although studies have investigated the impact of specific family-level factors on child health in South Africa, the particular aspects of family life having the greatest influence on children have not been examined in a holistic fashion. In the next section, we put these differentials into perspective by considering a variety of family characteristics that affect child survival.

Household structure

Organisation of family units has implications for child health. In particular, the absence of fathers from households may have detrimental effects on children. Studies of paternal involvement tend to focus on fathers' financial contributions to their households (Teitler 1999). But aside from providing economic resources, fathers can give their children the time and attention of which they are often deprived in single-parent families. Studies from developed countries suggest that, in addition to monetary contributions, fathers play a unique role in child development that greatly benefits the cognitive and emotional maturation of young children (Harris et al. 1998; Parke & Sterns 1993). Household size is an additional component of family structure. In large households, social and financial resources may not be adequate to accommodate each individual's emotional and economic needs.

Household size is particularly critical in poor areas, where the demands placed on large families are often difficult to absorb because of widespread impoverishment. A child's health can be compromised in large families through malnourishment, failure to recognise illness, inadequate attention, unsanitary living conditions and failure to take a child to see a doctor. Furthermore, the risk of disease spread and cross-infection is heightened whenever a large number of people live within close proximity to one another (Justeson & Kunst 2000). Family structures and patterns of family interaction vary substantially in South Africa as a result of the different race and ethnic groupings' unequal access to socio-economic resources in society. In this study, family structure and household size are measured by whether or not the household is female-headed and the total number of persons living in the household.

Rural/urban residence

Research indicates that child mortality is lower in urban areas than in rural areas (Forste 1994; Gupta & Baghel 1999). Urban women often have fewer children than rural women, and typically have greater access to contraception and education, have higher socio-economic status, and frequently have more family decision-making power (Dodoo & Tempenis 2002; Kirk & Pillet 1998). Additionally, women living in urban areas usually have more immediate access to healthcare than rural women. In their study of African and coloured families, Romani and Anderson (2002) found that fewer than 20 percent of coloured children lived in rural areas compared to 69 per cent of African children. Of African households, some 43 per cent were more than 5 km from a medical service, true for only 14 per cent of coloured households. In the present study, rural residence was included in the analysis as a dichotomous measure.

175

Household socio-economic status

The relationship between economic resources and child health is well documented (Aber et al. 1997). Families of higher socio-economic status are able to provide better healthcare for their children. Higher socio-economic status is also tied to sanitary living conditions. Such amenities as latrine facilities, piped water, and electricity are critical to children's health (Defo 1997). Furthermore, families with higher income can more easily spend money on warm clothing and on food to ensure family members stay warm and protected and receive the proper nutrients they need (Barrett & Browne 1996).

In a study that examined the factors influencing infant and child survival among African and coloured children in South Africa, Anderson et al. (2002) observed a striking contrast between the overall conditions of life of African and coloured children, with coloured children enjoying a better-off and healthier life than their African counterparts in every area of life. For example, they found that a substantially larger proportion of coloured households – 93 per cent – had access to running tap water in the dwelling or on site; this was true for only 42 per cent of African households.

Educational resources

Maternal education is one of the most important factors accounting for differentials in child mortality (Caldwell & McDonald 1982; Peña et al. 2000). Education improves child health in several ways. Maternal education is closely linked to household socioeconomic conditions (Barrett & Brown 1996). Women with more education increase their likelihood of securing steady, high-paying employment and are more likely to marry husbands with higher educational attainment and higher-paying jobs (Barrett & Brown 1996). With more money in a household, living conditions are generally better and are more conducive to good child health. Maternal education also brings about changes that result in better child health. Educated women wield significant decision-making power and control over resources (Frost et al. 2002).

Women with authority are more likely to draw attention to their children's illnesses, and to take a sick child to the health clinic (Caldwell 1993). Education also equips women with greater health knowledge (Bhuiya et al. 1990) and influences women's attitudes about health (Castro Martin & Juárez 1995). Education is often associated with a break with tradition, making women more likely to accept modern medicine, and use preventive health services (Bicego & Boerma 1993). Education also affects reproductive behaviour conducive to child health: higher education is linked with lower fertility, reproduction at low-risk ages, and longer birth intervals (Cleland & Van Ginneken 1988). Paternal education has also been shown to increase the probability of child survival (Gourbin & Wunsch 1999).

In some cases, the effect of paternal education is independent of maternal education (Baya 1998). Bailey (1993) hypothesises that better-educated fathers are more involved in childrearing because they are more knowledgeable about child health and development. As far as South Africa is concerned, Anderson et al. (2002) found comparable race differences also existed in the level of educational attainment of mothers, with 11 per cent of African mothers having no education as compared to five percent of coloured mothers. Perhaps most striking were the differences between the two groups in access to safe water supplies and sanitary facilities. However, a preliminary analysis of SADHS data from 1988–1992 found that in Gauteng province the IMR for the African population was much higher than that for the coloured population (34 versus 9), even though educational attainment, medical attendance at birth and use of antenatal care among the two groups were almost identical (Rossouw & Jordaan 1997).

Socio-demographic factors and child mortality

Table 8.1 shows the results of the Cox regression models for child mortality. The first series of models reports regressions for each of the demographic and socio-economic characteristics. Then a restricted model (see Table 8.3) includes only the statistically significant variables that account for race group differences. Model 1 shows comparative rates for the racial and ethnic groups considered. The most disadvantaged group of Africans is the comparison group. Coloured people and the more advantaged group of Africans have substantially lower rates of child mortality, followed by the Asian group. White people have by far the lowest rates of child mortality. Socio-economic variables have a substantial impact on infant mortality. Consistent with other research, more educated mothers have lower rates of child mortality. Access to flush toilets, clean water and media also reduce the risk on infant mortality. Higher socio-economic status as measured by the possessions index and husband's education are also associated with lower mortality.

Husband's occupation (not shown) did not have a statistically significant association with child mortality and data was not reported for a substantial number of husbands so this variable was not included in the model. Women who work and have control of the income they earn actually report higher rates of child mortality. Residence in more urban areas is associated with lower mortality. Finally, children are at greater risk in smaller households. Sex of the household head does not have a large association with child mortality. Even though several of these variables are important predictors of infant mortality, a few do not account for racial/ethnic differences; the degree of impact is assessed by comparing the race/ethnic group variable before (Model 1) and after each other characteristic is included in the model. Thus, urban residence, household size and female employment account for very little of the group membership effect. White and Asian children have lower mortality, in part because the women and their partners are more educated, households have more resources, and they have more access to the media. Male education and access to toilets and clean water are the most obvious explanations for the somewhat lower mortality among coloured children. But these variables do not account for the mortality differences between the two groups of African children.

Table 8.1: Cox regression models predicting child mortality: demographic and socio-economic conditions

Group	1	2	3	4	5	6	7	8	9
African-advantaged	–.498*	–.481*	–.441*	–.469*	–.462*	–.439*	–.482*	–.492*	.511*
Coloured	–.389*	–.316*	–.245*	–.315*	–.292*	–.315*	–.422*	–.359*	–.389*
White	–1.556*	–1.000*	–1.350*	–1.358*	–1.146*	–1.386*	–1.596*	–1.475*	–1.688*
Asian	–.689*	–.331*	–.487*	–.514*	–.514*	–.535*	–.775*	–.557*	–.373*
Maternal education		–.558*							
Living conditions									
Piped water			.541						
Well-open water			.327*						
Flush toilet			–.233*						
Latrine			–.072*						
Dirt floor			.107						
Possessions index				–.073					
Husband's education									
None					.276				
Primary					–.009				
Secondary					–.516*				
Higher					–1.251				
Media						–.130*			
Maternal employment									
Works, control $							.227*		
Works, joint control							–.083		
Works, no control							–.135		
Residence									
Large city								–.201*	
Small city								–.215*	
Town								.119	
Household size									–.071*
Female head									–.023
X²	107.92*	466.67*	148.20*	123.10*	275.04*	134.81*	124.69*	127.02*	171.97*
d.f.	4	5	9	5	8	5	7	7	6

*p<.05

Reproductive behaviour

Various reproductive behaviors strongly influence child survival in developing regions. Many women in developing countries marry early and have children in their teenage years when they are physically immature and do not have access to prenatal and obstetric care. A key reproductive behaviour in determining child health outcomes is birth spacing (Curtis et al. 1993; Forste 1994). A short birth interval is strongly correlated with mortality (Lindstrom 2000; Manda 1999; Miller et al. 1992). Boerma and Bicego (1992) attribute the relationship between birth spacing and child health to three mechanisms. First, short intervals between births do not allow a woman sufficient time to replete her nutritional status (maternal depletion syndrome). The child following the short interval is disadvantaged as a result of foetal malnutrition. Second, sibling rivalry occurs between children close in age that must compete for resources and maternal care. Third, short birth spacing is associated with an increased exposure to infectious disease by the younger child.

The older sibling is more likely to bring infections into the home, putting the youngest sibling at risk of becoming sick. Another reproductive factor proven to influence child health and survival is birth order (Alam 2000; Bai et al. 2002; Forste 1998; Sommerfelt & Stewart 1994; Sullivan & Rustein 1994). As family size increases, resources such as food, clothing, and parental attention must be shared among more children. High-order births may be more susceptible to mortality and poor health in instances of maternal depletion, or if the presence of more children creates a greater risk for the spread of infectious disease (Brittain 1992). In this study, reproductive behaviours were measured by whether the child was a first, or higher-order birth, and duration of the preceding birth interval which is coded 0 for fewer than nine months, and up to 7 for more than four years. First births were coded 7 – the mean – on the preceding birth interval variable.

Medical care

Both pre- and post-natal health practices are critical to child survival and development. Visiting a medical doctor before giving birth is critical, as trained physicians can prevent and/or detect pregnancy complications. In many developing countries, women may first seek the help of faith healers or religious curers, which may have adverse effects on the mother and unborn child (Suwal 2001). In many settings, a large proportion of births are carried out in private residences. Unhygienic conditions, coupled with untrained traditional birth attendants, are partially responsible for high IMRs in poor countries. Health risks of both mother and infant are significantly reduced if delivery occurs in hospitals or is accompanied by trained birth attendants under sanitary conditions. Proper medical attention and delivery conditions reduce the overall risk of infection and complications that may arise during birth (Paul & Rumsey 2002).

Feeding practices

Child feeding practices encompass a broad range of interrelated behaviors known to impact child health. Breastfeeding has repeatedly been established as one of the strongest predictors of child health (WHO 2000). Low prevalence and duration of breastfeeding increases the risk of infant and childhood mortality in both developed and developing countries. However, the effects of breastfeeding are strongest in poor and developing regions, where economic development is limited and resources are not evenly distributed (Forste 1994).

Other important feeding practices include introduction of solid foods, feeding nutrient-dense complementary foods, and frequency of feeding. Because feeding practices are manifest through several different behaviours across several months, efforts to measure their association with child health have been hindered by methodological problems (Ruel & Menon 2002).

The breastfeeding variable attempted to measure breastfeeding for at least six months. It was coded 2 for children who were breastfed for at least six months, and 1 for those who were under six months and still breastfeeding, or who died before six months, but were breastfed until the month of death.

Health and reproductive factors and child mortality

Table 8.2 shows the results of the logistic regression models after we have considered health and reproductive characteristics. The baseline model is repeated to simplify comparison. These variables are also associated with higher mortality. Families with birth characteristics such as multiple births, first births, and births after a short interval are all associated with higher risks of dying . Acceptability and use of family planning reduce the risk of mortality. Finally, access to pre- and post-natal medical care dramatically reduces the mortality rate. Of these variables, contraceptive use and access to medical care appear to account for noticeable shares of the race/ethnic group difference. Babies who were breastfed have lower mortality. A large part of the breastfeeding effect is an artifact due to missing data for the infant group with high mortality rates, but it appears that breastfed babies have mortality rates half as high as those who were not breastfed. Nonetheless, groups with higher child mortality are more likely to breastfeed their children. Their rates of mortality would be even higher if they did not breastfeed, which gives them some advantage over white mothers, and to a lesser degree Asian mothers.

As the final step in our analysis, we estimated a model including the variables that appeared to make a difference in racial/ethnic group patterns of infant mortality. The first column of Table 8.3 reports results of this model. Results suggest that utilisation of pre- and post-natal medical care is by far the most important factor. The breastfeeding variable is not included because of the high number of missing cases and the fact that it does not account for higher mortality among African children. Moreover, utilisation of medical care may be a consequence of resources, education and so forth. Thus, we estimated a second model excluding medical care. Results from this second model indicate that education and contraceptive use are also relevant.

Table 8.2: Cox regression models predicting child mortality in South Africa: reproduction and health

Group	1	2	3	4	5	6
African–advantaged	–.498*	–.483*	–.495*	–.429*	–.233*	–.370 *
Coloured	–.389*	–.336*	–.383*	–.225*	–.038	–.174*
White	–1.556*	–1.807*	–1.467*	–1.395*	–.515*	–1.016*
Asian	–.689*	–.743*	–.601*	–.465*	.331	–.115
Birth characteristics						
Twin		.658*				
Female		–.165*				
Order		–.143*				
Interval		–.292*				
Family planning index			–.087*			
Ever used birth control				–.691*		
Medical care					–1.797	
Breastfeeding						
Some						–2.522*
6+ months						–4.568*
X²	107.92	602.62*	125.34*	318.92*	3490.41*	4283.48*
d.f.	4	8	5	5	5	6

*p<.05

In short, three variables account for an important share of group differences as far as child survival is concerned in the country, namely utilisation of medical care, contraceptive use and education. We show the distribution of these three characteristics in Figures 8.2, 8.3 and 8.4. As Figure 8.2 shows, white people have a clear educational advantage, followed by Asian people. Differences between coloured people and various groups of African people are relatively small in comparison with the white and Asian advantage. Moreover, there is more group variation in contraceptive use as shown in Figure 8.3. White, Asian, coloured and African people who speak English or Afrikaans show the comparatively higher levels of contraceptive use of 70 per cent or higher. Some African groups have rates between 60 and 70 per cent, including Sotho, Tswana and Swati. The Xhosa and Pedi have rates below 50 per cent. Finally, as is clear from Figure 8.4, white mothers also have the clearest advantage in utilisation of medical services when the child is born. As with contraceptive use, the Xhosa and Pedi are relatively low on use of medical services.

Table 8.3: Cox regression models of child mortality: summary model

Group	1	2
African–advantaged	-.224*	-.442*
Coloured	-.049	-.267*
White	-.523*	-1.035*
Asian	.271	-.348
Maternal education	-.009	-.393
Possession index	.048	.043
Husband's education		
None	.122	.701*
Primary	.175	.617*
Secondary	.120	.299*
Higher	-.217	-.160
Living conditions		
Piped water	.120	.242
Well-open water	.168	.222
Flush toilet	-.038	.074
Latrine	-.034	.049
Media	.025	.038
Contraceptive use	-.114	-.503*
Medical care	-1.767*	
X^2	348.13*	710.71*
d.f.	17	16

*p<.05

Figure 8.2: Maternal education by race/ethnicity

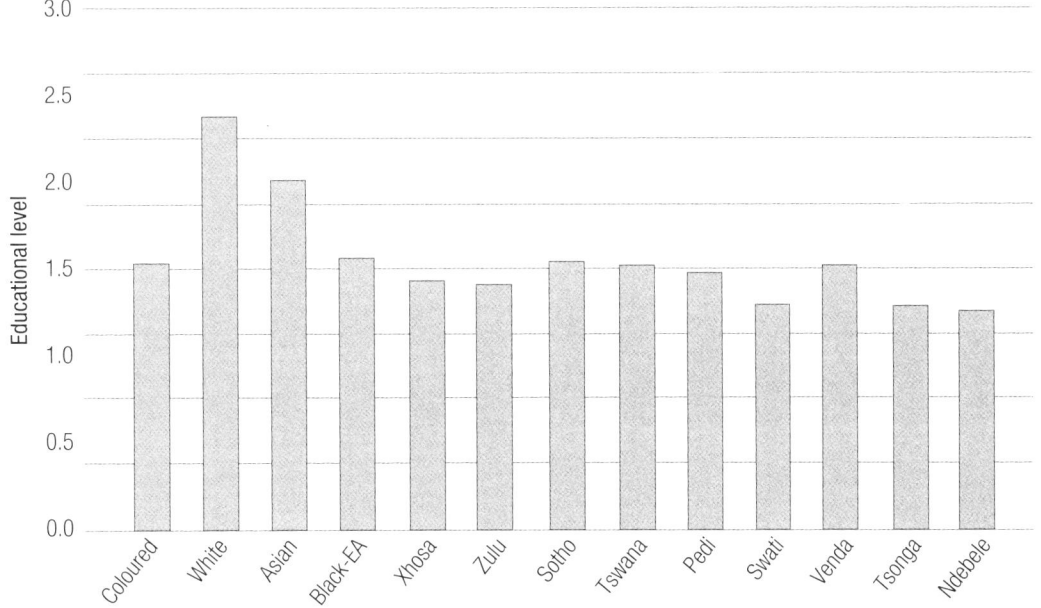

Figure 8.3: Contraceptive use by race/ethnicity

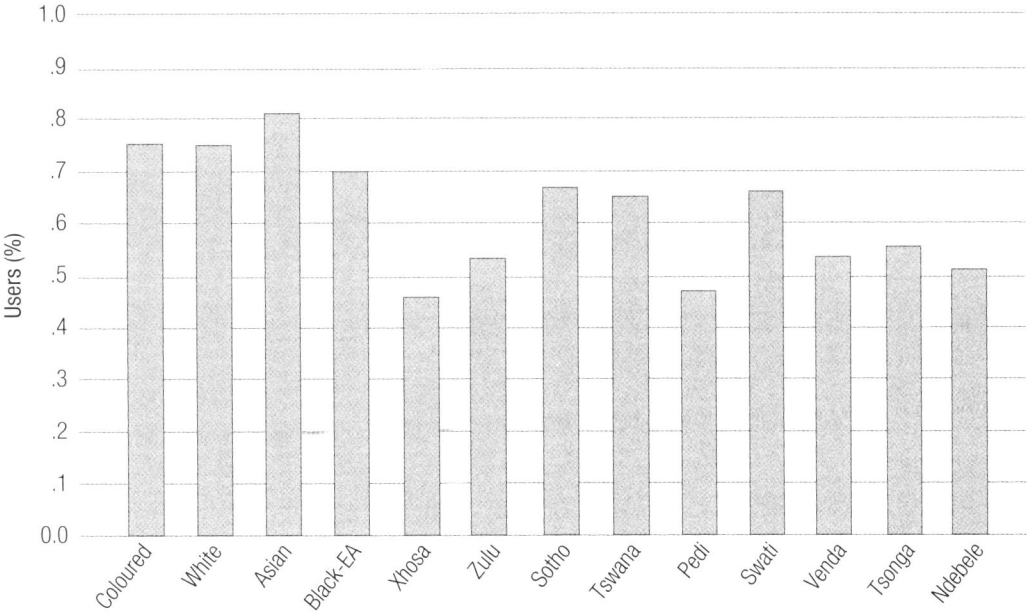

Figure 8.4: Utilisation of pre- and post-natal healthcare by race/ethnicity

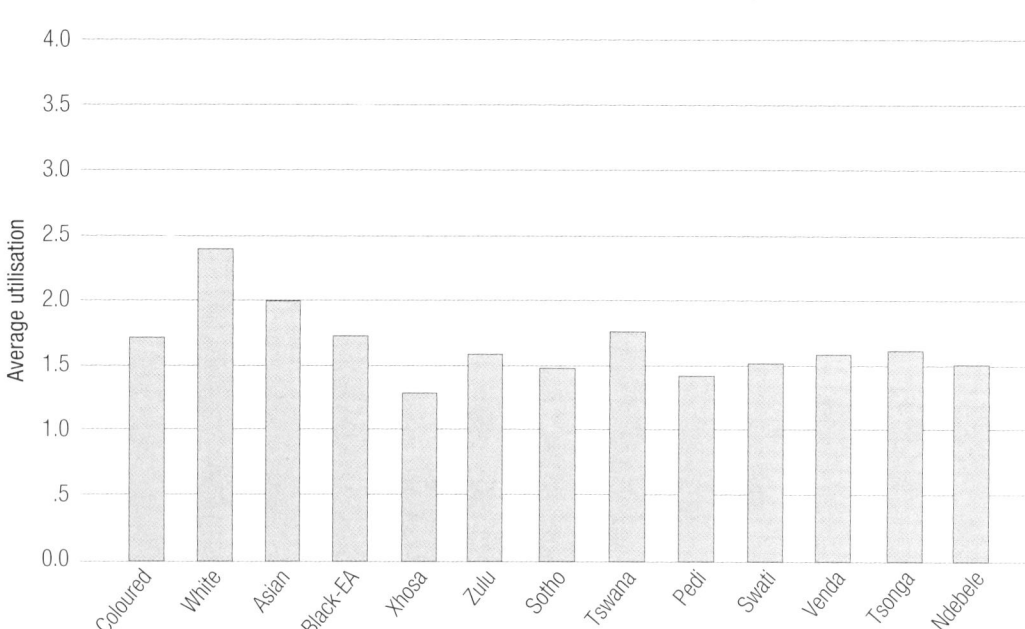

Conclusion

Our aim in this study was to examine the impact of the family context on child survival in South Africa. To this effect, we examined such family characteristics as household structure, household size, socio-economic resources such as education of wives and husband, flush toilets, clean water, and sanitation. We also examined characteristics such as access to medical care, reproductive health, contraception and feeding practices for the four major race groups and the several African ethnic groups in the country. We found that socio-economic, environmental and demographic factors like flush toilet, clean water, maternal education, urban residence, household size, female employment and household possessions were associated with higher probabilities of child survival, although a few of these did not account for racial/ethnic differences in these probabilities.

We also found that such birth characteristics as multiple births, first births, and births after a short interval are all associated with higher risks of dying. However, a multivariate analysis to assess the impact of these factors revealed that of all the factors we examined in our study, contraceptive use and access to medical care accounted for noticeable shares of the race/ethnic group difference in infant and child mortality. In fact, utilisation of pre- and post-natal medical care was by far the most important factor. Thus, three factors accounted for an important share of group differences as far as child survival is concerned in the country, namely utilisation of medical care, contraceptive use and education.

References

Aber JL, Bennett NG, Conley DC & Li J (1997) The effects of poverty on child health and development. *Annual Review of Public Health* 18: 463–483

Alam N (2000) Teenage motherhood and infant mortality in Bangladesh: Maternal age-dependent effect of parity one. *Journal of Biosocial Science* 32(2): 229–236

Anderson BA, Romani JH, Phillips H & Van Zyl J (2002) Environment, access to healthcare, and other factors affecting infant and child survival among the African and coloured populations of South Africa, 1989–94. *Population and Environment* 23(4): 349–364

Bai J, Wong FWS, Bauman A & Mohsin M (2002) Parity and pregnancy outcomes. *American Journal of Obstetrics and Gynecology* 186(2): 274–278

Bailey WT (1993) Fathers' knowledge of development and involvement with preschool children. *Perceptual and Motor Skills* 77: 1032–1034

Barrett H & Brown A (1996) Health, hygiene, and maternal education: Evidence from Gambia. *Social Science and Medicine* 43: 1579–1590

Baya B (1998) Parents' education and child survival in Burkina Faso: The case of Bobo-Dioulasso. Les dossiers du CEPED No. 48

Bhuiya A, Streatfield K & Meyer P (1990) Mother's hygienic awareness, behavior, and knowledge of major childhood diseases in Matlab Bangladesh. In J Caldwell, S Findley, P Caldwell, G Santow, W Cosford, J Braid & D Broers-Freeman (Eds) *What we know about health transition: The cultural, social, and behavioural determinants of health.* Canberra: The Australian National University Printing Service

Bicego GT & Boerma JT (1993) Maternal education and child survival: A comparative study of survey data from 17 countries. *Social Science and Medicine* 36(9): 1207–1227

Boerma JT & Bicego GT (1992) Preceding birth intervals and child survival: Searching for pathways of influence. *Studies in Family Planning* 23(4): 243–256

Brittain AW (1992) The effect of parental age, birth order and other variables on early childhood mortality: A Caribbean example. *Social Science and Medicine* 35(10): 1259–1271

Caldwell JC (1993) Health transition: The cultural, social, and behavioral determinants of health in the Third World. *Social Science and Medicine* 35: 125–135

Caldwell JC & McDonald P (1982) Influence of maternal education on infant and child mortality: Levels and causes. *Health Policy Education* 2: 251–267

Castro Martin T & Juárez F (1995) The impact of women's education on fertility in Latin America: Searching for explanations. *International Family Planning Perspectives* 21: 52–80

Cleland JG & Van Ginneken JK (1988) Maternal education and child survival in developing countries: The search for pathways of influence. *Social Science and Medicine* 27: 1357–1368

Curtis SL, Diamond ID & McDonald JW (1993) Birth interval and family effects on postneonatal mortality in Brazil. *Demography* 30(1): 33–43

Day RD, Gavazzi S & Acock A (2001) Compelling family processes. In A Thornton (Ed) *The well-being of children and families: Research and data needs.* Ann Arbor Michigan: The University of Michigan Press

Defo BK (1997) Effects of socioeconomic disadvantage and women's status on women's health in Cameroon. *Social Science and Medicine* 44: 1023–1042

Dodoo FN & Tempenis M (2002) Gender power and reproduction: Rural-urban differences in the relationship between fertility goals and contraceptive use in Kenya. *Rural Sociology* 67(1): 46–70

DoH (Department of Health South Africa) (1999) *South Africa Demographic Health Survey 1998*. Pretoria: DoH

Forste R (1994) The effects of breastfeeding and birth spacing on infant mortality in Bolivia. *Population Studies* 48(3): 497–511

Forste R (1998) Infant feeding practices and child health in Bolivia. *Journal of Biosocial Science* 30: 107–125

Frost MB, Haas DW & Forste R (2002) Maternal education and child nutritional status in Bolivia: Finding the links. Presented at the Annual Meetings of the Population Association of America, Atlanta, Georgia

Gourbin C & Wunsch G (1999) Paternal age and infant mortality. *Genus* 1-2: 617–72

Gupta H & Baghel A (1999) Infant mortality in the Indian slums: Case Studies of Calcutta Metropolis and Raipur City. *International Journal of Population Geography* 5(5): 49–68

Harris KM, Furstenberg FF & Marmer JD (1998) Paternal involvement with adolescents in intact families: The influence of fathers over the life course. *Demography* 35(2): 201–216

HST (Health Systems Trust) (1998) Health and development. In *South African Health Review* 1997. Durban: HST

Justeson A & Kunst A (2000) Postneonatal and child mortality among twins in Southern and Eastern Africa. *International Journal of Epidemiology* 29: 678–683

Kirk K & Pillet B (1998) Fertility levels, trends, and differentials in sub-Saharan Africa in the 1980s and 1990s. *Studies in Family Planning* 29(1): 1–22

Lindstrom DP (2000) The effects of breastfeeding and birth spacing on infant and early childhood mortality in Ethiopia. *Social Biology* 47(1–2): 1–17

Manda SO (1999) Birth intervals, breastfeeding and determinants of childhood mortality in Malawi. *Social Science and Medicine* 48(3): 301–312

Macro International (2002) DHS and World Bank use wealth index to measure socioeconomic status. *DHS+ Dimensions* 4(2): 1–2

Miller E, Pebley A & Vaughan B (1992) Birth spacing and child mortality in Bangladesh and the Philippines. *Demography* 29(2): 305–318

Parke RD & Sterns PN (1993) Fathers and child rearing. In GH Elder, J Modell & RD Parke (Eds) *Children in time and place: Developmental and historical insights*. New York NY: Cambridge University Press

Paul BK & Rumsey DJ (2002) Utilization of health facilities and trained birth attendants for childbirth in rural Bangladesh: An empirical study. *Social Science and Medicine* 54(12): 1755–1765

Peña R, Wall S & Persson LA (2000) The effect of poverty, social inequity, and maternal education on infant mortality in Nicaragua, 1988–1993. *American Journal of Public Health* 90(1): 64–69

Population Reference Bureau (1980) *World Population Data Sheet.* Washington D.C.: Population Reference Bureau

Population Reference Bureau (1984) *World Population Data Sheet.* Washington D.C.: Population Reference Bureau

Romani JH & Anderson BA (2002) *Development, health and the environment: Factors influencing infant and child survival in South Africa.* Cape Town: HSRC Publishers

Rossouw J & Jordaan A (1997) *Infant mortality and child health in South Africa 1988–1992.* Pretoria: HSRC

Ruel MT & Menon P (2002) Child feeding practices are associated with child nutritional status in Latin America: Innovative uses of the Demographic and Health Surveys. *Journal of Nutrition* 132: 1180–1187

Sommerfelt AE & Stewart MK (1994) *Children's nutritional status.* Demographic and Health Surveys Comparative Studies No. 12, Macro International, Calverton MD

Sullivan JM & Rutstein SO (1994) *Infant and child mortality.* Demographic and Health Surveys Comparative Studies No. 15, Macro International, Calverton MD

Suwal JV (2001) The main determinants of infant mortality in Nepal. *Social Science and Medicine* 53: 1667–1681

Teitler J (1999) Father involvement, child health and maternal health behavior. Paper presented at the Urban Seminar on Children's Health Safety, Harvard University, April 23–24

Thornton A (Ed) (2001) *The well-being of children and families: Research and data needs.* Ann Arbor Michigan: University of Michigan Press

UN (United Nations) (1999) *World population prospects. The 1998 revision* Vol I: Comprehensive Tables. New York: UN

UN (2001) *World population prospects: The 2000 revision* (Highlights and Tables). New York: UN. Also available at http://www.un.org/esa/population/unpop.htm

WHO (World Health Organisation) (2000) Effect of breastfeeding on infant and child mortality due to infectious diseases in less-developed countries: A pooled analysis. *Lancet* 355: 451–455

Yach D (1994) Health status and its determinants in South Africa. *Africa Health* 3: 5 8

CONTRIBUTORS

Professor Acheampong Yaw Amoateng is a family sociologist and Director of Research in the Child, Youth, Family and Social Development Research Programme of the Human Sciences Research Council (HSRC). His research interests are in the areas of family formation and dissolution patterns, and adolescent development.

Dr Daniela Casale is a lecturer in the School of Economics at the University of Natal. Her research interests include labour and development economics, including aspects of labour force participation; poverty, inequality and human development; issues around household composition and welfare; gender and the aged.

Chris Desmond is a research specialist in the Child, Youth, Family and Social Development Research Programme of the HSRC. His work has covered a number of aspects of the economic impact of HIV/AIDS and the planning for responses to such impacts. Recent work has focused on methods of costing childcare and measuring the effectiveness of different options for its provision.

Professor Tim B Heaton is a Professor and Research Associate at the Center for Studies of the Family at Brigham Young University in the United States. His research interests are family change in less developed countries, marriage and divorce.

Professor Ishmael Kalule-Sabiti is a professor of Demography and Director of the Population Research and Training Unit, North West University, Mafikeng Campus. His research interests are migration, marriage and divorce.

Dr Monde Makiwane is a research specialist in the Child, Youth, Family and Social Development Research Programme of the HSRC. His recent publications are in the areas of fertility and adolescent reproductive health.

Dr Martin Enock Palamuleni is a lecturer in Population Studies at the Population Training and Research Unit (POPUNIT), North West University, Mafikeng Campus. His research interests include demographic analysis, fertility transition in southern Africa and reproductive health issues in the region.

Ms Sharmla Rama is a research specialist in the Child, Youth, Family and Social Development Programme of the HSRC. Her areas of research interest include child well-being and rights with a focus on child-centred statistics, children's patterns of time use, and children's transport and mobility issues.

Professor Linda M Richter is the Executive Director of the Child, Youth, Family and Social Development Research Programme of the HSRC. She holds a Chair in Psychology and is an elected Fellow of the University of KwaZulu-Natal. She is an Honorary Professor in the Department of Paediatrics and Child Health at the University of the Witwatersrand, a consultant in the Centre for the AIDS Programme of Research in South Africa (CAPRISA), and an Honorary Fellow in the Department of Psychiatry at the University of Melbourne. She has published more than 150 papers in the fields of child adolescent and family development, infant and child assessment, protein-energy malnutrition, street and working children, and the effects of HIV/AIDS on children and families, including HIV prevention among young people.